Generations

Essays by

Noel Annan
Douglas Bush
Mary Douglas
Tamara K. Hareven
Harold R. Isaacs
Morton Keller
Annie Kriegel
Jonathan Lear
Shirley Robin Letwin
Laura L. Nash
Matilda White Riley
Carl E. Schorske
Robert Skidelsky

Generations

Edited by STEPHEN R. GRAUBARD

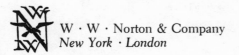
W · W · Norton & Company
New York · London

Library of Congress Cataloging in Publication Data
Main entry under title:
Generations.
    1. Peer groups—Addresses, essays, lectures.
2. Age groups—Addresses, essays, lectures.
3. Identity (Psychology)—Addresses, essays, lectures.
4. Conflict of generations—Addresses, essays, lectures.
I. Graubard, Stephen Richards.
HM133.G45   1978   301.43   79–21410
ISBN 0–393–01268–9
ISBN 0–393–95093–X pbk.

This book was printed and bound by Vail-Ballou Press, Inc.

1 2 3 4 5 6 7 8 9 0

Contents

Preface

THERE ARE FEW TERMS that have been as frequently invoked—but as little studied—over the last twenty years as the term "generations." In the scholarly world, in the social policy professions, and in the press, the concept of generations has become one of the most adaptable themes of contemporary discourse. Yet, in trying to apply the concept to these last two decades themselves, one realizes how elusive and difficult the idea of generations is, whether used as a tool of historical or intellectual analysis. How ought one to read the record of the last twenty years? Do they indeed provide a record? Is it the record of one generation's thinking, of two, or more? Where can one generation be said to end and another begin? Are these terminal points the same without regard to subject?

Is there any reason to believe, for example, that 1968 was a significant date in world history—comparable perhaps to 1848—and that it helped shape a generation's thinking? If so, which generation, and how? Or was 1973, with its oil embargo and substantial increase in fuel prices, a decisive moment of change? Again, for whom, and with what intellectual and other consequences? Or, are these events essentially parochial, almost trivial, of little consequence beside certain others which have entailed a vast expansion in the number of nation states, a massive proliferation of nuclear weapons, and the development of wholly new nationalisms, not to speak of new ethnic and racial identities? How did these and other like developments shape a generation? Did they? Which generation? When? Where?

A volume on the theme of generations should begin by acknowledging the many ambiguities that attach to the concept. Indeed, there is no substantial scholarly literature on the subject. It is the very popularity of the concept, of the term itself, that requires explanation. There is reason to believe that the idea may be more congenial today than it has ever been. It is certainly more variously used—sometimes almost to the point of caricature—by those whose interest is to emphasize how much has changed recently, and how much they (and their generation) have contributed to the changes.

Yet, it is Annie Kriegel who raises the heretical question whether, for all the "breathless succession of revolutions and restorations of all kinds: demographic, technical, economic, cultural, religious, social, political" that have occurred since the eighteenth century and that have unquestionably contributed to our legitimate preoccupation with generations—whether there have been any major universal happenings since World War II, anything that would merit permanent international attention. Kriegel writes: "Paradoxically . . . we may wonder whether, since 1945 and thus for more than thirty years, it is not rather the absence of a universal event likely to unify the memory of the whole of humanity that has given the search for generational identity its almost desperate character."

If there have been no recent universal events—nothing even remotely approaching the French Revolution or the Russian Revolution, nothing at all like World War I or World War II—then most of humanity has lived recently with more parochial happenings, with groups investing certain of these more purely local incidents with an importance they never merited. Thus, for example, the American antiwar demonstrators in 1968, milling around the Democratic party convention hall in Chicago in protest against the Johnson administration's policies on Vietnam, wanted to identify both themselves and their cause and shouted to the television cameras, "The whole world is watching; the whole world is watching." What was sad about the spectacle was that the whole world was not watching; only miniscule numbers are in the habit of sitting before their television screens, watching news clips from abroad; and even among these few, many do so from a safe emotional distance, casually and unconcerned, almost apathetic. The next day this same audience, or one very much like it, will be watching another "media event," with the same degree of detachment. The sheer evanescence of so much of recent history—the ephemeral character of incidents made to seem important for a day, a month, or a season by the genius of the mass media—leaves many individuals with a sense of living in undifferentiated time, without significant or substantial links with those living elsewhere, untouched by experiences other than those provided by their immediate environment.

Yet, there is a passionate wish to belong, to insist that one is part of a world-historical process, that one is not isolated, that one is in fact having significant influence. Again, it is Annie Kriegel who reminds us that "no writer of memoirs, no chronicler, no autobiographer seized by the furious desire to reduce reality to the world of the 'I' can resist the temptation to justify his undertaking by making it appear collective, and to introduce his subject by stating that 'to belong to the generation that . . .' "

Ours is a generation-minded time, and it is well to understand why it is, why indeed the theme has asserted itself so insistently in modern times. This is not to say that others did not also think in generational terms, but only that the use and meaning of the idea are markedly different today from what they were in the past. Others appear to have invested less sentiment in the concept; they probably needed it less.

As this collection makes abundantly clear, the idea of generations has immense appeal and considerable utility. Its uses in explaining political phenomena and, indeed, in providing quite new perspectives on significant social change may be only slightly more apparent than what it accomplishes in illuminating changing preoccupations and interests in art, literature, and scholarship more generally. Whether the subject be Homer or Trollope, Quine or Ayer, Fraser or Lévi-Strauss, the generational perspective forces us back to new considerations of the role of style and fashion, of influence itself.

Mary Douglas, in quoting from E. H. Gombrich's *Art and Illusion*, pays particular heed to what he says about the artist's struggle "to win freshness of vision." She reminds us of the significance of this, of what Gombrich writes about the difficulty of achieving innovation. Would it be too much to say that one of the more obvious evidences of the hubris of modern man is his insistence that this is not so, and that innovation not only is possible, it is relatively easy? Is this not the century of men and women who have sought to persuade others and who have themselves believed that they have created a new vision—unique to their own generation—and that theirs was a vision sufficient to transform society? One is reminded of Alfred North Whitehead's wise dictum, that "the introduction of a reform does not prove the moral superiority of the reforming generation," and one wonders how often this is understood. Reform, innovation, change—all are accomplished by devices and procedures, often protracted and generally more complex than is commonly acknowledged today. To study "generations" is to study change, but to study it critically and dispassionately.

The essays in this volume first appeared as an issue of *Daedalus*, the Journal of the American Academy of Arts and Sciences. Thanks are due to the Ford Foundation for making the volume possible. Its support of interdisciplinary inquiry has never seemed more warranted.

S. R. G

LAURA L. NASH

Concepts of Existence: Greek Origins of Generational Thought

WHAT MARKS A GENERATION? When the term categorizes a group of people unrelated by blood, the critical criteria defining a generation are endlessly variable, from the nearly meaningless numerical division by decades (the "sixties generation," for example) to the mutual participation in a specific event as profound as Vietnam or as trivial as drinking Pepsi-Cola. Age itself may mark a generation, with specific physical characteristics (gray beard and stooped posture) or behavioral patterns (as in Gibbon's "brisk intemperance of youth") providing the definitive signals. But our most secure standard for defining a generation rests on the Greek root of the word, *genos*, whose basic meaning is reflected in the verb *genesthai*, "to come into existence"; until 1961 the first definition of the word in Webster's unabridged dictionary[1] was still "procreation." That moment when a child is born simultaneously produces a new generation separating parent and offspring—*gonos* ergo *genos*—and the very concept educes the paradox of an ever-shifting threshold in time.

I

Even within a familial context the boundaries of the collective generation—that "body of living beings constituting a single step in the line of descent from an ancestor"—are not easily fixed. Like a single point on a line, the individual generation operates in another dimension and is perceived with difficulty except as a constituent part of the entire pedigree. Homer plays on this elusive and ambiguous quality of the concept in the sixth book of the *Iliad*. Diomedes, one of the strongest warriors of the Greeks, who in his enthusiasm and combative prowess wounds even two gods at Troy, is brought up sharp in the midst of battle when he comes face to face with Glaucus, a Trojan ally. Awed at his opponent's glorious might and daring, Diomedes asks him who he is. Addressing Diomedes by his patronymic, Glaucus replies:

> Greathearted son of Tydeus, why do you question my lineage [*genea*]?
> As is the generation [*genea*] of leaves, so too of men:
> At one time the wind shakes the leaves to the ground,
>   but then the flourishing woods
> Gives birth, and the season of spring comes into existence [*epigignetai*];
> So it is of the generations of men, which alternately
>   come forth and pass away.[2]

1

Glaucus uses the same word for the collective generations (lineage) and an individual's life (birth to death). The opening question of his reply might appear at
first to be a rebuttal, a scornful dismissal of Diomedes' inquiry on the grounds
of irrelevancy. But in fact the simile is an affirmation of lineage, formulated in a
dismissal as prelude to what follows.[3]

Unlike the negative force of the Christian simile, "Behold, all flesh is as the
grass . . . for lo, the grass withereth, and the flower thereof decayeth," the
Homeric comparison stresses continuity and cycle, death and birth, birth and
death. Glaucus questions the question, as it were, because the details of his past
are unnecessary in that the quality of his ancestry should be self-apparent: one
generation grows out of another, and shares its characteristics. The tree loses its
leaves, but puts them forth again; "spring comes into existence" specifically
applies to the young warrior, whose prowess is the natural extension of his past
ancestry.[4]

The positive aspect of the simile is affirmed by the speech that follows.
Glaucus more than answers Diomedes' inquiry by tracing his ancestry five male
generations back to the god Aeolus (Aeolus-Sisyphus-Glaucus-Bellerophon-
Hippolochus-Glaucus). The exploits of his grandfather, Bellerophon, are told
in great detail and Hippolochus's virtues recounted before the recital ends in
ring composition with a reaffirmation of lineage: "Hippolochus begat me . . .
and when he sent me to Troy he charged me always to be bravest and preeminent, and not to shame the race [genos] of my fathers who were the noblest in
Ephyre and wide Lycia. Of this lineage [genea] and blood I swear I am." Diomedes is delighted, for he realizes that his father and Bellerophon were guest-
friends, and so he is prevented from fighting the fair Glaucus. The power of
lineage suspends war itself, and the two jump down from their chariots to shake
hands and exchange armor.

In his opening simile Glaucus uses the same word genea, for lineage and the
cycle of life which is marked by birth. Like the English usage, ancient Greek
and Latin terms for generation (genos, genea, genesis, gonē, genus, generatio, etc.)
carry a wide scope of meanings, from birth and reproduction to age, time of life,
cycle of life, race, family, or even species. All these words stem from a common
Indo-European root, *gen- (o-grade, *gon-; zero grade, *gn; cf. Sanskit jánah)[5]
the fundamental signification of which is "to come into existence." But even
when it is closely tied to its primary meaning, the concept of generation maintains an ultimate relativity: the child forms a generation only with respect to his
parents, or when children are in turn born to him. Generation, then, is the
reference point, in ancient usage as well as today, for a multitude of concepts, a
very metaphor for existence. Like the verb to be, generation requires an adjective
of context, a predicate of relativity, before it takes on meaning. Used sometimes
with complacency ("my generation"), sometimes with belligerence ("your generation"), and even with affection, as when Telemachus vows his friendship to
Peisistratus by reason of their similar ages,[6] generation marks allegiance, time of
life, span of years, sameness with one group and otherness from the rest.

In the Iliad, Nestor, the eldest Achaean at Troy, stands as the living embod-
iment of the generational process. He has already witnessed "two generations of
men, who were born and reared contemporaneously [hama] with him, pass

away," and now, still vital, he rules a third.[7] In the *Odyssey* he is said to have ruled over three generations.[8] While the two statements are somewhat discrepant with respect to the exact span of Nestor's regnant years,[9] they stand for approximately the same idea, and in both passages the word for generation is the same (*geneai*). If we take "born and reared contemporaneously with him, they passed away" to signify the cycles of generation which Glaucus compared to the leaves of a tree (they pass away and come forth, they come forth and pass away), then Nestor's three "generations" are easily understood: the first generation would be those born to his father and his contemporaries, of which generation Nestor is the youngest; the second generation would consist of their children, and the third of their grandchildren. While Nestor's precise age, like that of any other Greek hero, is totally irrelevant and never supplied (despite the calculations of the mathematically minded Porphyry and later scholiasts),[10] his vitality and longevity are given prominence and have protracted his own generational (procreative) abilities so that his sons are equal in age to his contemporaries' grandsons.

In describing Nestor, generational awareness surpasses the narrow bounds of family to encompass simultaneously general stages of heroic accomplishment. Generation still rests partly on family (the father as a distinct generation from his son, the son of the same generation as his brothers), but more strongly on one's contemporaries in battle. Nestor's extraordinary vitality both in youth and old age allow him to fight alongside three different sets of warriors: as a very young man with his father Neleus in local disputes with the Eleans and Epeians, as a young adult in the prime of warriorhood with the Lapiths against the Centaurs, and now in his old age at Troy.

As the two world wars set a generational standard for the first half of the twentieth century, so the event of Troy became the primary reference point for the generations of the Heroic age. Nestor, by his participation in pre-Trojan, Trojan, and post-Trojan events, stands for heroism and time itself. He would have been young Churchill charging with the Twenty-first Lancers at Omdurman, leading the expedition to Antwerp in World War I; the respected counselor at Troy would have been prime minister in World War II, and the venerable statesman who delivered the White Paper on Defense in the postwar period.

Nestor's sons at home in Pylos would be analogous to the "air-raid generation"[11]—too young to participate in battle, but permanently affected by the war. If ever there was a "lost generation" in Greek mythology, it is that of the post-Troy heroes, the sons of those who sacked Priam's city. Their tales are tarnished in comparison to the brilliance of the Trojan struggle—Orestes murders his mother, Neoptolemus comes late to Troy, murders Priam at the altar, and later dies at Delphi in a fight with the priests.[12] Their tales betray a general disorientation of the heroic code in the disillusionment of the post-Troy years. Even Telemachus's heroism, emergent in hand-to-hand combat in his father's halls, has its weird culmination in the hanging of the women servants. The heroic code is so shattered after Troy that one story has Orestes slay Neoptolemus in a dispute over Menelaus's daughter.

Nestor, however, escapes the aftershocks of Troy, and while for others the longest period of life is adulthood (see table below), for Nestor the venerability of old age remains his throughout the Trojan and post-Trojan periods. It is possible to schematize a relative chronology of heroes with Nestor as the reference point:

Heroic Generation	Nestor's Familial Generation	Relative Chronology of Nestor's Contemporaries
	⌈ Neleus	⌈ Herakles
Pre-Troy	Eleven sons	Eleans, Epeians
		Lapiths, Centaurs
	⌐ Nestor	
Troy		Agamemnon Odysseus
		Achilles, Ajax, Diomedes
	⌊ Antilochus	⌊ Neoptolemus
Post-Troy	Nestor's other sons	Orestes Telemachus

If generation is a threshold, then both Nestor and his son Antilochus are special embodiments of generation in that they mark the boundaries of both the familial and contemporary generational scheme. Nestor is the last brother, but eldest of those at Troy as well as the post-Troy generation of the *Odyssey*. Antilochus is among the youngest who fight at Troy, but the eldest of the post-Troy generation (had he lived) to which his younger brothers belong: they are contemporary with the sons of Odysseus, Agamemnon, and Achilles.

II

As our own generational standards blur, we seek even harder to define—hence control—the stages of life. If the success of Gail Sheehy's *Passages* is any indication, our perception of a lifetime has become increasingly recherché; no longer content with divisions by decade, we regularly recognize at least fourteen stages of life: newborn, infant, toddler, child, preteen, teen, early twenties, late twenties, midthirties, forties, midforties, fifties, early sixties, senior citizen. Greater precision ironically heralds greater confusion. Generational uncertainty derives not from lack of definition but lack of relativity: like the monotonous and frequent format to which the world events, many and varied, are daily reduced (two minutes or two columns), personal definitions of the events of one's life or the stride of one's psyche lack a sense of history. Activities of the present have no relative value to the past and no predictive value for the future self.

In contrast, ancient Greek generational categories are fewer in number, hierarchical, and have a primarily relative meaning. Numerical age is meaningless except in the designation of life expectancy (Mimnermus, Solon, and Pythagoras set the normal lifespan anywhere from sixty to eighty years); even the age categories for competition at the Olympian games were flexible enough to allow for unusual rates of physical development. As A. W. Gomme notes, there were only three generally recognized divisions of a life: the child (*pais nēpios*), the youth (*hēbē*),[13] and the old person (*geraios, gerōn*). While the *anēr* "man" clearly represents adulthood, the term does not signify stage of life per se, and there is no term for middle age. When Thucydides wishes to designate the generation of men contemporaneous with Pericles, whose military prime occurred in the years after the Persian and previous to the Peloponnesian wars, he must employ a circumlocution, *hē kathestēkuia hēlikia*, or "the 'settled' stage of life."[14] Plato later calls it the "settled and middle stage of life," which Cicero translates "constans aetas quae media dicitur."[15]

There are some exceptions to this scheme, most notably Solon's division of a lifetime into ten stages of seven years each, a division often quoted in later antiquity.[16] But the ten categories must be acknowledged as a product of the period (Archaic quantification) rather than the cultural expansion of generational definition. Solon's Greek can not accommodate ten stages with as many abstractions, and the generic terms are still limited to three: child (*pais nēpios*) for the first stage, adolescence (*hēbē*) for the second and third stages, and man (*anēr*) for the fourth through sixth stages. The last four ages carry no term at all besides numerical designation even though Solon had a word for old age, *gēras*, in his vocabulary;[17] *anēr* is understood or replaced by the indefinite pronoun *tis* as the subject of the sentence.

Pythagoras, on the report of Diogenes Laertius, attempted to divide a man's life into four numerical groups of twenty years each. Diogenes attributes the categories to the seasons of the year, but the sacredness of the Pythagorean *tetractys* may equally have influenced the division.[18] Vocabulary again proves inadequate: Pythagoras's abstractions are roughly equivalent in English to "child," "youth," "young man," "old man."[19] Archaic attempts to define the stages of life in absolute terms or numerical sets had little basis in traditional Greek thought; the idea was both revolutionary and unsuccessful from the point of view of language. Their terms were not adopted even though the sayings were quoted.

As Solon's and Pythagoras's divisions indicate, the general stages have no one set name. Categories of childhood, adolescence, and adulthood overlap, and the terms for stage of life, like "generation," usually depend on context for precise meaning. The simple formulaic grouping of *genea* or *genos* in the dative with a comparative adjective in Homer underscores the relativity of the abstraction.[20] Menelaus is "younger in age" than Odysseus (*genei husteros*) but a fluent speaker nonetheless.[21] Agamemnon asserts, "Let him [Achilles] submit to me, inasmuch as I am more kingly, and avow that I am elder in age [*geneai progenesteros*]."[22] In each case age is explanatory; the comparison has value in that certain qualities of action (speaking in the assembly) or character (kingliness) are especially appropriate to and validated by one age more than another.

Despite ambiguities of designation, generational identity (stage of life) is easily recognizable in ancient Greece, for the ages have a distinctive character and set associations. Youth, for example, is a time of action, while contemplation and counsel are for the aged (Solon is reported to have said, "I grow old, learning more and more").[23] Age has a certainty about it that makes it a stable cultural value, and in natural opposition to that stability is its transgression, which by its very clearness provides an effective device for underscoring exceptional ability or humor. The seemly eloquence of young Telemachus at Nestor's court[24] is perceived as unusual for his age, understood as an inheritance of his father's genius. Only genetic determinism overcomes the limitations of age; exchange of behavioral and physical attributes between young and old is impossible to the degree that veneration of youth and the miracles of hair dye have transformed today's generational categories.

If there is any sense of transgression of the appropriate in the sixty-year-old actress playing the ingenue offstage at Studio 54, or the thirty-two-year-old mayor of a well-known Midwestern town "retiring to write his memoirs," it is lost in the general confusion of generational affiliation. "Life begins at sixty" would be incomprehensible to the Greek, or better yet, a joke. When old Strepsiades decides to join the youths of Socrates' thinking-school in Aristophanes' *Clouds*, his generational limitations—*paideia* is for the *paides* (education is for the young)—are at once apparent and the butt of several outrageous showpieces of sophistry. A famous visual joke by the Andocides painter portrays a very young boy assuming the role of judge over two wrestlers, one of whom is clearly an older man, while a second set of athletes parodies the hold of a Zeus and Ganymede, with the younger boy holding the elder man aloft.[25] If humor is the setting up of a recognizable context only to introduce the totally out of context, then it is easy to trace the stock theme of Old Comedy, impossible rejuvenation, to the fixed generational associations of ancient Greece. The primal joke—old and certain—still provokes a laugh: even if the humor is cheap, granny on a motorcycle is *funny*.

Nestor, ever the touchstone for heroic standard, makes the distinction between old and young clear in the ninth book of the *Iliad*. His favorite young warrior, Diomedes, offers an opinion to the assembled Achaeans. In response to Agamemnon's faintheartedness, the youth advises action: "Go if you like, but Sthenelus and I will stay here and fight until we achieve the goal of Ilium." Nestor rises and compliments Diomedes first for his prowess in battle (action) and secondly for his words (counsel), which, he says, are best *for one of his age*. "But," he continues, "you didn't reach the end of your speech." Though his instincts are right, the intensity of youth prevents Diomedes from seeing the whole situation and offering workable advice; Nestor asserts, "I aver to be older than you and will speak forth and outline the whole." The details of Nestor's advice continue the distinction between ages; he orders the young to post sentinels while Agamemnon should prepare a feast for the elders (*gerousin*) so that they can devise counsel.

In Homer, physical prowess and the needs of war are in large part the determinative factors of the age distinction. Old age is "grievous" because it weakens the limbs, but longevity has the positive qualities of cumulative wisdom and broad perspective. Experience of the past is recognized as true and essential, especially for success in warfare. Thus the hierarchy in battle as Nestor describes it takes strategic advantage of the age distinction. The strong wage war while the aged—revered administrators whose advice is drawn from experience—arrange the battles and keep order among the troops. The sixth-century poet Tyrtaeus outlines the same order by age in an exhortation to Spartan youths to fight for their country:

> O youths, abide with your fellows and fight,
>   and do not begin shameful flight nor be fearful,
> but make the spirit in your breast great and strong,
>   and do not be cowardly when fighting men.
> And the aged, whose knees are no longer nimble,
>   do not leave them in the front, the aged.

For this indeed is shameful: falling among the vanguard
    the aged man lies before the youths,
head already whitened, and beard gray,
    breathing out his strong spirit in the dust,
holding his bloody genitals in his hands—
    a sight so shameful and indignant to the eyes—
and his skin all exposed. But to the young all is seemly,
    while the bright flower of lovely youth remains
for men a wonder to behold, and a desire [lit. object of *eros*] of women,
    as long as he lives, and fair when he falls in the vanguard.
So let each one plant himself firmly and abide,
    both feet set on the ground, biting his lip with his teeth.[26]

Tyrtaeus turns the traditional portrayal of youth into a moral standard for battle. Set within the conventional framework of praise-blame poetry, the action of youth is a seemly thing, all the more attractive for its heightened contrast with old age. It is shameful behavior when the old are allowed to be the doers; their death in the vanguard, ugly and castrating, is set up as foil to the lovely, courageous, sexually vital generation to which the exhorted belong. As an incentive to youthful heroism, age is cast in as negative a light as possible, but the unbalanced emphasis on one age over another is clearly influenced by the genre. Erotic poetry of the same period suppresses the positive qualities of old age to underscore the attractiveness of youth, and the persona of the enfeebled (or rejuvenated) old man admiring the vital adolescent recurs throughout Archaic poetry.

The young are sheer energy rather than strength, but like an overloaded electric line, they tend to short-circuit in their impetuousness, and require the steadying direction of the elderly. The adult, mature in strength and possessing the common sense of experience, bears the brunt of war. This generation is the least well-defined, but most abundant in heroes. Unlike today's association of youth with novelty, individuality marks, if anyone, the man (*anēr*) rather than the youth. But while the "adult" stands out as self-contained, heroic, individual, and generationally unaffiliated, the more fixed categories of youth and old age recover in complement what they lack in isolation. Types of the older and younger hero, whatever the actual age difference, are frequently paired in battle at Troy: Nestor with Diomedes, Patroclus with Achilles. Even in the controversial *Doloneia*, often assumed with the Townsley Scholia to be an interpolation,[27] the pairing is conventional: Odysseus is the calculator of stealth to Diomedes' reckless action. Menoetius summed up the conventional behavioral distinctions in his advice to Patroclus before he and Achilles left for Troy: "My child, Achilles is nobler than you in birth [*geneei*] but you are older. He is far stronger in might yet you must speak to him shrewd counsel and make things clear."[28]

Behavioral age distinctions, perhaps the strongest generational pattern in Greek thought and standardized in Homer, operate with a proverbial force in the fifth century, coloring everything from dramatic characterization of the king and statesman to historical analysis of military strategy. Both Herodotus and Thucydides play off the conservative, antiaction (antiwar) wisdom of the old with the risk-taking impetuousity of the young.

Herodotus's report of the Persian deliberations before the second invasion of Greece refracts into intensely age-specific opinions. Artabanus, aged counselor to Xerxes, warns him against "always giving in to (his) youthful spirit," which is motivating the king to engage the Greeks in war ten years after his father's unsuccessful attempt on Hellas in 490. Xerxes rages at the advice, but afterwards apologizes, blaming his temper on his youth: "For I have not yet attained the fullness of wisdom . . . When I heard Artabanus's counsel, immediately my youthful spirit boiled over [lit.] so that there burst forth an unseemly word against a man older than myself."[29] And yet they go to war. Xerxes is pursued by a vision which demands war, and when he at last persuades Artabanus to dress up in the king's robes (become king and become young) the vision visits Artabanus as well, and he accedes to Xerxes' ambition (which proves disastrous).

Thucydides also sets the opposing deliberations before the Sicilian expedition into categories by age. Nicias, older, cautious, anti-imperialistic, argues against the expedition, and warns the Athenians not to listen to one who is too young to command and has a monetary stake in the war (Alcibiades). "For this is a weighty matter, and not for a young man to decide or rashly undertake."[30] Alcibiades in turn accuses Nicias of trying to set the young against the old in contrast to the allegedly traditional unity of generations whereby "united in counsel, old and young together, they brought our affairs to their present height."[31] A brilliant general and attractive athlete, Alcibiades reminds the Athenians of his "success" at Mantinea and the glory which his Olympic victories brought to Athens. Sarcastically, he turns Nicias's words around again: "Thus my youth and unnatural folly did meet with appropriate words the might of the Peloponnesians." The Athenians unwisely follow the young man's fallacious advice, and afterwards they compound their mistake with a second violation of age category: they recall Alcibiades and put the older Nicias in charge of the action. His physical debilitation and mental hesitancy prove fatal to the Sicilian expedition.

Generational categorizations such as these, occurring at crucial stages in the reporting of contemporary events, are further evidence of the social pervasiveness of the generational definitions as well as of the historian's reliance on poetic patterns for historical analysis.

Throughout Greek literature, obvious physical distinctions place the old and young in contraposition: spent strength, gray beard, canescent hair have their counterpart in the untiring vitality, flowing locks and newly-sprouted beard of the young man. The setaceous bud of early puberty blossoms into a stock comparison of the down on an adolescent's cheeks to flowers or fruit (preserved in our term "peach fuzz"). Pindar compares the youthful bloom to the soft down on a grape leaf, while Aristophanes likens it to the bloom on apples.[32]

Hair has a particular association with youth, derived perhaps from the ritual dedication of a lock of hair "for nurture" to the local river upon entering manhood. The association of hair-cutting and adolescence is so strong that the Suda offers a false etymology for *kourosunos-on* (youth) from *keiro* (to cut hair), basing the linguistic analysis on such homonyms as *koura* (lock of hair) and *koura* (maiden), punned in Aeschylus's *Choephoroi*,[33] or the similar *kouros* (youth) and *kourias* (one who wears his hair short).

Nursling of the river, fructification of the beard, the springtime of life—the metaphors of youth have an easy affinity with nature. Nowhere does the trope turn more felicitously than in the vehicle of the horse. In Archaic poetry, the gangly filly captures the attractive awkwardness of the young maiden: "Thracian filly, why do you eye me askance? Why do you shun me and take me for a fool? . . ."[34] Spartan maiden choruses are called "herds" and individual singers are compared to various breeds. So Alcman describes Hagesichora, "second in beauty only to Agido—a Colaxean steed behind an Iberian."[35]

For young males the horse is an appropriate accessory, a symbol of heroism and high spirits. So the charioteers at Troy are often young squires; so in the *Doloneia* it is Diomedes who gets the horses of Rhesus while Odysseus retains the Thracian king's armor. Paris's vibrant exuberance finds perfect representation in a horse simile: "Even as when a stabled horse, well-fed at the manger, breaks his halter and thunders over the plain—intent on bathing in the fairflowing river—and exulting; on high he holds his head, his hair flowing around his shoulders; and sensing his own splendor, brisk knees bear him to the haunts and pastures of the mares—even so Paris son of Priam strode down from Pergamum's height . . . laughing, his swift feet bearing him on."[36] Greek agespecific metaphors and behavioral traits are not formed on exclusive preposession—heroes of all ages are seen with horses—but rather on a tendency toward classification and appropriateness that is in large part generational. For example, warriors of all ages compete in Patroclus's funeral games, but when Agamemnon *characterizes* the contests, they are the realm of the young: "You've attended the funerals of heroes, seen when a king dies how the youths gird themselves and prepare for the contests."[37] An age-specific activity today would be listening to rock music. Many people of various ages listen to rock music, but in a characterization of a teenager, the music to which he listens will be rock.

From the downy cheeks and undeveloped strength of the young it is a short distance to effeminacy. In Homer the womanly is that which is outside war, synonymous with the unheroic, and confined to the rebuke: Hector angrily replies to Ajax's taunting, "Do not make trial of me as if I were a puny boy or woman, unacquainted with the deeds of war." The world of peace and women are one, and inappropriate to the Homeric hero, but in Archaic poetry the erotic potential of adolescent effeminacy is fully explored. Anacreon addresses a boy "with maiden glance,"[38] and as Hermann Fraenkel notes, love is directed less toward an individual than a type, sensuality of imagery a primary function of the erotic portrait.[39] In the *Bacchae*, however, for Pentheus's harbored sexual ambiguities the hermaphroditic Dionysus, the young god with his pale skin and long curling locks, holds a sinister fascination which entices the prince to his doom.

The hallmarks of youth have their darker side. Generational attributes take on two kinds of moral value; the high spirits and impetuousness of the young erupt into a hubristic arrogance, well-documented in tragedy (as in Sophocles and Aeschylus),[40] but this same earnestness of spirit, passionate and uncompromising, is the bulwark of heroic self-sacrifice. In Euripides, especially, the impetuous heroism of youth shines with painful intensity: Hippolytus's youthful lack of perspective and almost mystic identification with nature compels his exclusive devotion to Artemis and consequent destruction by Aphrodite.

There is an intrinsic mistrust of a young man's wisdom throughout Greek literature, and it was claimed that one of the objections to the Sophists was that they taught the young *euboulia*, ability to give good (persuasive) counsel. It is with the driest irony that Socrates enjoins Gorgias's young protégé Polus "Colt," who had already published at a young age a treatise on rhetoric, to be so good as to correct him and Gorgias should they make some mistake in their reasoning: "It is for this that we possess companions and sons, so that when we, becoming older, should stumble, you younger ones may be at hand to set our lives straight in words and deeds."[41]

Central to generational categories is the peer group; one's companions are those like in age to oneself. The Greek word *hēlix*, "of the same age," frequently occurs in the plural to designate "companions," *hēlikes*. The second usage asserts itself as independent of its original age connotation, and the wide occurrence of the word in both ways makes it an undependable indicator of generational affiliation. Intensified to *homēlix*, however, the root continues to be age-significant. To compare someone by age is to make their character predictable. In tragedy the hero or heroine stands outside the familiar and accepted; heroic identity is to be other, unlike in mind and extraordinary in action. Interestingly, *homēlikia* occurs nowhere in the extant plays of Aeschylus or Sophocles, nor is it preserved in the tragic fragments. Only in Euripides, where "the common opinion holds value," is this epic-lyric word for a contemporary reintroduced.

The opposition of affiliation to one's own generation and exclusion from others (as well as their concomitant behavioral associations) gives the Homeric and lyric character an almost arcane security of identity, which is reinforced by the operating reality that the peer group is homologous in action, thought, and emotion. Like in age, like in mind, hence contemporaneousness generates a special empathy and affection. So Telemachus's affection for Peisistratus is motivated by their similarity of age: "Guest-friends of old from our fathers' friendship we avow to be, and moreover we are of the same age [*homēlikes*] And this journey will confirm our oneness of heart [*homophrosunēisin*] still more."[42] Aristophanes parodies such affection in a wonderful crisis in the *Acharnians*. Dikaiopolis seizes a charcoal burner and holds it hostage from the Acharnians, whose livelihood is gained from the manufacture of charcoal. Upon his threat to slay the scuttle, the feisty old Acharnians cry, "Then you will slay this lover-of-charcoal, its equal in years!"[43]

At its root, generational affiliation is a humanistic impulse, the affirmation that being born at the same time identifies one man with another. In the emotionally charged moment when Priam suddenly appears at Achilles' feet and kisses the hands "which had slain his many sons," his crucial appeal for Achilles' tolerance rests on likeness of age: "Remember thy father, godlike Achilles, and how I am of like age, on the threshold of grievous eld."[44] Generational identity, the legitimate assurance of character, at once transfers Achilles' affection for his father to the aged Priam. The hero's empathetic response to Priam's likeness of age runs deep and true: Peleus, too, will soon lose his son.

III

The widespread extent of age paradigms in ancient Greek literature testifies not to an immaturity of character development (which is already quite sophisticated in Homer), but to the Greek tendency to preserve simultaneously the type and its specific variation; the tension between the two is the essence of what we call the Classic.[45] Moreover, this terribly strong notion that generation (age, time of life, ancestry) has its own independent force underscores a basic stability in the society; the stages of life have an enduring reality, a continuity of development, which can be categorized and characterized. The paradox of the concept—that generation marks similarity to one group and difference from others—gives it its strength. Generational awareness is strong because old and young are recognizably distinct, but also complementary.

In the steady state of Greek family and social order, the young are subordinate to their elders, whose guidance and superior strength (military and political) place them in a dominant position. Belief in inherited talent and assumption of predictable social order determine that the son is, ideally, a lighter carbon copy of his father. In this framework, deliberate separation or dissension (youthful rebellion) are incomprehensible,[46] as is the independence of the young which would be a necessary quality of heroic character. Thus the paradigms of youthful heroism have a profoundly tragic potential and feature a separation of parent and child which is compelled by external event. Action is at once the youth's rite of passage into manhood (hēbē) and heroism, but that action usually involves the death of the parent or child. Orestes, the paradigm of youthful heroism in the Odyssey, must murder his mother and her lover. If neither parent nor child die in the performance of the adolescent heroic act, then the parent is most likely to be dead already (Neoptolemus is brought to Troy after Achilles' death). Telemachus provides one of the few examples where father and son are reunited.[47]

A second pattern of youthful heroism is far more common and far more pathetic than the death of the parent: the death of the young. Antilochus is a representative figure; he loses his life rescuing his father Nestor, who gets tangled in his horses' reins. The combination of filial piety and tragic death became paradigmatic for youthful valor, and the poignancy of untimely death a favorite poetic theme. The bereaved parent has a particularly powerful pathos and symbolizes the profoundest grief.

This motif caps the supernatural night watch over Patroclus's pyre, which is the climax of Achilles' mourning (afterwards he will sleep for the first time since Patroclus's death). All night long the north and west winds howl around the pyre, while Achilles pours libations and mourns his lost companion. In a summary description, the intensity of his grief is articulated by a simile which turns on the youthful-death motif: "As a father wails for his son as he burns his bones, a bridegroom [=young][48] who in death brings sorrow to his wretched parents, thus Achilles wailed for his companion as he burned his bones, making his heavy way about the fire, ceaselessly groaning."[49] The intensity of a father's grief, which heightens the pathos of youthful (untimely) death, is so powerful that the motif readily asserts itself not just in similes, but also to the subordination of accuracy. In the Iliad young Harpalion, who had come with his father to Troy, is killed by Meriones.[50] He dies in the arms of his comrades, who take his body back to Ilium, and the vignette closes with his sorrowing father Pylaemenes following the bier. Pathos is at its fullest, but Homer has nodded: Pylaemenes is already dead, slain a hundred lines earlier, and yet the pathetic motif of the father mourning the dead youth is so vivid that it intrudes on the narrative sequence to cap Harpalion's death.

At times untimely death attaches to the young hero as the appropriate (and vividly poignant) *topos*: Orestes' pretended death at the Pythian games in Sophocles' *Electra* is a sophisticated manipulation of youthful motifs which simultaneously advance his character (exemplary youthful hero) and the plot (Clytaemestra is deceived into dropping her guard). Untimely death, though false, is an appropriate characterization largely motivated by the strength of Orestes' age identity in myth. At other times, however, the youthful death motif is applied to less appropriate (that is, older) characters, functioning less as an indicator of age than to intensify the pathos of an untimely death. Failure to recognize this technique has led to a confusion of the age of some heroes, a confusion which results from the emotional translation of untimely death into death of the young.

For example, *hēbē* (youth) attends the elder Patroclus on his death: "his soul, flitting from his limbs, went off to Hades, wailing its fate, leaving manliness and *hēbē*."[51] Because Patroclus cannot possibly be a youth, *hēbē* is usually translated "the strength of youth." But *androtēta* "manliness" is the word which describes his strength and valor—*hēbē* adds a particular pathos to his death. So, too, Andromache begins her lament for Hector, "Husband *[aner]*, you are perished from life, a youth *[neos]* . . ."[52] The power of the motif, which is metaphorical, is so assertive that it characterizes without regard to accuracy, and the figurative time of life becomes reality.

Nowhere is this more apparent than in Homer's characterization of Achilles. His age is especially difficult for various reasons, but particularly for the discrepancy between his past experience and his fate. His many battles before Troy, his son, his pairing with Hector—all define him as beyond the youthful stage of life, and yet the intensity of his prowess (which is most like Diomedes'), the language of his fate (*ōkumoros* "short-lived"), and the pathos of his death define him as a young hero. But the effective transference of untimely death into young death in other places in Homer suggests that the same phenomenon happens with Achilles and results in his ambiguous generational identity. His heroism at Troy is a constant anticipation of his death ("you will be old and inglorious or glorious and short-lived; once Hector dies you will die soon after, etc."), so that the motif of the youth dying—applied to Achilles' untimely death for heightened pathos—effects a transformation of his identity during his entire career at Troy. Youthful traits in his character are highlighted in disproportion to the rest.

Such a distortion need not be conscious. A similar cultic transformation occurred at the death of John F. Kennedy. As youngest president of the United States he was seen as young but certainly not a youth, for he had a war career, a family, a political career already behind him. But the profound sense of tragedy which was felt at his untimely death could only be expressed in the most pathetic image, hence the almost instantaneous perception of it as the death of a very young man. The accounts reflecting this transformation of youngest president into very young man range from the austerity of *The Times'* obituary (which begins with a studied deference to his political acumen in the Cuban missile crisis but turns in the first subhead to "Youngest Ever"; eighth subhead,

"Youthful Appearance") to the maudlin diminutive, *Johnny, We Hardly Knew Ye*.[53]

IV

The mind in old age is wont to attend to and plan the necessary—

Sophocles[54]

The physical qualities intrinsic to youth and old age easily translate into behavioral characteristics. The physiologically enforced inactivity of old age leaves time for the contemplation and broad perspective which together make up sound judgment; weakness reinforces the advisory role, posing no threat of personal involvement. Hence the tragic chorus is frequently a group of old men, reflective and helpless in the face of heroic energy.

If the heroism of youth—though celebrated—entails tragic loss and is re-garded as an ambiguous good, the heroism of old age is clearly more positive. Throughout the archaic and classical periods the commonplace recurs that hap-piness is to live moderately (that is, not as a *tyrannos*) and long enough to see one's children survive to have children, which is, after all, the final duplication of one's own life and ultimate evidence of continuity (Plutarch later standardizes the definition of a generation to be the time between the birth of a son and a grandson). As the body decays, the mind strengthens, and age is a living asser-tion of cumulative wisdom and constancy of values.

Age is a measurement not only of wisdom and temperament, but also ac-complishment. Diodorus Siculus reports how Darius was intercepted by an Egyptian priest when he was about to erect a statue at Memphis in front of that of Sesoösis.[55] The priest claimed that the Egyptian had far surpassed Darius in accomplishments and his statue deserved prominence. Darius countered that when he equaled Sesoösis in years, then he assuredly would not be behind him in deeds, and that the priest should judge the deeds of each at the same age (*hēlikiotis*), for this was the fairest test of worth (*aretē*). So too, Plutarch admires Pericles for undertaking and completing in the acme of his political influence projects that would have taken other men many successive "generations."[56]

The assessment of the accomplishments of Darius and Pericles by their age, that is, the premise that as one ages one not only knows more but also accom-plishes more, underscores the unique relationship to action which each stage of life has. Authority of age rests on more than the special sagacity of the old, for the authority of age has an immediacy arising out of the *active* participation in the deeds of the past. The strength of tradition has a normative value; it shapes the present to such an extent that to call on the past is to introduce reality into the uncertain and elusive present. The manifestations of this surety are wide-spread. On a linguistic level, certain words for the past and future assert a fundamental fixity on the past which approaches the physical. While we "look ahead" to the future in our progressivism and "back" to the past, Greek does just the opposite: the word for the past, *prosthen* (or *prosō*), is a preposition which means "in front of," while *opisthen* (*opisō*), "the future," is "behind," at one's back, unknown. A vestige of this directional attitude to the past is unconsciously preserved in our prepositions "before" and "after," but the directional idea inherent in these time words is not in current usage.

If the past is sure, if what is true is the reassertion of past values, then the past is "living" and has the special problems of access that the recent past poses today. Apart from the divinely inspired memory of the poet (the ability to commemorate), the past is preserved by its participants, who order it chiefly by generations (*genea*). As Troy becomes a primary focal point in later time for the heroic "age," so too the heroes at Troy mark the past by other wars and exploits, but particularly those in living memory, that is, previous generations. Generational order reclaims the past as experience rather than verisimilar reconstruction. So too we designate what is still in living memory a generation (the First World War generation, the sixties generation), but the more remote past is methodically worked up by history into an "age." No one refers to the Generation of the Enlightenment because the distance of the eighteenth century allows for a perspective which spans more than a generation.

From a Homeric viewpoint, the heroic "age" (*genos* admits this meaning as well as "generation") has an immediacy of value and reality that defies the larger perspective of the historian, and is largely generational. Nestor, of course, is the chief access to pre-Trojan times in the *Iliad*. Eyewitness to the events preceding Troy, he is respected by the Achaeans as the incontrovertible authority of tradition (with a contingent of ninety ships, the second largest at Troy, he has the military clout to match). Like Mark Twain's Captain John Nye, Nestor "had a good memory, and a tongue hung in the middle."[57] He draws constantly on the experiences of his youth to advise the Achaeans at Troy. In the first book of the *Iliad* he breaks up the heated quarrel between Achilles and Agamemnon by trimming them both down to size: "Listen to me, for you are both younger than I. And before now I mingled with more heroic men than you, and they never set me at naught. And never since have I seen—nor shall see—such warriors, . . . They hearkened to my counsel and were persuaded by my words. Even so, do you also listen to me, since to be persuaded is better."[58] Far from obsolescent, the events of the past set the heroic code, and Nestor's argument rests on a general belief in the degeneration of the generations. He tells of a generation of monsters and superheroes, the Lapiths and the Centaurs, whose presence on earth is now permanently in the past. Absence of a Panhellenic mythological authority and conflicting local claims to past heroic contact prevent methodical chronology of the heroic age, but Nestor's appeal to the degeneration of the generations reflects an overall consonance in the progressive direction of heroes and mankind away from the gods. Hesiod attempts to order this regression by *genea* in the *Works and Days*.

Five ages record the decline of man from his close proximity to the gods to his present physical and moral decrepitude. Each age is called a *genos*, "generation," but generational affiliation is neither to contemporaneous birth nor shared participation in battle, but to a timeless period which appears and disappears spontaneously without explanation. It is the *process* of degeneration, the inevitable if not rhythmic thrust of mankind towards ineffectual toil and moral contention, that affixes each *genos* except the heroic age to a metallic substance which devaluates from gold to silver to bronze to iron. Hesiod's account is neither internally logical nor unified. The generations decline and revive only to decline again, and yet the scheme is not really cyclical. Eschatalogical visions of the spirits of the past ages (above ground, below ground, in Hades, and the Islands of the Blest) combine with a confused progression and regression of war and peace, justice and internal strife. Plato was so disturbed by the statement that the earth covered the golden race and their spirits roam the surface, that he emended *gaia* (earth) to *moira* (fate).[59] Possible Near Eastern sources for some or all of the metallic ages are a matter of wide speculation, as is the general thrust of the account.[60]

Despite these tremendous difficulties, the overall conception seems clear; the reality of the heroic past, which operates throughout Greek thought as normative but idealized (no longer possible on earth) has a traceable history. E. Meyer and more recently T. Rosenmeyer both insist on the historical integrity of Hesiod's account, that the poet has selected and schematized an assortment of traditional stories with a perception of order and significance.[61] Generational awareness has expanded from an ordering of living memory to an arrangement of the primal and cosmic.

That Hesiod's view of the *genea* has its root in the general belief in the superiority of the past is as clear as the seventeenth-century relationship between traditionalism and the observation that nature decays in old age. But whereas quality of the mind, especially the scientific mind, concerned Goodman and Bacon, the ancient Greeks are more concerned with quality of the physical and social body, from the heroic code to legal constitution. Hesiod's degeneration of the generations, Nestor's constant *exempla* from his youth, Odysseus's refusal to vie with men of old, the basic hierarchy of gods, heroes, and men, introduces the sticky question of progressivism in Greek thought and its influence on generational attitudes.[62] The poetry of Xenophanes or Thucydides' dismissal of Homer have a complex and frequently obscure relation to the rest of Greek thought. To pose the idea of progress is not to accept it; nowhere is this more apparent than in the reflections on technological innovation.

Thucydides' observation that "as in technical skill so in politics, the innovative prevails"[63] suggests a fundamental progressivism, but though the commonplace is advanced as positive, the consequences of Athenian *polupragmasunē* (compulsive activity) are nothing less than disastrous by the end of the Peloponnesian War, and the encomium of her restless energy and innovative spirit carries with it the certain knowledge that it has led to inevitable and self-destructive imperialism. Paradoxically, the youthful nature of technological innovation defies the normal generation hierarchy, and yet ultimately proves less powerful. Daedalus devises the wings that will surmount human limitation, but the simpler behavioral categories by age still whisper their power: cautious and knowledgeable, the old man survives, but he loses young Icarus, who in his reckless youth flies too close to the sun. In Hesiod's five ages, toil and with it technology are a response to the world's decline, as is social innovation, the civilized bestiality of the post-Golden *genea*.[64]

V

In the *logos* of the five ages, neither was generation genetically continuous nor did it have a fixed lifespan. With such immaturely defined characteristics, the notion of the *genos* failed to create a satisfactory historical methodology. But as a concrete term for the span between two births, or one generation, *genea* marks the passage of time itself and is the first tool for its rational ordering. Out of the three generations of a lifetime evolves the systematic ordering of the remote familial past: genealogy, the account (*logos*) of the generations (*genea*).

Hesiod employs the genealogy as the prime organizational element of his account of the race of gods and demigods, the *Theogony*. Time is loosely systematized into paternities and maternities and is nonlinear; successive generations of peer groups—the reigns of Earth and Heaven, Cronus, and Zeus—interrupt the familial succession of physical and metaphysical forces of nature (Night, Ocean, Brilliance, Sun) in Cronus's period, which includes some of the Olympians who wed their children and grandchildren. Generation, then, is an organizational tool, but as in Homer, the two very different criteria for classification—procreation or mutual participation in an event—introduce an intrinsic disorder into the account.

And yet the schematic potential of the genealogy is strong, both to explain the nature of things ("coming into existence")[65] and to organize long periods of time. In the early fifth century Hecataeus of Miletus traced the pedigree of the Spartan kings back to Herakles' immediate progeny, calculating forty years to a generation. But the measuring stick was impossible in that it attempted to reconcile two different kinds of time. There was the immediate past, remembered and mortal, and then there was the heroic past (roughly nine hundred years earlier), commemorated and immortal. The attempt to draw a continuous line from the present to the past was doomed to an impossible paradox, for it was an attempt to unite two modes of existence.[66] And yet belief in divine ancestry was unquestioned; aristocratic claims to an immortal progenitor were legitimized by familial priesthoods and political influence.[67] Despite obvious contradictions between different genealogies, elaborate chronological schemes continued to be worked out as late as Ephorus.

Herodotus makes full use of genealogical reckoning; Herakles is the relatively fixed point (about nine hundred years back) for the Lydian, Median, Egyptian, and Spartan chronologies. However, modern analyses of the rise of historical writing, which is traditionally attributed to Herodotus, take special care to emphasize the difference between Herodotus and the logographers.[68] Apart from stylistic differences (the prose of Hecataeus and Pherecydes being rather simple and monotonous), the genealogical tables differ from history in that they were limited to the reconciliation on a linear scale of the mythological and factual ancestry of kings and aristocratic clans, but attached no further interpretative evaluation to their material. History, however, moves outside any one clan or period, and finds a significance and coherence in widely disparate events.

For Herodotus the subject for historical inquiry is the Persian War, the conflict of East and West in the first part of the fifth century B.C. If Troy was the major event of the heroic past, Marathon—when the Athenian army against all odds and without Spartan hoplite forces charged down the hill and drove the Persians into the sea—was the paradigmatic battle for Athens, and the Persian War became the generational focal point for all Hellas. If not exactly an era, the onslaught of Persian imperialism at least overrode local affiliations and provided a chronological reference point that was more universal than personal memory.

For the historian the determinative effect of an event on a group of people only roughly the same age and from different places becomes a useful categorizational tool. Generation by participation in an event abstracts into metaphor: the city's "ancestry," marked by the generational steps of participation in wars, preserves—or creates—a historical record. So the public eulogy imitates the private; praise of the *progonoi* (ancestors), the funeral oration's stock *topos*, is turned by Thucydides into a "generational" record of Athenian development into a major imperialistic power: "I shall begin with our ancestor . . . they dwelt in the country without break in the succession from generation to generation, and handed it down free to the present time by their valor. And if our more remote ancestors deserve praise, much more do our own fathers, who added to their inheritance the empire which we now possess, and spared no pains to be able to leave their acquisitions to us of the present generation. Lastly, there are few parts of our dominion that have not been augmented by those of us here, who are still more or less in the vigor of life [the "settled age"]."[69] The state's metaphorical genealogy records and orders in concise and recognizable fashion the events which made it great and defines the men who participated in those conflicts as a group.

This special combination of peer group and ancestral generation may in fact partly explain the origins of history. Herodotus's "inquiry" (*historiē*) into how the nations of the East and West grew to be great, and how they came to war against each other takes its ethical lead from tragedy (the fortunes of a state or king are in constant flux; the small become great and the great insignificant). But the ordering principle by which tragic reversal is made coherent within a prose genre is not so much tragic motif as generational *schema*. Generational awareness (mutual participation in an event) was particularly strong after Marathon and Salamis. At the same time organized records of ancestral generation (genealogy) were well established in a prose format. Generation, the classification of ancestors or affiliation by peer group, was already a familiar notion as far back as Homer and was an ordering principle in Hesiod. But Herodotus took the brilliant step of compounding the generational concepts, to adopt the genealogical ordering by steps in ancestry to the events in the birth and stages of the life of a nation, events which were not successive (ancestral) but definitive of the peer group (generational). Just as ancestral genealogy records not all the members of the family but only the first sons, history isolated the first sons of a nation, whether they were kings or wars. Since generation of the state is not a natural occurrence, the historian must trace and explain its origins through whatever methodology seems valid, from king lists to inherited curse, but the orignal choice of subject—how the nations came to be (*genesthai*)[70] and how their rise inevitably led to conflict (criteria for generation)—is fashioned on the traditional Greek concepts of the *genos*. Generational awareness, then, so strong after the Persian War, seems to be the first principle of historical thought.

VI

Generational age distinctions, the claim of aristocratic ancestry, and identification with peer group continued to be asserted throughout the Classical, Hellenistic, and Classical Roman periods. These notions are not unfamiliar; they form the intellectual history of our own conceptual approach to this abstraction just as, linguistically, "generation" preserves its Greek root. There were important rejections and reversals of the traditional beliefs, from Aristophanes' biting parodies of Euripides' genealogical predilection[71] to the philosopher's debunking of common admiration of the long pedigree.[72] Such objections are evidence not only of a new evaluation of generational ideas, but also of the strength of the tradition. Aristocratic affiliation to clan, continuity of the generation from inherited character to inherited occupation, set an ethical and religious standard for the whole society. If generation is a metaphor for existence, generational continuity (of ancestry, stages of life, measurement of the nature of things) is a touchstone of the remarkable stability of tradition throughout the changing ancient world.

Familial continuity and hierarchy of appropriate age distinctions precluded the equivalent of today's wunderkind. The fifteen-year-old tennis star competing against adults, the twenty-four-year-old program manager at NBC, the tenured professor at twenty-nine(!) are matched in Greek literature only in caricature (infant Hermes besting Apollo in mischief) or tragedy. Haimon's "rebellion" from his father in the *Antigone* is, after all, a symptom of extrasocial values; the mode is tragedy, the way of life a tyranny—conventional preconditions of family discontinuity and identity reversal.[73] Ancient Greek attitudes of generational behavior are so fixed that they admit no socially viable alternative.

It would be absurd to argue for a return to the rigid age categories of the past. Vitamins and technological obsolescence have conspired to force a whole society, not just its tragic heroes, to transgress traditional generational definitions. Qualitatively, wisdom has changed: the assertion of novelty, so common that it has lost its newness, negates cumulative perception. In 1963 Susan Sontag wrote of the "inhuman acceleration of historical change"; in 1978 Elizabeth Hardwick notes the "severe reduction" of history itself, which makes people "products" of their decade or half-decade.[74] From the sixties to the seventies the pendulum did not simply swing, it jumped back and forth like a convulsed railroad signal, complete with warning bells and flashing lights. It was quite possible in 1972 for a graduate student to see himself as a wholly different generation from the postdraft undergraduate—a time span of three to five years.

Time has shown that the signals were misleading. Vietnam and post-Vietnam make little difference now to those who never had to fight. The widely various activities of the Class of '70, from doctoral work to political exile, fail to operate as distinctively age-specific or the mutual endeavor of a generation. Instead of identifying stages of life with the seasons as Pythagoras did, we define ourselves generationally by the administrative divisions of the university—undergrad, graduate, pretenure, posttenure, emeritus—or by the *cursus honorum* of the bureaucracy—graduate, junior exec, senior exec, chairman of the board, retired. The categories are at best fuzzy measures of identity; the professional activities of the graduate student and the professor emeritus are basically the same; the twenty-four-year-old vice president shares experience with the sixty-year-old senior executive. Is income bracket the new generational standard?

Greek conceptions of the *genos* view generation as a life sign. But even our ultimate touchstone of generational definition—the birth of sons and daughters—has become insecure: we are refusing to have children. Far more stable is the perception of generations of computers than generations of humankind.[75] The generational concepts on which the Western world grew up, and which until quite recently were still familiar, may have lost their validity in 1978—or at best, generation has lost its reference point.

REFERENCES

[1]*Webster's New International Dictionary*, 3rd ed. (Springfield, Mass.: Merriam, 1961).

[2]Homer, *Iliad*, book 6, lines 145-149. (In subsequent references to classical works, the books, sections, and lines will be cited by number only, e.g., *Iliad* 6.145-149.)

[3]Cf. Achilles' words to his mother, *Iliad* 1.365f.: "You know, why should I tell you who know everything?," which are immediately followed by the whole story. For the possible chronological displacement of the Glaucus episode see Cedric H. Whitman, *Homer and the Heroic Tradition* (Cambridge, Mass.: Harvard University Press, 1958), p. 265.

[4]*Tēlethoōsa*, "flourishing (woods)" forms on the root for *thalos*, which, like the English word "scion," signifies either a new shoot of a tree or a young man. So Pericles compared the state's loss of its young men in battle to the year losing its spring (Aristotle, *Rhetoric* 1.7 and 3.10; cf. Herodotus, 7.162).

[5]Pierre Chantraine, *Dictionnaire Etymologique de la Langue Grecque* (Paris: Klincksieck, 1968-), vol. 1, s.v. *gignomai*, pp. 221-224.

[6]Homer, *Odyssey* 15.196f.

[7]*Iliad* 1.250.

[8]*Odyssey* 3.245.

[9]Donald Wilson Prakken, *Studies in Greek Genealogical Chronology* (Lancaster, Pa.: Lancaster Press, 1943), p. 7ff.

[10]Hartmut Erbse, *Scholia Graeca in Homeri Iliadem* (Berlin: De Gruyter, 1969), vol. 1, A 250a-b.

[11]Dame Rose Macaulay, *Staying with Relations* (New York: Liveright, 1930), p. 57: "I remember an air raid. They woke me up and carried me down to the basement. I am the air-raid generation."

[12]For variant versions of the Neoptolemus/Pyrrhus myth see Joseph E. Fontenrose, *Python* (Berkeley, Calif.: University Press, 1959), pp. 397-401, 418-426.

[13]Adolescence generates the widest vocabulary of all; just as "adolescent, youth, juvenile, teenager, and young adult" may all describe an eighteen-year-old today, *neos*, *bēbē*, *pais*, *kouros* (masc.)/ *kourā* (fem.), *hoploteros*, and later *meirax* (fem.)/*meirakion* (masc.) may indicate the same stage in Greek.

[14]A. W. Gomme, *A Historical Commentary on Thucydides* (Oxford: Clarendon Press, 1956), vol. 2, p. 105.

[15]Cicero, *de Senectute* 20.76.

[16]Solon 27 with ancient citations in M. L. West, *Iambi et Elegi Graeci* (Oxford: Clarendon Press, 1972), vol. 2, pp. 135-137.

[17]Solon (West's numbering), fr. 24.10.

[18]Diogenes Laertius, 8.10.

[19]The middle stages are nearly identical: *neēniskos* and *neēniēs* are both variations of *neos* (young, youth) and are synonymous in Herodotus 3.53 and 4.72; cf. Plato, *Symposium* 211D, where boys (*paides*) and youths (*neāniskoi*) are paired. In short, neither term is especially relevant to persons aged twenty-nine to fifty-one, inclusively.

[20]Pierre Chantraine, *Grammaire Homerique* (Paris: Klincksieck, 1953), vol. 2 p. 75.

[21]*Iliad* 3.215.

[22]*Iliad* 9.160f.

[23]Solon (West's numbering), fr. 18.

[24]*Odyssey* 3.79ff.

[25]Red-figured amphora, Staatliche Museen, Berlin; for an example of the regular distribution of age groups in athletics, see red-figured wine cooler (in the manner of the Phintias painter) Museum of Fine Arts, Boston. Both vases are reproduced in Ludwig Drees, *Olympia* (New York: Praeger, 1968), plates X and 33 respectively.

[26]*Tyrtaeus* (West's numbering), 10.15-32.

[27]See Whitman, *Homer and the Heroic Tradition*, p. 353, n. 70, for full bibliographical reference; cf. H. T. Wade-Gery, *The Poet of the Iliad* (Cambridge: University Press, 1952), p. 70, n. 43.

[28]*Iliad* 11.786f.

[29]Herodotus, 7.13.

[30]Thucydides, 6.12.2.

[31]Thucydides, 6.18.6.

[32]Pindar, *Nemean* 5.6; Aristophanes' *Clouds* 978; and see especially, E. K. Borthwick, "The

'Flower of the Argives' and a Neglected Meaning of *Anthos*," *The Journal of Hellenic Studies*, vol. 96 (1976).

[33] Aeschylus, *Choephoroi* 226.

[34] Anacreon, fr. 417 in Denys Lionel Page, ed., *Poetae Melici Graeci* (Oxford: Clarendon Press, 1962).

[35] Anacreon (Page's numbering), 1.58f.

[36] *Iliad* 6.506f.

[37] *Odyssey* 24.87f.

[38] Anacreon (Page's numbering), fr. 360.

[39] Hermann Fraenkel, *Early Greek Poetry and Philosophy*, trans. Moses Hadas and James Willis (New York: Harcourt Brace Jovanovich, 1962), p. 294.

[40] Sophocles, fr. 718.3; Aeschylus, 7182 in August Nauck, *Tragicorum Graecorum Fragmenta*, ed. Bruno Snell (Göttingen: Vandenhoeck and Ruprecht, 1971).

[41] Plato, Gorgias, 461C. Cf. *Iliad* 3.108f.: "Ever unstable are the minds of the young, but in whatever an old man takes part, he examines the before and after, that the issue may be best for both sides."

[42] *Odyssey* 15.196f.

[43] Aristophanes, *Acharnians* 336.

[44] *Iliad* 24.486f.

[45] John H. Finley, *Three Essays on Thucydides* (Cambridge, Mass.: Harvard University Press, 1967), pp. ix, 79-82. Cf. Plato, *Phaedrus* 240C: *hēlix hēlika terpei* "age enjoys its own age."

[46] Meyer Reinhold, "The Generation Gap in Antiquity," Introduction to *The Conflict of Generations in Ancient Greece and Rome*, ed. Stephen Bertman (Amsterdam: B. R. Gruener, 1976), which I was not able to see until after this article was written.

[47] The author is currently undertaking a study of youthful heroes and heroines in Greek and Roman mythology.

[48] Cf. Sophocles, *Antigone*, 876.

[49] *Iliad* 23.212f.

[50] *Iliad* 13.643f.

[51] *Iliad* 16.857.

[52] *Iliad* 24.725.

[53] *The Times*, November 23, 1963; reprinted in *Obituaries from "The Times" 1961-1970* (Reading, England, 1975); Kenneth O'Donnell and David Powers, *Johnny We Hardly Knew Ye: Memories of John F. Kennedy* (Boston, Mass.: Little, Brown, 1972).

[54] Sophocles (Nauck's numbering), fr. 239.

[55] Diodorus Siculus, 1.58.

[56] Plutarch, *Pericles*, 13.

[57] Mark Twain, *Roughing It*, chap. 35.

[58] *Iliad* 1.259-274.

[59] Plato, *Cratylus* 397E.

[60] See especially, Jean Pierre Vernant, *Mythe et Pensée chez les Grecs* (Paris: Maspero, 1969), pp. 19-47.

[61] Thomas G. Rosenmeyer, "Hesiod and Historiography," *Hermes* 85 (1957): 257-284; Eduard Meyer, "*Hesiods Erga und das Gedicht von den fuenf Menschenge schlechtern*," *Kleine Schriften* (Halle: 1924), vol. 2 pp. 34ff.

[62] In the past two centuries modern scholarship has veered from one side of the issue to the other. Most recently, Ludwig Edelstein, in a posthumous publication entitled *The Idea of Progress in Classical Antiquity* (Baltimore, Md.: The Johns Hopkins Press, 1967), reviews the evidence of Rohde, Comte, Bury, and others in an attempt at a more balanced understanding of ancient progressivism, but he omits such antiprogressive studies as B. A. Van Groningen, *In the Grip of the Past* (Leiden: E. J. Brill, 1953).

[63] Thucydides, 1.71.3.

[64] For the antithetical conception of civilization and nature in Greek thought, see Charles Paul Segal, "The Raw and the Cooked in Greek Literature: Structure, Values, Metaphor," *The Classical Journal* 69 (April-May 1974): 289-309.

[65] So Semonides bases his satire on the nature of women on the notion of *genea* and progenitors; Hugh Lloyd-Jones, *Female of the Species* (London: Duckworth, 1975).

[66] E. g. Chester G. Starr, *The Origins of Greek Civilization* (New York: Knopf, 1961), p. 67.

[67] It has been impossible to discuss the extremely complicated clan structure of ancient Greek society in this article, but see A. R. W. Harrison, *The Law of Athens* (Oxford: Clarendon Press, 1968), vol. 1; and S. C. Humphreys, *Anthropology and the Greeks* (Boston, Mass.: Routledge Kegan Paul, 1978).

[68] E. g. Charles W. Fornara, *Herodotus. An Interpretative Essay* (Oxford: Clarendon Press, 1971), pp. 2, 13ff., reworks the developmental hypothesis, tracing the maturation of the author from

inheritor of genealogical tradition to artistic and sophisticated historical analyst.

[69]Thucydides 2.36, trans. Crawley, *The Complete Writings of Thucydides. The Peloponnesian War* (New York: The Modern Library, Random, 1951).

[70]For evidence of the metaphorical "coming-into-existence" of the nations, see the deliberate repetition of *genētai* in the Prologue to Herodotus's *History* (cf. *gegone*, 1.5.4), or the relative "ages" of each nation, e.g., Scythia is the "youngest" nation.

[71]*Acharnians* 37f.

[72]Plato, *Theataetus* 175A.

[73]Archaic *topoi* associating tyranny with a surfeit of wealth and inevitable collapse of family are collected by David C. Young, *Three Odes of Pindar* (Leiden: E. J. Brill, 1968), p. 9ff.

[74]Susan Sontag, "The Anthropologist as Hero," *The New York Review of Books* (1963), reprinted in *Against Interpretation and Other Essays* (New York: Dell, 1966); Elizabeth Hardwick, "Domestic Manners," *Daedalus* (Winter 1978): 2. Cf. Alexis De Tocqueville in 1835: "If the changes which I have described were gradual, so that each generation at least might have time to disappear with the order of things under which it had lived, the danger would be less; but the progress of society in America is precipitate, and almost revolutionary." [*Democracy in America*, trans. Henry Reeve (Oxford: Galaxy, 1947)].

[75]E. g. Charles J. Elia, "Heard on the Street," *The Wall Street Journal* April 19, 1978); early usage of generational categories for computers cited in *A Supplement to Oxford English Dictionary*, ed. R. W. Burchfield (Oxford: Clarendon Press, 1972), s.v. generation: *Computer Journal* 6.144/1 (1963).

ANNIE KRIEGEL

Generational Difference: The History of an Idea

The fateful act of living in and with one's generation completes the drama of human existence.

Martin Heidegger

Un jour, à Göttingue, dans une brasserie, un jeune Vieille-Allemagne me dit qu'il fallait venger dans le sang des Français le supplice de Conradin de Hohenstaufen que vous avez décapité à Naples (au XIIIème siècle). Vous avez certainement oublié cela depuis longtemps mais pas nous.

Henri Heine

I *Genesis*

IN THE BEGINNING, it was only the simple recognition of a demographic fact: three generations in a century—this was the average yield of the precarious flow of the stream of human life through the ages. One generation meant the time that sons needed to become fathers. And then, by Littré's definition in 1863, it became the *cohort*—the sum of all men of flesh and blood who make up the abstract thickness of time thus carved out; or else, if time was narrowed to a point (the point of departure, or of arrival), the generation became the promotion—of all those who had, in the same year, passed the same test.

It is only at the turn of this century that the generational rift intrudes into social practice and is transformed from a primitive means of accounting into one of the tools for decoding reality. Simultaneously comes a tendency to shrink the concept of the natural space of a generation. More and more, this space becomes confused with a decade—particularly in the American world, where the division into decades (the twenties, the thirties) seems to compensate for both the enormity of territorial space and the thinness of recorded history.

In traditional societies, whose movement is so slow that they seem in retrospect almost immobile, what purpose could a division into generations serve? Reproducing themselves identically, with the same replacing the same, these societies seemed to follow a cyclical pattern—the yearly cycle of the seasons, and the timeless cycle of the gods. When such societies had to conceptualize discontinuity, a possible rupture of the cycle, they had no way to imagine middle solutions: thought turned at once to Apocalypse. And even when the pace of change increased somewhat, when mankind in its entirety truly entered history, these societies encountered innovation only from time to time; in-

23

stances of realized potentialities for change were too few and far between. One generation was much too short a time. More substantial units had to be employed; hence, the era (Christian), the epoch (modern, defined in contrast to the ten centuries of the Middle Ages), the century (of Louis the XIV).

By the eighteenth century, the times for which a century was an adequate yardstick came to an end—even Daudet's formula about the "stupid nineteenth century" can only reflect his ill-temper. The century can no longer measure a reality overflowing the boundaries of such a constraining concept.

Once more, we are led back to the decisive turning point of the Enlightenment, and to the revolutions which followed it, in order to examine the new conditions which gave social effect to the generational theme.

First, life expectancy, although more widely varied by social class and shorter than today, nevertheless had become a largely collective reality. Life was no longer an adventure whose evils were so totally individual that one could not think in terms of a life expectancy about the same as one's general age group. Duration, the considerable increase in one's personal chances to survive for a calculable period of time, thus engendered reasons to settle down and form links with others of one's own age range. At the same time, confusion and disorder, sharp disparities in age groups within the family or local community, due to the extreme unevenness in lifetimes, were disappearing. Agnès and her old fogey were a commonplace occurrence when the state of matrimony was so frequently interrupted by the death of one spouse, when it was fully expected that widowers would remarry, and when such remarriage entailed, for women as well as for men, looking to the pool of available single boys and girls for a new mate. The reduction of the age difference between spouses (a difference that today has all but disappeared, even when a second marriage follows a divorce, because of the lack of available prospects of a really different age) thus contributed to the objective creation of age groups, clearly demarcated and separate, because their members are destined to go together through the basic steps of childhood, adolescence, marriage, parenthood. Contemporaneity, once approximate, has become strict.

If the generational fact has emerged as one of the more constraining social parameters, it is also because other attributes that previously nurtured a sense of individual identity have, in modern society, lost some of their structuring significance. The decline of the automatic inheritance of condition, of estate, and of status, which meant that everyone had a perceptible and stable social identity from birth, has led us to search for another principle to help us classify our individual destinies intelligibly. Moreover, since the dynamic sector of the new society not only was supposed to, but, in fact, did rest on selection by a certain type of merit—by ability as one used to say—what could be easier than to evaluate one's personal trajectory, one's career, by comparing it to that of one's friends who started at the same time? In France, for instance, we know well the role played in the formation of political, economic, or cultural elites by *les Annuaires*, in which successive classes of alumni of the Grandes Ecoles carefully list the level of grade achieved by their members on a hierarchical scale. To be happy, to have "succeeded," one must have climbed each step at a given age. To climb it six months earlier than the norm is cause for elation; six months later, feverish alarm.

This is also probably one of the ways in which the modern state has penetrated social life, to regulate and to legislate it. Obsessed by the thought of rationalizing process in order to maximize the effectiveness of its social investments, the state would not rest until it had fixed, uniformly and compulsorily, the age at which one must enter kindergarten, learn to read, graduate from high school, serve time in the army. This practice is rendered all the more meaningful by the simultaneous and increasing uncertainty of the Catholic Church, whose relationship to modernity is particularly problematic, about the "right age" for receiving successive sacraments, particularly baptism and first communion.

Lastly, it must be recognized that the advent of division by generations comes not just by the high probability that each of us may live a "whole" life, nor even by the transformation of the most dynamic sector of society from a roughly hierarchical *fact* of status to a network of hierarchical *paths*, though restricted by the differences of wealth or prestige. This change is also a result of the fact that in the past two centuries the problem of the succession of age groups has become a key question. This succession, while it remains in part the replacing of same by same, is more and more the replacing of same by other, by displacement or by innovative addition. The distance between age groups then is no longer simply a passage of time, filled by nothing except the passage of life itself and its ability to produce in turn new life, but a sum of changes which impose singularity on a generation by its mores and behavior. A generation is now defined as the generation of electricity, of television, or of blue jeans.

And at the same time, the birth of generational difference is coupled with another birth: that of the intelligentsia, insofar as the latter marks the intersection of two distinct groups which, in fact, are both producers as well as consumers of change—intellectuals and revolutionaries. We must recall here that, at the beginning of the nineteenth century, slogans and programs in which key words refer to age enter the political vocabulary for the first time: "Young Italy," "Young Germany," "Young Europe." Only a little earlier, in Germany, the spiritual climate and its devotees—intellectual, artistic and literary—were divided by, incarnated in, and imbued with the idea of generational succession and generational conflict: the generation of *Sturm und Drang*, the romantic generation. And meanwhile, from about 1825 onward with the Decembrists, and then about every twenty years—1840, 1860, 1880—Russia registered its moods and its changes of course through the dialogue, often brutal and sometimes frightful, of Fathers and Sons.

II *Connotations*

It is well known that Mannheim was the first thinker who attempted to integrate the generational theme into a theory of social function in which other types of conflict relationships—notably class struggle—were seen as the driving force of progress. Robert Wohl, in a fascinating study,[1] has since examined in great detail the emergence, just before the First World War, not only of the generational fact itself, but of the awareness of its importance that writers, men of letters, and essayists in the different European cultures manifested at about the same time.

Yet, whether it takes the form of a static situation—the existence and coexistence of distinct generations; or whether it takes the form of conflict—intragenerational or intergenerational struggle; it seems to have been impossible to extricate the very concept of generation from the web of connotations that obscured it.

FIRST CONNOTATION: GENERATION OR YOUNG GENERATION?

In traditional societies, the only truly meaningful age discontinuity was that which isolated the elders. Still they did not yet represent an age grouping (after all, the sad "retirement" of today is not comprised of the *elders*, but rather of the *old*). The elders then were happy members of society. Far from embodying the frightful threat of physical and mental decline (old age as "shipwreck"), they finally had reached harmony, wisdom, and even triumphant fecundity. Philémon and Baucis for harmony, Abraham and Sarah for fecundity; these couples are smiling (the former) and laughing (the latter), proclaiming the privileges of grand old age.

We must wait until the nineteenth century to observe, in Europe, the reversal of sensibilities through which a generation became not so much men who shared the same age as men who shared youth.

At this point, the mechanisms and social supports that, in the nineteenth century, contributed to the elaboration of an ideology of youth are becoming better understood—how youth came to be seen as a period of time at once ephemeral, specific, and privileged.

The fact is that such an ideology arose first of all out of new conditions. The development of industrial society both demanded and allowed a space of time between childhood (freed of economic obligations) and adulthood (the time to settle down into marriage and work)—a kind of interlude devoted to apprenticeships, whose economic consequences could be deferred, and which therefore had to be supported by family or society.

In a rather paradoxical way, the increasing differentiation and complexity of professions, trades, and technology within the process of industrialization swelled the ranks of those considered young—apprentices and students—even at a time when the age groups between fifteen and twenty-five were in overall decline.

It is therefore not surprising that it was students, including those going to the Grandes Ecoles—young gentlemen—who offered the first model of "Bohemian life," a life-style appropriate for an interclass group. The women these students had as their mates were not students, except, after 1880, in the Judeo-Russian student circles; they were wage workers from the popular classes, these "Mimi Pinsons"—seamstresses, laundry women, milliners. Yet they were a one-generation group, as the song points out:

> And hurray for students, mother!
> Hurray for the students,
> They have women, but they don't have children.

Within this framework, the school and the conscription army were institutions which measured time (either time largely defined as the duration of studies or of military service, or internal time, broken down into classes, terms, or years crowned and blessed by final examinations); these institutions greatly contributed to a division of their population founded in time.

Moreover, the school and the army, by initiating pupils and recruits in the most recent scientific discoveries, in the latest technical inventions, in the most modern works of art, reinforced the two virtues which have been considered as the very essence of youth: its *purity*, which stemmed above all from protection against the contaminating influence of money since, even if poor, youth was not expected to make money its concern, and its *enthusiasm*, which stemmed from freedom from any routine or repetitive tasks since youth had no role other than to acquire knowledge.

By the same token, the school and the army bestowed upon the sons knowledge to which the fathers had not had access: the effects of this reversal have gradually come to upset all relationships between familial strata. No longer is familiarity with the world and its ways the privileged prerogative of adulthood; on the contrary, adulthood has come to mean increasing banishment into a status of stranger to modernity.

However, neither the school nor the army were truly new institutions, except insofar as they now involved an important proportion, or even the totality, of the age group they mobilized and enrolled. In order to manifest its congruence with youth itself, the ideology of youth had to produce an institutional form exclusively its own inspiration. Thus arose the *youth movement*—archetypically represented by the German and Austrian *Ingendbewegung*, foreshadowing a great but suspect destiny. Whether patterned on a military model, eventually adapted to colonial war (from the military man to the militant, from the scout to the boy scout), or whether modeled on educational forms adapted to after-school or extracurricular activities (from schooling to education)—youth organizations are a new form in associative life, since they are based on the segregation of one segment of the age pyramid. As they multiplied, either as specialized appendages organically linked to adult bodies in each spiritual, cultural, or political family, or as radically independent organs able to focus the innovative zeal—even in time the rebellious or revolutionary zeal—of those soon expected to "enter a career," youth movements contributed to the consolidation of "generational consciousness."

Youth movements were particularly well suited to this task because they had to define their particular place among the various movements which, at the turn of the century, represented the *social* movements for which the labor movement, in its cooperative, unionist, and political forms, was the model and the federator. It became obvious that since the social movements in general aimed at leading a general process of emancipation or, later, of liberation—with the labor movement dedicated to the emancipation of wage-earners, with nationalist movements dedicated to the liberation of oppressed nationalities and the creation of independent national states, with feminist movements and minority movements of all kinds—youth movements had as their purpose the emancipation of those called the young. Such an emancipation has as its adversary, to define it roughly and abstractly, the whole of established society. In these conditions, youth movements, while they essentially drew their membership from the middle social strata, aligned themselves almost automatically with the forces

of protest and revolution. The latter did not necessarily benefit from this align-
ment. Young people—among whom students or those who resembled them
held on to positions of leadership—served, albeit not always knowingly, as vehi-
cles for the ideas, the values, and the interests of the middle class strata from
which they came. Moreover, even if they intended to take on society in general
in its oppressive and decadent aspects, they were inevitably drawn into the
pitfall of equating the daily incarnation of the enemy with, simply, adults. It is
not by chance that in nearly all countries of Western Europe socialist youth
movements ended up substituting for the distant figure of Capital the very present figure of the adult Party as the target of their attacks and protests.

SECOND CONNOTATION: FROM AGE COMMUNITY TO COMMUNITY OF SENIORITY

Age is only a countable objective datum; seniority is the result of steps at
least partly voluntary. It implies joining, personal affiliation. The date of birth
is mere fate; but the date of entry into any sort of institution, particularly if the
latter is meant to give a meaning to life, or even to transform it, represents the
choice of one's destiny. No one can escape the reality of belonging to an age
group. It is a fact established once and for all, but it yields little meaning, being
absolutely general and passive. Seniority, on the other hand, forces us to look
back to a significant selection between alternatives, choices the person had to
make. It is worth noting that in communist terminology there are no *old* people
but only *seniors*, as though every person, even without particular commitment or
claim to fame, deserves by the evening of life the final and modest reward of
seniority.

It is all the more true that seniority binds generational communities more
strongly than age because of the fact that, since the nineteenth century, both
social and geographical mobility have vastly increased. Whole societies built
upon successive waves of immigration, as in American or Israeli society, have
based at least one of their internal hierarchies—and certainly not the least operational—on the date of arrival in the country, either that of the individual or that
of his lineage or group. Within global societies apparently tied to the soil for a
long time, microsocieties of immigrants—from one continent to another, from
countryside to city, from old town to new town, from one occupation to another, from one corporation to another—define and organize themselves according
to the wanderings of their members.

One of the most curious manifestations of the advantage of seniority over
age is the compensation which seems to operate between the different types of
mobility: while long-distance geographical mobility increases, the mobility of
the labor force, once it is integrated into a given enterprise, regresses considerably. It is as though after a few necessary experiments early in professional
life, the norm becomes to "dig one's heels in," to stay put. Membership, no
longer in a craft or a trade, but in a corporation, is so laden with meaning that
even the labor union press, when addressing its workers, uses the corporate
name of the employer to signify their unity as workers: they are called "les Lip,"
"les Michelin," "les Boussac." What would the proletarians of the Belle Epoque
have thought of that: they who held that the pride of the worker meant that he

should hand in his resignation, if not every other day, at least as often as he saw fit, to show that "men are free in a Republic"; they who would never have accepted the loss of their individual identities (much less the nickname given to them by their workmates) in favor of such a collective identity, and the boss's at that!

The shift from age to seniority as the cement of generational unity can finally be captured in the move from the term *jeune classe* to the expression *young generation*. Today, jeune classe is an antiquated expression, evoking nostalgia. Yet, it was a cruel expression when it described the enrollment of the conscripted, the *drafted*, those drafted into the war. Veterans of the First World War were still defined by the class to which they belonged: it had been bad luck to be in the class of 1914 or 1915. And when a republican grade-school teacher would summon his pupils by clapping his hands and calling out, "Come on, the Jeune Classe!" the "blue line of the Vosges" could be seen in his eyes, because his students were also "the soldiers of Revenge." In the thirties of the Popular Front, the call to the "young generation" rang more peaceful; the appeal was to *the union of the young generation*, which could show the way and complete the union of the working class and of the masses.

THIRD CONNOTATION: GENERATION—MASS OR COLLECTION OF CHOSEN TYPICAL INDIVIDUALS?

In theory, a generation could only be the sum of all those who reach the same age or the same seniority at the same time; thus the concept of generation should be biased toward the mass, individualized only by age or by seniority. In fact, things are quite different. The concept of generation is fundamentally elitist. In social practice, it does not refer to an interval of time, but to an energy field that provides a framework for one or several experiences held to be crucial and worth remembering. A generation is only constituted when a system of references has retrospectively been set up and accepted as a system of collective identification. From the plurality of undertakings which may have aroused the interest and held the attention of members of the same potential generation, only one or two undertakings have a chance to be selected a posteriori, and their protagonists chosen to represent their contemporaries. To speak of the generation of the Résistance in France or of that of the Independence in Algeria is—unlike that of the *alioth* in Israel—neither to speak only of the résistance fighters, who were in limited numbers, nor to generalize excessively and imply that everyone in France was a "résistant" and everyone in Algeria a "patriot." Rather, it is to consider that the label for general use has been imprinted by an elite, which has imposed its model. The issue of whether the *gauchistes* of the sixties are entitled to embody a generation has been much disputed, because in real numbers (even for all tendencies taken together) they were so few—representing less than 5 percent, it seems, even within the most favorable of groups, the students. But the legitimacy of paradigmatic representation has no quantitative basis. It stems purely from the ability to achieve recognition by providing the maximum differentiating identity.

Under these conditions, the generational rift appears to be an intermediate structuring mechanism between the macro-group, the total age group, and the subgroups, too numerous, dispersed and transient, like bands—particularly bands of youths. Certainly, nothing can completely take away the arbitrary and even manipulative aspect built into the definition of each particular generation. The history of literature is full of such excesses, which consist in the very subjective presentation of the whole creative output of a period as belonging to one given school. For instance, the writers of the period immediately following the First World War are collectively referred to as "the generation of the surrealists"; this is all very well, as long as one remembers that the two geniuses of that time, Proust and Kafka, had nothing to do with surrealism.

III *Effectiveness*

If, despite the uncertainties suggested by these diverse connotations, we resort inevitably to the use of the generational theme, it is because it is undeniably effective.

In a society fascinated by the search for a way to eradicate inequalities, intergenerational inequalities actually appear likely to threaten the progress made in the area of social inequalities. The equalization of income, of status, of interests may conceivably be brought nearer by global yet differentiated policies. Even the equality of opportunities within a given generation may be increased through certain measures—though it is as yet unclear whether such measures may not have extremely unfortunate side effects. The current debate on the means used to fight race and sex discrimination through quotas—themselves inversely discriminatory—illustrates the difficulty in resolving the abstract universalism of law, equal for all and thereby a principal condition of democracy, with the concrete uniqueness of actual equality, which presupposes taking into consideration initial inequalities.

But this difficulty is slight compared to the intergenerational inequalities resulting from the irregularities of the demographic flow. All Western countries are dominated today by the very long-range effects of the alternate weighting and unweighting, since the beginning of this century, of small classes—classes depleted by historical cataclysms such as wars or revolutions—and of full classes—classes left intact by historical circumstance.

In a medium-size country like France, the relatively sharp changes from the small classes of the early twentieth century, to those brutally deprived of their male members by the First World War, to the even more depleted classes of the interwar period, to the fuller classes since 1935, to the very full ones from 1945 to the early 1960s, and finally again to smaller classes since 1964, and even smaller since 1973—these changes have produced successive generations whose destiny has been partially formed and unified by their weight in relation to that of the preceding and following generations.

For those belonging to the classes of the immediate post-World War I period, the massacre of the young officers who had graduated in the classes of 1912, 1913, and 1914 meant that countless positions, jobs, and roles had become vacant in all spheres of society; this led to an ephemeral but marked shift to a more youthful establishment; hence, the Roaring Twenties.

For those belonging to a smaller class when, after World War II, the education and care of the baby-boom children created vast personnel needs, this demand represented a collective good fortune for their generation—born at the turn of the thirties—and substantially repaid them for the hardships of their childhood and adolescence.

On the other hand, the full classes born in the fifties, today reaching the age of responsibility, find themselves, after an adolescence generally protected from hunger and great hardships, caught between the preceding classes, smaller but by now firmly entrenched and benefiting from a longer life expectancy, and the new smaller classes which follow them, and who require no more than the replacement of present equipment and institutions.

These are major demographic facts whose importance is coming to be correctly weighed and generally taken into account in the choice and direction of professions. Thus, in the sixties, the teaching profession attracted, all at the same time, persons of the same age, whose simultaneous aging is beginning to create serious problems, particularly that of promotion into the few desirable positions—which of course gives rise to constant competition between the aging applicants. Of course, this fact could not by itself explain the overall allegiance of teachers to political options on the left and extreme left of the political spectrum; however, it may be one factor which contributes to the persistence of this allegiance.

These major demographic facts bear equally on the evolution of mentality and mores. For instance, the appearance of a new type of woman—the *garçonne* of the twenties, with her short hair and freed waist—is best understood as linked to the massive entry of women into the industrial-labor force caused by their becoming heads of household as wives of enlisted men or as war widows. Even if peace, and the homecoming of soldiers, brought many of these women back home, their return did not turn back the clock. Women have learned that they should prepare their daughters to be able to raise a family single-handedly (hence the expansion of women's education), and that in any case the prosperity of the household is greatly increased when the woman, instead of restricting herself to domestic tasks, diverts some of her energy away from motherhood toward an economically rewarding occupation. Inhabitants of the working class districts of a city like Paris remember that the first beauty salons for women opened in 1916-1917, at a time when women were working in the war industries in large numbers.

The influence of the reversal of the age differential between spouses on the pace of the evolution of mores, and the role it played in the emergence of a new type of young couple within which the demarcation between masculine and feminine roles began to blur, is perhaps less well understood. This reversal in age differential came about because a significant number of women from the doubly depleted class of the Second World War had to look for their spouses in the fuller classes that followed them, and thus they married men younger than themselves.

Not only do intergenerational inequalities make a case for the effectiveness of the concept of generation, generational consistencies do also. Here, one should cite the data from public opinion polls and electoral analyses, but such data are well known. The age variable is perhaps not the one which produces the largest differences, but it is never negligible in any area.

However, I would prefer to emphasize the effectiveness of the concept of generation in a field which belongs to it exclusively; I have in mind the creation of a collective memory and the building of a tradition.

It is no accident that the generational dimension seems best adapted to a contemporary history. For one thing, history now unfolds itself globally, although it springs from unevenly developed sectors, situated at unequal distances from the most active centers and foci, and operating with different value systems. This creates encounters, violent or peaceful, interpenetrations, submersions, persisting patterns of all kinds. All these phenomena trace lines of fracture and discontinuity manifested by expansions, regressions, start-ups, catching-ups, blockages, and a whole gamut of mixtures. From all these new events, the protagonists and their contemporaries have drawn part of their own identity as well as the collective experience which makes them a generation, such as the generation of "awakenings" or that of "Independences."

On the other hand, elements of change now prevail over the slow, heavy movements of classical history. Since the eighteenth century, history has been characterized by a breathless succession of revolutions and restorations of all kinds: demographic, technical, economic, cultural, religious, social, political. Three types of events have especially provided the major milestones between which generations have been sacrificed: war, depression, and revolution. From that point of view, World War I has been the ultimate event: it broke world history in two and, of course, not only European history. It should not be surprising that it provided the framework on which a generation emerged, a generation officially proclaimed to be the "Génération du Feu."

Paradoxically, however, we may wonder whether, since 1945 and thus for more than thirty years, it is not rather the absence of a universal event likely to unify the memory of the whole of humanity that has given the search for generational identity its almost desperate character. No writer of memoirs, no chronicler, no autobiographer seized by the furious desire to reduce reality to the world of the "I" can resist the temptation to justify his undertaking by making it appear collective, and to introduce his subject by stating that "to belong to the generation that . . ."

An event in fact as limited as May 1968 in Paris has, a decade later, been subjected to an exegesis which inevitably had to start off by situating itself in relation to the "generation of 1968": a generation which, incidentally, had at the time chosen its own models, its heroes and its titles from the "generation of the Résistance," even speaking of a "New Résistance," although never truly spelling out what and whom this New Résistance was fighting, except in a metaphorical way.

This rather artificial insistence on dates which may rather quickly lose their meaning and their resonance still has one advantage: it allows us to outline the three segments which any event, limited as it may be, produces as soon as it has become a "knot," that is, a point of origin and of reference for a generation. A first segment, the narrowest, remains faithful to the event in its literal segregation. Struck by the event as by lightning, this group will rearrange the rest of its life according to what it feels it has immutably learned at that time. A second segment, a little larger, will retain the event's imprint, will turn it into a personal object of nostalgia, of anniversary celebration, of thought or of knowledge, but will cease to define itself in relation to it. We can find this group, enriched and matured by the experience, integrated into the best adapted strata of the larger society. Finally a third segment, the biggest, has retained practically nothing from the event and has become woven into the uniform texture of the social fabric.

IV Wear

This proliferation of the generational idea and its vulgarizing, are they not in the end signs of some sort of premature wear? Do we not mistake for a new generation what is in fact only a *new wave*, easily recognized when it is emerging, but basically destined to be covered by the next wave and to disappear very quickly into the human ocean?

Let us examine, for instance, what is really meant by the cliché of the impossibility of intergenerational communication. On the one hand, it is true that we feel that each generation can only speak to and for itself. Those who were, for a season, called the New Philosophers were not revealing anything previously unknown about the germs of barbarism bred by the Soviet socialist system; however, they were saying it in their time, in their turn, and for a generation which, according to some, had at first accepted the idea that socialism deserved to be the end of history.

Nothing is ever said once and for all. Nothing is ever learned beyond the need for relearning. Experience is not transmissible, and the worst consequence of death is that it annihilates in one blow this form of primitive accumulation—acquired culture. But what of it! This sort of catching up which each generation in fact has to do for itself, and which thus forces it to speak to itself, to teach itself, does not do away with the general discourse which is that of a whole society, not of one generation. In this discourse, the voices which are blended, which answer each other or struggle against each other, do not represent generations, but spirited "families." Yet, there is indeed a manner of speaking and of writing which comes recognizably from a generation which learned Latin and Greek, in which one rubbed shoulders with "good authors" and the noble rhythms of their prose, and another manner that tells of a generation that learned to read with "modern teaching methods" and phonetic spelling, and whose easy-going styles of thought and of dress match their sloppy style of comic-strip writing. And so what! The way in which things are expressed is worth something, but it is not everything. In the end, anyone who likes to read will read authors from all generations—though some will be better liked than others—because, while generations may differ about second-rate authors which are peculiarly their own, they unite and agree on which minds and works truly capture their time. For the thirties and forties who else but Céline—alas—could be hailed as the common writer of genius?

The point is that it takes time and distance to appreciate and discern what is really a break from that which only appears, episodically, to be a break. We may think we are observing the spirit of a generation when we are only witnessing a fashion—a fashion so impertinent that it denies having any purpose except that of giving a charming disguise to what is—and would be even more were it not for its adornments—a vale of tears. Is it worth reminding the reader of the grotesque sociological musings on the relation between miniskirts and women's liberation?

Generational specificity is itself a fiction: in truth, all successive generations resemble each other in their laments as in their triumphs. Is there even one which, in times of depression, has not called itself a lost generation? From Barrès to Remarque, from Remarque to Hemingway, disenchantment has the same ring of bitterness or of anger.

At one time, there were attempts to test out the validity of the generational theory by envisaging it, not at the level of one generation only, but as a series made up of three successive generations. According to anthropologists and sociologists, this represented the total time and the stages necessary for an immigrant community to become assimilated and blended into its new society, whether or not it had enriched the latter with traditions from the old country. This "trigenerational" view was in fact spontaneously systematized as early as 1840 when an observer named Ben Levi wrote in the *Archives Israélites*, which were published in Paris:

> The Grandfather believes, the father doubts and the son denies. The grandfather prays in Hebrew, the father reads the prayer in French, and the son does not pray at all. The grandfather observes all festivals, the father only observes Yom Kippur, the son does not observe any. The grandfather is still a Jew, the father has become an Israelite, and the son is simply a deist . . . unless he is an atheist, a Fourrierist, or a Saint-Simonist. [2]

As it happens, the first problem is that the time and type of acculturation and assimilation seem to vary considerably between different immigrant groups and different societies. A young French historian, J. P. Brunet, has studied in great detail the formation of the population of a fairly large city in the greater Paris suburbs.[3] Saint-Denis, which had only 22,051 inhabitants in 1861, before industrialization, had 71,759 by 1911. By 1891, barely 20 percent of the city's population was native-born. For most people from the provinces (from Northern France, Alsace and Lorraine, from the Massif Central, Burgundy and the Nivernais), and for most foreigners (Belgians, Germans, Swiss, or even English), integration is almost immediate since, from the first generation on, they intermarry without taking into account their place of origin: what counts is that they live in Saint-Denis. There are two important exceptions to this rule: for those from the provinces, migrants from Brittany; and for foreigners, Italians and Jews, who for the most part maintain the practices of endogamous marriage and grouped residency.

The second problem is that in communities which strongly resist absorption, the three generations have long since passed, and the expected assimilation has not been completed. In the case of France, where we know the vast assimilative power of a society and a culture which demand a high degree of unity and centralism in their rules and values, the Jewish community started on its way toward integration or—as it was called in the nineteenth century, its assimilation—190 years ago. This represents at least ten generations, including the three or four living today. And yet, the feeling of belonging to a separate community is much stronger now that it was fifty years ago. Jewish identity is so laden with meaning that it is claimed even as primary identity by the children of mixed marriages; indeed, even the percentage of these intermarriages has declined markedly from the level it had reached immediately after World War II.

Clearly, certain exceptional events may have disrupted what should normally have happened. The Dreyfus Affair, the Holocaust, the massive stream of immigrants first from Eastern Europe and then from North Africa have ensured that forgetting would be impossible. On the other hand, the decline of the nation-state, or its reorganization in relation to other institutional levels, which were becoming newly, or again relevant—the supranational European level, the infranational level of once submerged regions and provinces—has contributed to the fading of the fascination for Jacobin-like Frenchness.

However, one curious fact must be pointed out. The oldest component of the Jewish community in France, the Jews of Alsace-Lorraine who, moreover, had spearheaded the drive for assimilation since the early nineteenth century, are a group whose singular identity and coherence now seem to have reached some kind of "cruising speed." It is as if, as a first stage, contact with the dominant society and culture intoxicated and clearly won over a more or less important fraction of the minority group, depriving it of its most marginal or fragile elements. The central nucleus, if it has resisted and persisted in its own logic (albeit at the price of internal rearrangements) and has retained its vitality, is then capable of maintaining itself as the focus of a lasting experience.

Thus was French Judaism drawn, for example, into a process of secularization which, since the Enlightenment, has penetrated all levels of the *civil* (as opposed to the state and the clerical); of the profane (as opposed to the sacred); of the laity (as opposed to the religious); of agnosticism, of free-thinking, of unbelief (as opposed to all forms and expressions of faith); as well as all shades of liberalism, of the private and individual (as opposed to the public and the collective). Following in the wake of this process, French Judaism was, on the one hand, forced to transform itself into a religion capable of coexisting with other, Christian, persuasions, and, on the other, constrained to give up its religious character. Deep and dangerous as these mutations may be, they still did not mean that the eventual crumbling of French Judaism could be predicted—as later events demonstrated. Other forces for persistence did, as it happened, replace the old disrupted patterns, particularly through the interplay between the religious and the national spheres.

In this way we reach an understanding of what enables a historical phenomenon to endure. Far from being its ability to command the identification of a generation, it is rather its capacity to get successive generations to accommodate to the logical nucleus which, for this particular phenomenon, ensures vitality. This nucleus can tolerate the emergence, within itself, of variants, but cannot withstand that which is truly incompatible with it.

In conclusion, if, on the one hand, the Socialist Party in Spain has a more certain future than the Communist Party, and if the French Communist Party, on the other hand, has a more secure present and future than the Socialist Party, it is because the Spanish Socialist Party and the French Communist Party have been roughly able to pattern their internal generational heirarchy to the generational distribution of the overall population in their respective countries. The French Socialist Party and the Spanish Communist Party show huge disparities between their own age pyramid and that of their nations.

REFERENCES
[1]Forthcoming. I thank the author, professor of history at UCLA, for having made the manuscript available to me.
[2]Ben Levi, in *Archives Israélites*, 1 (February 1847).
[3]J. P. Brunet, "Une banlieue ouvrière: Saint-Denis, 1890-1939" (Thèse, Doctorat d'Etat, Sorbonne, 1978), book edition forthcoming.

APPENDIX—WHO ARE THE LEADERS OF THE FRENCH COMMUNIST PARTY?

Once again, the question is asked: what really prevents the Communist Party from changing? How can we explain that a party—whose general secretary at the time, Pierre Semard, already called it fifty years ago, not without bitterness, a "flow-through party"—has managed to remain so constant and, one might say, as Stalinist as at the height of Stalinism even though its Stalinism is now sporting the French flag?

As is so often true, one element of the answer to this puzzle can be found in the data. We need only observe the radical difference between the pyramid of the political generations within the mass of party members, and the pyramid of these same political generations within the ruling group of the party.

The date of membership is not available for all members; however, for our purposes we may use as an approximation the report prepared by Claude Poperen, acting in the name of the *commission des mandats*, and given to the most recent Party Congress (the twenty-third, which took place in February 1976). Among the 1,522 delegates to this Congress, who represented the body of party activists, we find:[1]

Number	Percent	Membership date
77	5.1	1920-1944
184	12.1	1945-1957
328	21.6	1958-1967
475	31.2	1968-1972
458	30.1	1972-1976

Thus over four-fifths (82.9 percent) of delegates had been militants only under the Fifth Republic, and close to two-thirds only during the past ten years.

This pyramid of what we may call "political generations" (not defined by the *age* of members, but by their *seniority* in the party), seems at first glance to match roughly the pyramid of political generations within the ruling group.[2]

Thus, if one includes in the ruling group (in a broad sense) the members of the Political Bureau, the regular members of the Central Committee, the substitute members of this same committee, and the members of the Central Commission for Financial Control, we find, in relation to the date at which each of these members joined the above ruling group, a pyramid which looks as follows:

Number	Percent	Date of entry into the ruling group
4	3.1	1920-1944
19	15.2	1945-1957
36	28.5	1958-1967
42	33.3	1968-1972
25	19.8	1972-1976

The match between the distribution of political generations within the body of members and the ruling group seems to be a satisfactory one, given a natural staggering and the appropriate time needed to go from one to the other:

Date of Membership or Entry into Ruling Group	Members (percent)	Ruling Group (percent)
1920-1944	5.1	3.1
1945-1957	12.1	15.2
1958-1967	21.6	28.5
1968-1972	31.2	33.3
1972-1976	30.1	19.8

Deceptive illusion. In fact, if we take as a criterion for the generational pyramid of the ruling group, not the date of their entry into that group, but, as for members, their date of membership in the party, the results are quite different:

Date of Membership	Political Bureau		Central Committee (Regular)		Central Committee (Substitute)		Financial Control Commission	Total	
1920-1944	10	47.6%	29	39.1%	0		3	42	29.3%
1945-1957	8	38.5%	37	50%	11	45.8%	2	58	40%
1958-1967	3	19%	8	10.9%	11	45.8%		41	28.6%
1968-1972	0		0		2	8.3%		2	3.9%
1972-1976	0		0		0			0	

It now strikes the eye immediately that the figures do not correlate:

Date of Membership	Members (percent)	Ruling Group (percent)
1920-1944	5.1	29.3
1945-1957	12.1	40.0
1958-1967	21.6	28.6
1968-1972	31.2	3.9
1972-1976	30.1	0

Thus, although nearly two-thirds of the members have been in the party for less than ten years, it is only true of 3.9 percent of the ruling group. On the other hand, more than two-thirds of this ruling group joined the party *before* 1958, over twenty years ago. They came to a party which was then the pride of international Stalinism. They must have felt comfortable with it, since they stayed in it. Thus, the renewal of the ruling group has since then been a pseudo-renewal: it only takes place within categories of members who joined when the French Communist Party was the "best French Stalinist." Such is its stable nucleus.

REFERENCES

[1] Cf. *Cabiers du Communisme*, March 1976. The breakdown into the five generations used here is the one employed by the communist author of the report.

[2] All data concerning the membership dates of members of the ruling group as well as the date of their entry into that group were kindly provided by the Secretariat of the Communist Party to Jean Elleinstein, *Le Parti Communist* (Grasset, 1976), pp. 185 ff. The definition of the ruling group is that used by Elleinstein. The computations are mine.

Translated by Elisabeth Hirsch

MATILDA WHITE RILEY

Aging, Social Change, and the Power of Ideas[1]

> Individuals who belong to the same generation, who share the same year of
> birth, are endowed, to that extent, with a common location in the historical
> dimension of the social process.
>
> Karl Mannheim[2]

WE KNOW THAT DEATH IS INEVITABLE. And we are widely led to believe that
aging over the life course is also inevitable, that the process of growing up and
growing old must inexorably follow an immutable pattern. Yet a principal tenet
of the sociology of age, a newly emerging scientific specialty,[3] is that aging is
not inevitably prescribed, that there is no "pure" process of aging, that the ways
in which children enter kindergarten, or adolescents move into adulthood, or
older people retire are not preordained. In this view, the life course is not fixed,
but widely flexible. It varies with social change—not only with the changing
nature of the family, the school, the workplace, the community, but also with
changing ideas, values, and beliefs. As each new generation (or cohort)[4] enters
the stream of history, the lives of its members are marked by the imprint of
social change and in turn leave their own imprint.

The theme of this essay concerns the relationship between the life course
and social change. It concerns the dynamic process by which social change
molds the course of our lives and by which the course of our collective lives
creates social change. The essay touches first upon this theme in general and its
intellectual background, then focuses on one aspect of the theme, on the meanings of our lives as we age from birth to death. The meanings we attach to the
life course, the theories of aging we espouse, have power over individual lives.
For human lives in the aggregate, too, these meanings have power to shape
social norms and institutions, to guide social change. According to the well-
known dictum of W. I. Thomas, if situations are defined as real, they are real in
their consequences. A sociology of age points to the differing life situations that
arise with social change, to the differing definitions of these situations by successive cohorts of human beings, and to the consequences of these differing cohort
definitions for further social change.

Aging and Social Change: A Sociological Perspective

For the past fifteen years, a number of us have been at work in the sociology
of age,[5] formulating and specifying the conceptual scheme that underlies this

essay. The aim has been to integrate and to reinterpret two seemingly disparate strands of work on: first, the aging process as individuals move through the social structure; and second, changing social structures as they environ successive cohorts of human lives.

In recent decades, scholars in several social science fields have been concerned with selected aspects of the aging process. Many have focused on discrete stages of the life course, and there are substantial literatures on childhood, on adolescence, on social gerontology, and more recently on middle age. In psychology, the predominant emphasis on childhood "development" or on old age "decrements" has been countered by attention to the entire lifetime among "life-span psychologists" (including Warner Schaie, Paul Baltes, John Nesselroade, and others), whose intellectual roots can be traced back to Quetelet and other eighteenth- and nineteenth-century scholars.[6] Current attention is being turned to the interaction of social, biological, and psychological aspects of the aging process,[7] and sociologists like Brim[8] and Clausen are examining the connections between the full life course and the social structure. In an extended treatment, Clausen has described the sequence of roles within the changing society in which the individual makes continual adjustments during his lifetime, to which he brings his accumulated stores of past experience and future aspirations, and through which he seeks to preserve some sense of personal continuity and identity.[9]

A very different set of studies has dealt with aspects of the changing age structure of society. Focusing on age structure, sociologists (like Parsons[10] and Eisenstadt[11]) and anthropologists (like Linton)[12] have noted that every society is stratified by age; thus people at varying ages differ in their capacity to perform key social roles, while the social system depends upon the continuing performance of numerous age-specific roles and functions. Karl Mannheim, in his seminal essay "The Problem of Generations,"[13] pays greater heed to the dynamic than to the structural aspects of social change. Subsequently amplified in the writings of Ryder[14] and Cain,[15] Mannheim's essay shows how each new cohort, starting its life course at a unique point in time, has unique characteristics because of the particular historical events undergone or the particular knowledge or attitudes acquired in childhood. Mannheim's concern with generations as contributing to "the dynamic of historical development"[16] has a close parallel in the current work of social historians and historical demographers who use reconstructed genealogies, biographies, or parish records to study changes in political ideology or in such age-stratified systems as the family or the school.[17]

Pondering over these diverse intellectual strands, each largely ignored in the other, we have devised a conceptual model[18] for continuing examination of their obvious, yet still unexplored, connectedness. In its most general form, this conceptual model comprises pivotal elements in the two types of interdependent changes I am discussing: changes in the society and its age-graded roles, and changes in people as they grow up and grow old. Two different dynamisms are involved, each with its own tempo. Society changes as it undergoes wars, famines, economic fluctuations; revolutions in beliefs and tastes; changes in the state of science and the arts; shifts in social norms, roles, and institutions; revisions in the age criteria for role entry and exit. Meanwhile, people change. They age over the life course from birth to death. And they are replaced by a succession of new cohorts, each composed of people who are aging.

It is useful to visualize this model schematically as a series of horizontal bars, staggered across the axis of historical time. Each bar represents a cohort of people all born during the same time period. Within each cohort, people are aging—socially as well as biologically and psychologically; moving through roles; accumulating knowledge, attitudes, experiences. In the meantime new cohorts are continually succeeding one another. This seemingly obvious schematic representation has the distinct use of forcing us to keep in mind that each cohort cuts off a unique segment of historical time—confronts its own particular sequence of social and environmental events. That is, because society changes, the modal life-course patterns of people in different cohorts cannot be precisely alike. This point, as initially formulated by Norman Ryder,[19] deserves the emphasis of repetition: because of social change, *different cohorts age in different ways.* Cohorts born recently in this country differ from earlier cohorts because of intervening social changes of many sorts: in education, in nutrition, in the occupational and income level at which people begin their careers, in the political zeitgeist surrounding their first voting experience. If for no other reason, then, the members of each new cohort *cannot follow precisely* in the footsteps of their predecessors. For example, as the Vietnam War has given way to such new critical issues as inflation and unemployment, today's cohorts of college students are more job-oriented, less dedicated to "causes," than the activist cohorts of the 1960s. Or, with reports of mounting crime and violence in the society, today's cohorts of young Americans are more likely to urge capital punishment than were their more humanitarian counterparts just a few years ago.

The scheme also illustrates societal elements in a sociology of age. It directs us to sequential cross-section views of all the coexisting cohorts. At any single moment of history, such as 1978 or 1928, a vertical slice through the staggered cohorts divides the population into age strata—the young, middle-aged, and old. These different strata are simultaneously acting out their respective age-assigned roles in society—as in an age-graded school. Comparison of several sequential cross-section slices (such as 1928 with 1948 with 1978) suggests how society is changing, just as longitudinal analysis of several sequential cohorts suggests how individuals age over their life course.[20]

The essence of this model centers in the continuing interplay between these two dynamisms: social change and the process of aging. Social change affects the situations in which people age. And the *way* in which people age—the process of aging itself—responds to these changing situations. Inherent in this interplay is the central problem of timing: the tension and strain produced by the difference between the tempo of mankind and the tempo of society. It is clear that cohorts of people follow one another in constant succession, even though particular races may eventually die out. And the biological lifetime of man has a definite rhythm from birth to death (albeit with secular variations in longevity within an apparently fixed total span). But the timing of societal process has no comparable rhythm or periodicity. The diverse ideas, beliefs, and artifacts of culture have varying lifetimes of their own, from the newspaper tossed away after one reading to the pyramids of Egypt. The wide range of social structures (from tribes or cities to nation-states) that concern us as sociologists also endure over varying periods of months, years, or centuries. Poets and philosophers, each in his own way, have attempted to define the course and the periods of societal time, from Heraclitus or Aristotle, through Ibn Khaldūn or Herbert

Spencer. And many early thinkers, including Hume and Comte, have made varying attempts to measure societal time in quantitative terms, seeking cyclical or "generational" or other rhythms—all such attempts dispatched as abortive by both Mannheim[21] and Sorokin.[22]

Whatever the nature of the processes of social change and stability—whether they are short-term or long-term, disintegrative or reconstitutive[23]—societal processes are certainly not synchronized with the lifetimes of the people progressing through the social structure in endless succession. As seen in the model, the society, itself moving through time, is the composite of the several unique cohorts—at varying stages of their journey, and often traveling divergent paths. Only by understanding this fact can we comprehend the sources of tension and pressure for change inherent in the differing rhythms of individual aging and societal change. Each individual must endure continual tension throughout his lifetime because, as he learns new roles and relinquishes others, he must adjust to shifting, often unpredictable and seemingly capricious, societal demands. And difficulties can beset the society because each new cohort that is born— characterized by its own size, sex composition, distribution of genetic traits and family backgrounds—requires continual allocation and socialization for the sequence of roles it must encounter within the prevailing social structure. Small wonder, then, that there can be no fixed process of aging!

As many of us continue to work with this conceptual model, to specify and adapt it, we find that a new window has been opened upon social reality. A fresh perspective is introduced—one that takes into account the human beings who are themselves changing as society changes.

Myths and Fallacies about Aging

The model has the further use of identifying many long-held and widespread myths, mistaken beliefs, and erroneous theories about age and aging. In an earlier reanalysis of the literature on older people,[24] we encountered numerous examples of myths that, on closer scrutiny, proved to be unfounded. We discovered the following to be true:

> Most old people are not (as the myth has it) destitute, dependent, or residing in
> nursing homes.
> Most are not seriously disabled.
> Work productivity does not invariably decline in old age.
> Most old people *do* feel adequate. Most are satisfied with their roles.

How then do such myths arise? Several types of fallacies or misinterpretations have been identified[25] and are becoming widely recognized as resulting from lack of such a conceptual model or inappropriate application of it. I shall mention only three. First, there is the "life-course fallacy," which erroneously interprets cross-section data as if they referred to the aging process. In cross-section, for example, old people have lower educational attainment than young people. This obviously does not mean that a person's educational level declines *because* of growing older. The apparent decline occurs because the more recent cohorts are better educated than their predecessors. In cross-section, too, teenagers generally score higher on intelligence tests than members of older age strata. Again, this obviously does not mean that an individual's intelligence necessarily declines *because* of growing older—although many psychologists thought so until a few longitudinal studies pointed to the life-course fallacy.[26] What had been overlooked were the cohort differences in life-course patterns. Second, there is the "fallacy of age reification," in which chronological age itself is treated as if it were a causal factor (one wants to "become one's own man" because he is age forty, according to Daniel Levinson,[27] or one "becomes re-signed" because he is age fifty, according to Gail Sheehy.[28]) Yet particular years of age (like particular historical dates) have no meaning in themselves; they are mere indexes, useful only as they reflect socially or theoretically relevant components of personal or social change.[29] (Preferable, perhaps, is the folk wisdom that forty is the old age of youth, fifty is the youth of old age.) And third, there is the "fallacy of cohort-centrism," which I shall discuss in some detail—the fallacy of overgeneralizing from the experience of a single cohort (usually one's own).

Thus there are many ways of being lured into erroneous ideas and theories of aging and the sequence of life events. Yet ideas and theories, no matter how erroneous or ill-founded, have their own power both over a person's life course and over societal change. They can, in Robert Merton's term, become "self-fulfilling prophecies."

Cohort-centrism: One's Own Theory of Aging

This brings me to the special focus of this essay, to definitions or theories of the life course and their consequences. Let us consider how such theories are formed, and to what extent they may be flawed by ill-founded myths and stereotypes and by the fallacy of cohort-centrism.

Each of us, moving along the trajectory from birth to death, constructs his own biography. We attach special meanings to past events. We look to the future with special hopes or anticipations, with special apprehensions or fears. Doubtless each of us also tends to generalize from this personal theory of one's own life—to treat it implicitly as *the* process of aging. Here lies the danger. For it can be stated as an axiom that each of us tends to define *"the* life course" as we have experienced it in our particular cohort. As William Graham Sumner suggested when he coined the term, we tend to be ethnocentric. I suggest that we tend also to be "cohort-centric." Yet, as the model reminds us, cohorts can age in different ways.

The absurdity of attempting to build a general theory of the life course from one's own experience seems clear enough. The meaning of life and of its sequence of life events is colored by the cohort to which a person belongs—and by the sex and class-segment of that cohort. In Mannheim's phrase, members of the same cohort share "a common location" in the social process. Those who reached the age of thirty in 1940, for example, had all experienced World War I and the Great Depression; they were currently exposed to World War II; and they confronted the future of the 1940s through the 1970s. At given stages in their lives, they were exposed to much the same zeitgeist; and they were finding their way into, and learning to play, roughly similar sets of roles. As Robert Merton puts it, "Structure constrains individuals variously situated within it to develop cultural emphases, social behavior patterns and psychological bents."[30] Thus any personal biography, or even the aggregate biographies of the members of a cohort, can only emphasize the constraints imposed by social structure and social change, by the social exigencies and prescriptions of the particular slice of history involved.

Obvious as the point seems, however, many definitions and theories on which we act—which are real in their consequences—are cohort-centric. As individuals, each of us is often guided by his own personal experience as he construes it. And when many of us in the same cohort are similarly affected by social change, we come to attribute similar meanings to our lives, to share similar assumptions about aging, to be beguiled or threatened by similar life events. Collectively, we develop "cohort definitions of the life course" that are implicit, unspoken. As each new cohort confronts a different set of social and environmental events, these cohort definitions subtly change. Thus one generation's folklore and "common sense" about the life course may no longer make sense to a later generation.

Even sophisticated philosophies, and the basic assumptions underlying professional practice or public policy, are sometimes beset by this potential danger of cohort-centrism. Erikson, whose ideas of the eight stages of life are widely influential in social science and psychiatry, derives his views from the "evidential field" of his own contemporary clinical observations.[31] Thus one wonders how universal are his postulated stages, how closely tied to particular ages, how inexorable their sequence (as from autonomy versus doubt, to intimacy versus isolation, to integrity versus despair).[32] One wonders also about the presumed universality and sequencing of Kohlberg's stages of moral development (also derived from contemporary studies).[33] One can question how certainly a man must "get into the adult world" precisely in his midtwenties or "become one's own man" precisely in his late thirties, as Levinson contends in postulating the "species-specific periods" that "have governed human development for the past five or ten thousand years" (conjectures based on recent studies of forty middle-aged men).[34] One need only look back at Freud's views of the life course—at the submerged hatreds and fears, the sublimated sexuality—to appreciate some respects in which even his theories are less pertinent today than to the Viennese cohorts of his own time.

To be sure, the danger of cohort-centrism is peripheral to the centrally important aim of many such theories of stages, patterns, stability and change over the life course. Their search is for *universals* in the aging process—for the similarities among cohorts rather than for the differences I have been emphasizing. This search can provide cogent insights. (It can also afford guidelines for counseling and therapy. In its popular versions, such as Gail Sheehy's *Passages*, it can offer reassurance, if sometimes misleading reassurance, to millions of readers undergoing life transitions of their own.)

Though there is little proof, a number of universal principles have been postulated. For example, there are the biologically rooted principles of *aging* and *cohort flow*. Mankind as a species invariably grows up, becomes fertile, grows old, and dies; and cohort flow persists as long as the society survives. There are certain empirical principles of the *sequencing of events* over the life course. For example, unlike such a socially prescribed (hence flexible) sequence as completing school, beginning to work, marrying, producing a child, it seems universally probable that a child cannot walk before standing, cannot solve moral problems before understanding words, or solve complex mathematical problems before understanding numbers. Of interest to us also has been a principle of *accumulation*.[35] By definition, the longer a person lives, the greater his chances of having acquired irreversible characteristics, such characteristics as a higher level of educational attainment or a chronic disease (if "chronic" is defined as "incurable").

How can the universality of such principles be tested? Which personal characteristics are inevitable, regardless of sociotemporal context? Which life sequences persist across time and space, rather than being culturally variable? One can only begin to answer such questions through studying and comparing many cohorts, not just one (as the increasing use of cohort analysis by social scientists attests). No "pure" process of aging occurs in any single concrete cohort observable in reality. A theory of aging, of universals, must be an abstraction from the experiences of many cohorts at many times and places.

Consider this example. Cumming and Henry concluded from the cohort they were studying that old people "naturally" disengage (withdraw) from society. But when we examined[36] another cohort, the cohort of young men who were unemployed during the Great Depression, we found that these young men also tended to disengage. Thus the cohort comparison indicated that not necessarily age at all, but exclusion from the labor force was the major precursor of disengagement.

This and many other findings point less to a fixed pattern of aging than to the ranges and variabilities in the ways people age. Indeed, that life-course patterns of successive cohorts are continually subject to change may prove to be another universal principle. There is intrinsic strain toward adjustment in the life course, because each new cohort must contend with the older cohorts that precede it; though they live as contemporaries, they are not coevals in age or experience. And there is the strain engendered by the differences in timing between social change and the processes of aging and cohort flow. Even in simple societies, where social change is deemed to be comparatively slow, the collective lives of successive cohorts are continually being altered as the society undergoes famine, pestilence, or conquest.[37]

The evidence is overwhelming that a person's life is not inexorably fixed, but highly flexible. The ages for beginning to learn, becoming a responsible adult, retiring from work, even reaching the onset of menarche are not irrevocably ordained. Declines over the past century in the age of menarche from seventeen to twelve or thirteen (attributed to changes in the social environment in the Western countries observed)[38] merely illustrate the variability in even the biological life-course patterns. Similarly, life constraints imposed by disease can be relaxed through medical advance, or biological processes involved in the aging of cells or of the brain may become modifiable as scientific understanding increases. Yet, despite the evidences of flexibility, misleading stereotypes and fixed-stage theories still abound. Just consider the consequences if a mother must assume abnormality in a baby that does not discover its own hand by age six weeks, if a man must expect a midlife crisis between age forty and forty-five, if a mathematician must assume at age thirty that he or she is necessarily past the peak, or if a worker at age sixty-five must be regarded as necessarily unable to earn a living!

Cohort-centric theories can produce such stereotypes. They can give each individual the false sense that the aging process is immutable. And, as such theories of the life course come to be shared within a cohort, these cohort definitions subtly alter the meanings and norms that guide our collective lives. Becoming self-fulfilling prophecies, they have consequences for social change.

Cohort Norm Formation and Social Change

As new cohorts, reflecting social change, differ from their predecessors, these cohorts in turn press upon the society for further change. Cohort definitions, even when false, can become institutionalized as new norms and new role expectations, crystallized as new customs or laws. For, according to the conceptual model, there is a continuing interplay, as in a feedback system, between social change and the life course. One can think of many examples of this interplay as it affects the nature and meaning of the life course, but I want to conclude with just two. Each example, described in highly simplified form, has potentially profound implications for us today and in the future—the first, for the meaning of death; the second, for the meaning of life.

First, consider the long-term decline in mortality in industrialized nations (commonly associated with societal changes in standard of living, nutrition, sanitation, recent medical advances, and so forth). As Kingsley Davis argues,[39] this decline in mortality (coupled with urbanization and industrialization) ultimately had an historic impact on fertility, both on fertility rates and on the meaning, the social valuation, of fertility. Instead of bearing enough children so that at least a few might survive, succesive cohorts of young people increasingly utilized whatever means of fertility control they knew (withdrawal, abortion, postponement of marriage) in order to reduce the number of children they bore. One can well imagine the motivating factors as the progeny were no longer winnowed by death: rivalry with their numerous surviving siblings; concern for the responsibility of rearing, educating, and launching their own children. The desire for high fertility in earlier cohorts tended to give way to the desire for low fertility in more recent cohorts. And in its turn, the reduced fertility of these new cohorts had still further societal consequences: smaller families, children with fewer siblings, parents with reduced responsibility for child-rearing, more time for mothers to take on new roles, and perhaps fewer children to support or care for parents in *their* old age.

Before continuing with this illustration, let me underscore the process I am describing. A social change in one factor (mortality) evokes a cohort response, a change in the life-course patterns of the new cohorts (reduced fertility), which in turn contributes to further social changes (smaller families, enhanced social status). Of central theoretical importance, such cohort response was not imposed from above. There were no birth control clinics when fertility began to decline in the nineteenth century in this country, no moral imperatives toward zero population growth or the "replacement level" family. The cohort response consists, rather, of countless separate but similar *individual* decisions (private

decisions by husbands and wives about whether to conceive another child). I
shall call this the process of "cohort norm formation," wherein these many sepa- ✓
rate decisions by cohort members gradually crystallize into standards or norms
that then govern decisions of future cohorts, or perhaps the whole society.

Returning to the example of declining mortality, I venture to suggest further
that the current continuing decline in mortality may now, by a parallel process,
be affecting the meaning of death. That is, just as the earlier decline in mortality
may have gradually diminished the positive value of fertility, the continuation
of this decline may be subtly diminishing the negative value of mortality. Mortality rates are now near a minimum among the young, where death seems most
poignant; in recent cohorts, most deaths occur in old age, near the completion of
a full life. Current deaths are both more protracted and require more decisions
than in the past. More deaths today result from chronic and lingering ailments
such as heart disease and cancer, and they typically occur in hospitals, where
the patients are apart from family and friends. Ironically, advances in biomedi-
cal science and technology, in saving life, are prolonging the process of dying.
Many decisions about when and how to die must now be made deliberately by
the human beings involved.[40]

How, then, are today's cohorts making these decisions? Is a process of new
norm formation at work? Are we seeing culture being made? Is the meaning of
death being reassessed? Here the answers are difficult to discern, for any drastic
change in the valuation of death could contravene deeply held ethical and moral
beliefs. Yet some evidence of cohort norm formation does exist. For example,
there is a movement to use a "living will" for protection in case of terminal
illness against heroic measures for life support. A major study of doctors shows
a widespread practice to acquiesce in the desire expressed by terminally ill patients to die.[41] A recent United States' survey finds a majority of the public
believing that "when a person has a disease that cannot be cured, doctors should
be allowed by law to end that patient's life by some painless means if the patient
and family request it"—an astonishing finding in view of earlier studies.[42]
There may even be an emerging acceptance of "social death," as observed in the
anthropological tradition, when old people, entirely bereft of meaningful roles
or solidary human relationships, without religious faith or dedication to a cause,
without the inner strength to live apart from social supports, lose the will to
live.[43] Despite the public mores against suicide, private mores may condone the
will to die.

If, under such conditions, death were to be more readily accepted, what
might be the societal consequences? One can only speculate. But there might
develop greater emphasis in the health professions on care of terminal patients
rather than on hopeless cures, more open discussion of the good death and
euthanasia, and the fact of death once again becoming a celebration of renewed
solidarity in family and community. Indeed, greater acceptance of death might
strengthen the links across generations, as generations seek to talk with one
another about this long-avoided topic. Most importantly, a change in the meaning of death might lead to changes in the meanings of life itself.

This brings me to my last example of the interplay between social change
and the life course, an example of equal concern to us all, I believe, if not
equally imponderable. Consider social change (past and future) as it relates to

the modal patterning over the lifetime of education, work, and leisure. In recent history, the case of women is more innovative than that of men, and may perhaps be instructive for the lives of men in the future. The rapid increases in female participation in the labor force over the past several decades is well known. What is less well known (revealed only by comparison of successive cohorts) is the complete reversal of women's work life: a shift from *declining* participation with age among cohorts coming into adulthood at the turn of the century, to *increasing* participation with age among those born more recently.[44] Here again one can look for concomitant social changes—rising educational attainment, expansion of demand for labor during World War II, emergence of the "empty nest" stage which produced leisure for middle-class women, and so on.[45] Here again, the *process* of change (in women's work life) consisted of millions of independent individual decisions by women in the affected cohorts, cohort norm formation that only now appears in its true light as a radical revision of the norms governing women's roles. Here the *consequences* for further social change are apparent in the drastic restructuring of both the family and the work force; in the diversity of the woman's combined work and family roles and the flexibility of accommodation required of her; and, significantly, in the pressure on the life course of men for complementary changes.

Contrast the situation of men. Unlike the varied options available to women, men's lives today (outside the family) are compressed into "three boxes"[46]: education in early life, work in midlife, leisure (more precisely, retirement) in later life. Historically, these sharp age divisions also arose from a gradual process of cohort norm formation. In those countries now classified as industrialized, there have been long-term tendencies for successive cohorts to stay in school longer, and to enter the labor force at increasingly *older* ages, but to leave the labor force at increasingly *younger* ages. In the United States, the proportion of men sixty-five and over in the work force has declined sharply from about two-thirds in 1900 to only one-fifth today. These striking changes in the age of retirement, and in the onset of long years of leisure, did not arise from any considered overall plan, but again because of millions of individual decisions, by employers to discharge, discourage, or fail to hire older men and by older workers to retire, to withdraw from the labor force. Only gradually did the norms crystallize, as ages of retirement became institutionalized in the United States through pension plans and (by 1935) through Social Security legislation (for which the choice of age sixty-five was made quite arbitrarily, and far above the average age of retirement today).[47]

What changes are now underway in the life-course patterning of work, education and leisure? One can imagine two scenarios for men and women alike. (Here one must keep in mind *all* the coexisting cohorts, each with its unique experience and its special normative claims, but all simultaneously pressing for differing changes in society.) In the first scenario, the cohorts starting out today might simply follow their predecessors, remain imprisoned in the "three boxes." With what future consequences? Predictably, there would be sustained age-based inequities in the burden of work and taxes placed on the middle-aged, in the exclusion from the labor force of both young and old (inequities exacerbated by the continuing increases in longevity). Predictably, too, age segregation in education and work would be accompanied by age segregation in the family, the community, and other social spheres; it would be accompanied by failures of empathy and communication across age lines; by anomie and aliena- tion in the excluded age strata. This is clearly a scenario of conflict, filled with intergenerational strains and tensions that could in their turn exert strong pres- sures for still further social change.

In the alternative scenario, new and more flexible life-course patterns might be introduced. (Here the implicit process of cohort norm formation might be given explicit direction through deliberate policy planning.) Many of us have been urging that education, work, and leisure be interspersed over the life course,[48] that social and economic structures be so modified that people of all ages might elect first, to work at one career, then to go back to school to learn another career; that leisure be apportioned more evenly from youth to old age, not concentrated at the very beginning and the end of life. And there are in- cipient changes that could be captured within such a scenario: older people going back to school for professional, vocational, or humanistic goals; legislation against a fixed age of retirement; pension plans for midcareer annuities; sabbati- cal leaves for all occupations; four-day work weeks; job sharing; flexible work hours; and models that have been set by women of combining many roles, as wives, mothers, homemakers, students, workers, all in one.[49]

What would be the future consequences if such a flexible integrative sce- nario were played out? At work, substitution of performance criteria for age ascription? Redistribution over the life course of challenge, responsibility, and usefulness? More options at every age? More equal sharing of child-rearing and bread-winning tasks? Greater solidarity in the kin network (in this era when there have never been so many generations of a family alive at the same time)? A closer integration of leisure into other life pursuits, with renewed evaluation of its seriousness and its purpose? Such questions currently press for answers. Cohort norm formation is underway.

Aging, the Power of Ideas, and Everyday Life

Thus a sociology of age makes clear that the meanings we attach to age have power. They become age stereotypes, shaping our personal plans, hopes, and fears. They become age constraints, built into the social structure, molding the course of our lives, directing social change. They are continually affecting the way we grow up and grow old and (as in my examples) modifying the values attached to life and death, pressing toward societal conflict or integration. Be- cause of this power, the sociology of age contains within it both responsibilities and opportunities.

We face a heavy scientific responsibility to broaden the base of understand- ing and to disseminate the soundest available knowledge to planners, profes- sionals, and the public. Age and aging as a topic of scientific concern is prematurely popular today, when there are best-selling books on how to rear the young, negotiate life's turning points, adjust to dying—treatments that too often pay little regard to potentially misleading stereotypes. Meanwhile much serious discourse, though burgeoning,[50] lies hidden in scholarly journals and arcane compendia. Yet serious students of the aging process have special access to the topic because of the principle of cohort flow itself: many different cohorts coexist at any given period of observation, and their past histories and future anticipations are available for comparison. Thus we are in a position to look with some dispassion upon the aging process, to help avoid the shibboleths of cohort-centrism, to assess the range of variabilities, and to anticipate the consequences of alternative policy decisions. And in looking toward the future, because of our focus on cohort flow we have a special advantage: we can make use of what has already happened, what is already knowable about the cohorts alive today who will become, respectively, the young, middle-aged, and old people of the future.[51]

We have an opportunity too to act upon the broadening knowledge base, to exert control over life course definitions as they develop. The meanings of age are not unchangeable. They respond to the pressures of each new cohort through the everyday interactions of cohort members, the millions of apparently unrelated individual decisions, the gradually emerging cohort definitions which then merge into new or altered norms, contracts, laws, social institutions. Whether we like it or not, age and aging *are* being defined. They will continue to be redefined and given new meanings. And each of us as we age (every day, every minute!) is playing an active, if often unwitting, part in this process of redefinition. As individuals, we can modify the remainder of our own life course by acting upon the best available knowledge. In a "self-help" society, each of us can, for example, heed current mandates from the medical profession to guard our health, or from social scientists to maintain our intellectual flexibility.[52] As citizens and policymakers, we can make explicit the potential personal and societal consequences of legislation aimed, for example, to postpone the entrance into adulthood, to alter the age of retirement, or to revise the pension level of the elderly.

In short, there is scope for us, personally and as members of the changing society, to benefit from the understanding that the process of aging is neither inexorable nor immutable, that to a considerable degree we ourselves are in control.

REFERENCES

[1]Portions of this article were delivered as a Presidential Address to the Eastern Sociological Society, Philadelphia, April, 1978.

[2]"The Problem of Generations," in Paul Kecskemeti, ed., *Essays on the Sociology of Knowledge* (London: Routledge, Kegan, and Paul), p. 290.

[3]For many of the ideas here, the author is indebted to her long-time collaborators, Marilyn Johnson, Anne Foner, Beth Hess, and Joan Waring; and for continuing suggestion and criticism to John W. Riley, Jr., Robert K. Merton, Orville G. Brim, Jr., and others.

[4]"Cohort" is used here to mean a set of people born at the same time. "Generation," reserved for the kinship context, indicates cohorts of relevance to particular individuals or families.

[5]This work began with the preparation of the Russell Sage Foundation volumes entitled *Aging and Society*: Matilda White Riley and Anne Foner, *I. An Inventory of Research Findings* (1968); Matilda White Riley, John W. Riley, Jr., and Marilyn Johnson, *II. Aging and the Professions* (1969); and Matilda White Riley, Marilyn Johnson, and Anne Foner, *III. A Sociology of Age Stratification* (1972). A small core of sociologists at Rutgers has gradually expanded into an "invisible college," spanning several disciplines in many countries, dedicated to this emerging sociological field.

[6]Paul B. Baltes, "Life-Span Developmental Psychology: Some Observations on History and Theory," address at annual meeting, American Psychological Association, San Francisco, 1977.

[7]See the volume edited by Orville G. Brim, Jr. and Jerome Kagan, *Constancy and Change in Human Development: A Volume of Review Essays* (in preparation). A Committee on Life-Course Perspectives on Middle and Old Age has been established by the Social Science Research Council to

address these and other neglected aspects of social research on aging.

[8]Orville G. Brim, Jr., "Socialization through the Life Cycle," in Orville G. Brim, Jr., and Stanton Wheeler, *Socialization After Childhood: Two Essays* (New York: Wiley, 1966), pp. 1-49.

[9]John A. Clausen, "The Life Courses of Individuals," in Riley, Johnson, and Foner, *A Sociology of Age Stratification*, chap. 11.

[10]Talcott Parsons, "Age and Sex in the Social Structure of the United States," *American Sociological Review* (1942): 604-616.

[11]S. N. Eisenstadt, *From Generation to Generation: Age Groups and Social Structure* (Glencoe, Ill.: Free Press, 1956).

[12]Ralph Linton, "Age and Sex Categories," *American Sociological Review* (1942): 589-603.

[13]First published in German in 1928, this essay appeared in English in 1952 in Kecskemeti, ed., *Essays on the Sociology of Knowledge*, pp. 276-320.

[14]Norman B. Ryder, "The Cohort as a Concept in the Study of Social Change," *American Sociological Review* (1965): 843-861.

[15]Leonard D. Cain, Jr., "Life Course and Social Structure," in Robert E. L. Faris, ed., *Handbook of Modern Sociology* (Chicago: Rand McNally), pp. 272-309.

[16]Mannheim, "The Problem of Generations," p. 320.

[17]See, for example, John Demos and Sarane S. Boocock, *Turning Points: Historical and Sociological Essays in the Family* (Chicago: University of Chicago Press, 1978); also the Spring 1968 issue of *Daedalus*, "Historical Population Studies," and the Winter 1971 issue, "Historical Studies Today."

[18]For further detail, see Riley, Johnson, and Foner, *A Sociology of Age Stratification*, chap. 1; also Matilda White Riley, "Age Strata in Social Systems," in Robert H. Binstock and Ethel Shanas, eds., *Handbook of Aging and the Social Sciences* (New York: Van Nostrand Reinhold, 1976).

[19]Norman B. Ryder, "Notes on the Concept of a Population," in Riley, Johnson, and Foner, *A Sociology of Age Stratification*, chap. 3.

[20]See Matilda White Riley and Edward E. Nelson, "Research on Stability and Change in Social Systems," in Bernard Barber and Alex Inkeles, eds., *Stability and Social Change* (Boston: Little, Brown, 1971), pp. 438-442.

[21]Mannheim, "The Problem of Generations."

[22]Pitirim A. Sorokin, *Social and Cultural Dynamics, Vol. IV, Basic Problems, Principles, and Methods* (New York: American Book Company), pp. 505ff.

[23]These are the dimensions used by Neil J. Smelser, "Toward a General Theory of Social Change," in Neil J. Smelser, *Essays in Sociological Explanation* (Englewood Cliffs, N.J.: Prentice-Hall), pp. 195ff.

[24]Riley and Foner, *Aging and Society, I.* as summarized on p. 7.

[25]Matilda White Riley, "Aging and Cohort Succession: Interpretations and Misinterpretations," *Public Opinion Quarterly* (Spring 1973): 35-49.

[26]Riley and Foner, *Aging and Society, I.*, p. 256.

[27]Daniel J. Levinson et al., *The Seasons of a Man's Life* (New York: Knopf, 1978).

[28]*Passages* (New York: Dutton, 1976).

[29]The current debate over "disentangling the effects of age, cohort, and period" verges upon reification unless the relevance of the concepts underlying these indexes is clearly defined. See Riley, Johnson, and Foner, *A Sociology of Age Stratification*, chap. 2; Karen Oppenheim Mason, William M. Mason, H. H. Winsborough, and W. Kenneth Poole, "Some Methodological Issues in Cohort Analysis of Archival Data," *American Sociological Review* (1973): 242-258.

[30]Robert K. Merton, *Social Theory and Social Structure* (Glencoe, Ill.: Free Press, 1957).

[31]Personal communication, 1976.

[32]Erik H. Erikson, *Childhood and Society* (New York: Norton, 1950). Note references in Erikson's more recent work to connections among the individual life cycle, the "cycle of generations," and "evolving social structure"; cf. Erikson, "Dr. Borg's Life Cycle," *Daedalus*, Spring 1976, "Adulthood."

[33]See, for example, Lawrence Kohlberg, "Stage and Sequence: The Cognitive-Developmental Approach to Socialization," in David Goslin, ed., *Handbook of Socialization Theory and Research* (Chicago: Rand McNally, 1969).

[34]Daniel J. Levinson et al., *The Seasons of a Man's Life*, pp. 41, 322.

[35]See Riley, "Age Strata in Social Systems."

[36]Matilda White Riley, Anne Foner, Beth B. Hess, and Marcia L. Toby, "Socialization for the Middle and Later Years," in David A. Goslin, ed., *Handbook of Socialization Theory and Research* (Chicago: Rand McNally), pp. 951-982.

[37]Anne Foner and David I. Kertzer, "Transitions over the Life Course: Lessons from Age-Set Societies," *American Journal of Sociology* (March 1978): 1081-1104. See also Riley, Johnson, and Foner, *A Sociology of Age Stratification*, chap. 12.

[38]J. M. Tanner, "Growing Up," *Scientific American* (September 1973): 17-28.

[39]Kingsley Davis, "The Theory of Change and Response in Modern Demographic History,"

Population Index (October 1963): 345-365.

[40]Among the relevant sources, see John W. Riley, Jr., "What People Think About Death," in Orville G. Brim, Jr., et al., eds., *The Dying Patient* (New York: Russell Sage Foundation, 1970), pp. 30-41; Robert M. Veatch, *Death, Dying, and the Biological Revolution* (New Haven, Conn.: Yale University Press, 1976).

[41]Diana Crane, *The Sanctity of Social Life: Physicians' Treatment of Critically Ill Patients* (New York: Russell Sage Foundation, 1975).

[42]National Data Program for the Social Sciences, General Social Survey 1977 (Chicago: National Opinion Research Center), computerized data file.

[43]Leo W. Simmons, *The Role of the Aged in Primitive Society* (New Haven, Conn.: Yale University Press, 1945), pp. 217-244.

[44]See Riley, Johnson, and Foner, *A Sociology of Age Stratification*, p. 56.

[45]Studying these phenomena in the 1930s, I expressed in an unpublished manuscript the hope that middle-class women would seize upon these changes as an opportunity to transform the definition of leisure, abjuring both its Romantic and its Utilitarian images as pure escape, and imbuing it with the more serious goals that men had been desperately seeking in work. But instead, those early—not yet "liberated"—cohorts of women merely followed men into the work force. Thus do the norms of particular cohorts have power over the trajectory of their lives!

[46]The expression "three boxes" was the tag used in an April, 1977, conference, called by the Center for Policy Process, on the topic of "Life Cycle Planning: New Strategies for Education, Work and Retirement in America." That this conference drew several hundred participants (including many outstanding scholars, professionals, and public officials) is just one indication of the mounting popular concern.

[47]Among the relevant sources, see Riley and Foner, *Aging and Society, I.*, pp. 42-43, 105; Riley, Johnson, and Foner, *Sociology of Age Stratification*, pp. 372-373.

[48]Matilda White Riley, "The Perspective of Age Stratification," *School Review* (1974): 85-91.

[49]Perhaps another term need be coined here, if these remarks sound "sex-centric."

[50]As one small example, a number of sociologists, psychologists, economists, physicians, and futurists participated in a January, 1978, symposium sponsored by the American Association for the Advancement of Science, entitled, "Aging from Birth to Death." These papers are to be published as a volume by the AAAS.

[51]For example, see Peter Uhlenberg, "The Impact of Demographic Change upon Three Generations of Old People," in Matilda White Riley, ed., *Aging From Birth to Death: Interdisciplinary Perspectives* (American Association for the Advancement of Science, forthcoming).

[52]See Melvin L. Kohn and Carmi Schooler, "The Reciprocal Effects of the Substantive Complexity of Work and Intellectual Flexibility," in Riley, ed., *Aging From Birth to Death*.

SHIRLEY ROBIN LETWIN

Trollope on Generations Without Gaps

WHILE TURGENEV WAS PRODUCING what is supposed to be the classic portrait of conflict between generations, his contemporary in England, Anthony Trollope, was describing a world where such a conflict is unknown. Not that there is any dearth in Trollope's novels of quarrels between parents and children, old and young. The subjects that provoke the quarrels range from religion and politics to the sinfulness of idleness, love-making, gambling, smoking, and the iniquity of penny newspapers, hunting parsons, and chignons and bustles. And of course marriages are the most common bone of contention: the Duke of Omnium was firmly opposed to the choices made by both his children—Lady Mary fell in love with a commoner and Lord Silverbridge with the granddaughter of an American dock laborer; Frank Gresham, who had been told daily that he had a duty to marry an heiress, became engaged to a penniless bastard; Nora Rowley chose a newspaperman whom her father regarded as a crook; Polly Neefit refused to marry the fine gentleman whom her father, the breeches maker, had labored to buy for her; Archdeacon Grantly's son decided to resist his father's disapproval of his marrying the daughter of a poor, half-crazed curate by selling a family estate. Throughout the altercations, we are reminded repeatedly that things have changed: the City is less suspect than it once was; bustles and chignons are worn by ladies rather than tarts; the clubs admit people like Major Tifto, who drops his aitches and spends his life on the turf; Parliament has been reformed and is full of "new men" who have no use for the niceties that preoccupy the Duke of Omnium; Mr. Grey, the old family solicitor, reflects sadly that men who regard the law as something to be outwitted are taking over; the Jew from the City, Mr. Brehgert, tells Mr. Longestaffe, who comes of an ancient family, that it is no longer inappropriate for a Jew to woo the daughter of a Longestaffe.

Yet most of the stories end happily. Though Lord Chiltern did not for many years speak to his father, they were reconciled by Chiltern's marriage to Violet Effingham. It is true that Mrs. Carbuncle drives her niece to madness and that Emily Hotspur dies of a broken heart. But mainly parents learn to accept their children's choices, and in only one case, that of Emily Wharton, does the yielding lead to disaster. Some readers have concluded that the happy endings are meretricious and that Trollope is more convincing when he is portraying the conflict that is the inescapable result of great changes. Others have argued that there was no fatal conflict between parents and children, because they lived in

53

an unchanging world where the young were disposed to conform to the ideals and conventions imposed by their elders and deviated only in trivial ways.

Both these conclusions are wide of the mark. What accounts for the harmony between old and young is not any absence of serious differences, but an attitude to disagreement and change, what might be called the attitude of a gentleman. As it is displayed in the details of personal relations, it is subtle and difficult to grasp quickly. We can, however, see the features of this attitude magnified, so that they stand out more boldly in Trollope's account of how, in politics, changes are introduced and accepted. Although the so-called political novels disclose very little about the political setup in nineteenth-century Britain, in the sense that we might expect to discover from a constitutional history, they nevertheless tell us something essential about it, the understanding that governed how politicians conducted themselves and responded to one another and to the opinions in the country in the making of innovations.

In *Phineas Redux*, Trollope gives an account of an attempt at a radical innovation—disestablishing the Church of England. It is a telling episode just because such an event never occurred, and yet might have, and the real significance of the episode is suggested by the fact that though today in England there is still officially an established church, in many respects the current position of the church is very like disestablishment.

The context of the episode in the novel is that the Conservative party was committed to defending the established Church, indeed that commitment was considered to be the essence of conservatism, while their opponents, the Liberals, were sworn to bring in disestablishment. The episode begins with a speech to his constituents given by the prime minister in a Conservative government, Mr. Daubeny. The speech included the following words: "The period of our history is one in which it becomes essential for us to renew those inquiries which have prevailed since man first woke to his destiny, as to the amount of connection which exists and which must exist between spiritual and simply human forms of government—between our daily religion and our daily politics, between Crown and Mitre." To Daubeny's immediate audience, the words carried pleasant intimations of "good old gracious times and good old gracious things," they liked the sound of the orator's voice, and they had no idea of what the words meant. But when the speech was reported in the press, the wise heads declared that something was afoot. Then came the leading articles in the newspapers which told everyone what the prime minister had really said. It took a few days for the "bran to be bolted," as Trollope puts it, and by the end of the week it was known everywhere that Mr. Daubeny had set his party on a course to disestablishment. Some Conservatives decided that the speech gave undeniable evidence of temporary insanity in the prime minister, and the squires and parsons, who were the backbone of the party, refused to believe that their leader could commit such an iniquity.

The truth about the affair, Trollope tells us, is that Daubeny had consulted no one before making the speech, that he had expected his constituents to miss the point, and had calculated that others would make the point for him within a week. When the expected clarification came, he readily explained his move to anyone who asked, but the explanations were many. Daubeny said that there was a storm approaching England and the most important thing was to save the land from being devastated by it, that he had done nothing but recognize what the current religious feeling in the country made inevitable, that it was preferable to have the Church disestablished by her friends than by her enemies. To colleagues who expressed outrage, Daubeny at once declared his willingness to resign, though he always added that such a terrible, drastic step might not, he hoped, be necessary. To some he confessed that he had known that his words would shock his followers, but that he had felt honor bound to declare his true opinion candidly to his constituents. Others were told that if they believed that the country would benefit from keeping the Conservatives in power, they had better let him satisfy the popular demand for disestablishment.

Daubeny's words were included in the Queen's Speech and in the Address to the Crown, thus becoming official policy for the government. There was a "long and stormy" debate on the address but by then, one Conservative after another rose to argue that the measure was designed to defend the Church, that the power of the Church would be increased by disestablishment, that good Churchmen ought to have taken this step long ago. In short, the Conservatives made it clear that by disestablishing the Church they would be restoring episcopal ascendancy.

A number of Liberals decided at once that although the Liberal party had always advocated disestablishment, they were now obliged to oppose the Conservative bill. Some Liberals acquired, for the first time in their lives, a real political conviction and declared themselves ready to die in defense of the Church. Some argued that it would be best to concentrate on attacking Daubeny himself and to ignore the issue. Others muttered mysterious words about how, "If we were all a little less in the abstract and a little more in the concrete, it would be better for us," which still others translated as meaning "men, not measures."

In the end, the leader of the Liberal opposition, Mr. Gresham, set out to bring down the Conservative government. Gresham declared that it was the greatest of all sins to let a measure be passed by men who, in voting for it, violated their consciences, which the Conservatives would necessarily be doing. No good could be achieved, he declared, from an army in which every man and officer was fighting against his convictions. As the discussion proceeded, it was repeated often that "the Church of England would still be the Church of England" until everyone grew weary of hearing about the Church, and moved on to quite another argument—about the wickedness of faction. Then that issue, too, melted away into a general knockabout on the relative merits of the two parties, which made everyone happy because it was a subject on which even the meekest and dimmest members of the House had something to say.

The climax came in the final debate between the two great gladiators, which held the House enraptured until ten in the evening. The next morning it was reported in some places that Mr. Daubeny had been too long and turgid, and Mr. Gresham too passionate, but elsewhere it was found to be an incontrovertible truth that Gresham had given his finest performance and that Daubeny had never been more lucid, and of course everyone agreed, as they always did on such occasions, that the "speeches of the day" were sadly inferior to "the great efforts of the past." The show ended with Daubeny's losing the vote. And in his speech of resignation he assured the country that it was doomed, because though he might have saved England, Mr. Gresham, backed by an unworthy House of Commons, would certainly ruin it.

If this were all that Trollope told us, it would be reasonable to conclude that the attempt at innovation was all pretence. Support for such an interpretation seems to come from the fact that Trollope not only tells the story throughout in an ironic tone of voice, but often likens the contest between the parties to a game. The dismay felt by the Liberals over Daubeny's sudden strike was, Trollope says, like that of a chess player mated "by some audacious combination of two pawns and a knight, such being all the remaining forces of the victorious adversary, when the beaten man has two castles and a queen upon the board." The Liberals believed that they owned Church reform, they considered it their legitimate property and most valuable asset, but they had not as yet used it because they were keeping it "in the background for some future great occasion." When Daubeny made his move, it was as if "the adversary had appropriated to his own use the castles and the queen of the unhappy vanquished ones."

The irony and the images seem to suggest that the only reality in the proceedings is a struggle for power, that the words used were but chips in a poker game with no truth in them, that the only real question was who bullied whom into giving way, and in short that though gentlemen may wear silk gloves over their brass knuckles, they play a dirty game. Grand reasons may be given for attempting, accepting, or rejecting innovations, but as some of the Liberals said, there was "no honesty in it," and the meanness of it all should make an honest man "sick of life."

What went on in the country at large appears to be just as devoid of seriousness and truth as what happened in Parliament. When the pundits began saying that "the disestablishment of the Church was only a question of time," they spoke on little or no evidence, as pundits generally do in order to attract attention. Yet before long, though no one knew precisely who had said what or why, the idea became familiar to the public. The press began to teem "with the assertion that it was only a question of time." There was the usual set of variations on the going opinion: "Some fervent, credulous friends predicted another century of life;—some hard-hearted logical opponents thought that twenty years would put an end to the anomaly;—a few stout enemies had sworn on the hustings with an anathema that the present Session should see the deposition from her high place of this eldest daughter of the women of Babylon." But despite all the predictions of instant disestablishment, "none had expected the blow so soon as this: and none certainly had expected it from this hand."

Much the same happened every time a new government was formed. While the great men were locked in consultation, it was being said outside that the difficulties in the way of forming a government would "be found to be insuperable." On Wednesday morning the prophets of doom wore "their longest faces" and were "triumphant with melancholy forebodings . . . there was a deadlock. Nobody could form a government." The newspapers carried detailed reports of wonderfully dramatic scenes—the Liberal leader had not only fallen on his knees before the queen; he had burst into floods of tears. It was said that the queen would be driven to implore the wildest of radicals to form a government. It was announced as an undisputed fact that in her desperation the queen had sent to Germany for advice. But by Wednesday night, the crisis was over, and "before the House met on Thursday every place had been bestowed, either in reality or in imagination." Not only had a government been formed, but it was precisely what everyone had always predicted, down to the last man. No one expressed any surprise; everyone behaved as if the week had passed in the same humdrum fashion as all other weeks.

Where in all this can any "reality" or "truth" be found? It appears to be a frivolous game in which anyone may say anything. Why or when it comes to be played, no one knows. The future in politics, we are told, is always obscure. It is "darker," the Duke of Omnium says, "than any other future . . . clouds arise one knows not why or whence, and create darkness when one expected light." The Duke seems to consider it almost indecent to deliberate about what should be done. When one of his ministers proposed that the cabinet would do well to "try and arrange among ourselves something of a policy," the Duke replied: "Things to be done offer themselves, I suppose, because they are in themselves desirable; not because it is desirable to have something to do." The Duke's words suggest that an innovation is and ought to be a random event. But there appears to be a contradiction between the Duke's attitude and that of Gresham and Cantrip, who are also gentlemen, and who praised Daubeny's deliberate audacity in bringing in disestablishment.

The difficulty disappears, however, once we recognize the conception of politics common to all gentlemen in Trollope's world. It is politics seen as an activity without a given goal or destination. Its purpose is simply to keep things "quiet and orderly" so as to enable everyone to go about his business in his own way, without fear of losing his liberty, his livelihood, or his property. The hallmark of such a condition of things, Trollope says, is habeas corpus—the "first and greatest shibboleth of a free people"—and habeas corpus has this importance because it signifies that communal life is governed by stable rules and procedures, without which men cannot be secure against arbitrary power and therefore cannot live as free men. In this picture, the only substantive objects that a politician ought to pursue are to preserve the rule of law, to keep taxes low, and to secure the country against enemies from without and hooligans within. And when people are governed in this manner, Trollope says, "good living" will spread through the whole of the nation. He defines good living in a homely fashion; it means "not simply beef and pudding, though they form no inconsiderable part of it. It is education, religion without priestcraft, political freedom, the power and habit of thinking, the capacity for enjoying life like a man, instead of enduring life like a brute." Certainly there is grandeur in politics, but it comes from the importance and not the amount of what is done by a government—more than any other activity, politics is essential to securing the enjoyment of private life.

In order to provide such security, the politician can never sit back. He must not stand up so violently as to rock the boat, but neither dare he omit to notice that it may be filling with water in a hidden corner. Constant change is therefore intrinsic to politics. But it is not change in the sense of initiating or founding great transformations or seeking "to rediscover the creative impulse." It is change in the sense of a constant adjustment, carried out with an awareness that while change is inescapable, there is nothing intrinsically desirable or noble

about changing things and it always carries grave risks. If an innovation re-
moves a troublesome dissonance in the established arrangements, it may be
considered useful. But there can never be any certainty about what needs to be
done, or by whom, or where, and judicious men will always be full of doubts
about what might or should happen, and even about the desirability of what has
happened. This breed of politician does not try to bring immortality into the
world, or to impose an ideal fixity on it. He is not out to capture a Holy Land or
to act as a merchant of salvation. Instead of wanting to inflame the passions of
men into accepting grand innovations, he strives to teach the public not to be
too anxious "to see some great effects come from our own little doings," to
recognize that, when "great measures" start coming fast, often "more is broken
in the rattle than is repaired by the reform." Far from supposing that it is the
business of government always to be making new laws, he believes that there is
much to be gained from "a lengthened period of quiet and . . . a minimum of
new laws." To "have carried on the Queen's Government prosperously for
three years" is for such a politician achievement enough. Trollope was genuinely praising Lord Brock when he described him as "the very model of an English
statesman" because he believed in letting "things take their way naturally—with
a slight direction hither or thither as things might require."

But because the objects of politics are so modest, the practice of politics is
complicated and difficult to understand. Trollope's politician lives in a world
where many different people are saying many different things and there is no
voice from heaven telling him whom to listen to. He is not at all in the situation
of a doctor who is brought a patient suffering from a distinct pain which he asks
the doctor to remove. The politician is faced with a bewildering array of candidates for the status of patient, some genuine, others more or less bogus, with
complaints in many different degrees and forms, and he has nothing even remotely resembling a pharmacopoeia. He is beseiged by many different groups,
each insisting that its interest should be held paramount or considered identical
with the good of the country, and each certain that "the welfare of the community depends upon the firmness with which they—especially they—hold to
their own." And yet governments are formed, questions are raised, laws are
framed, accepted, and rejected, and Englishmen go about their affairs in an
orderly fashion. How is this miracle achieved? Trollope's answer is: by an unpredictable coming together of intentions, motives, contrivances, and conflicts.

In this view of politics, the apocalyptic frame of mind does not signify insight. It belongs rather to the vulgar, the cads, the cranks, and the villains.
These are men like the scurrilous journalist, Quintus Slide, the self-appointed
"people's friend" who tells his readers that the "ruling powers" are the people's
enemies; or Turnbull, the Radical demagogue, who goes in "for everything in
the way of agitation," always carries a cause in his breeches pocket and sherry in
his carriage to "remedy the costs of mob popularity"; or Daubeny, the Conservative demagogue, who assures the people of England that decay, disaster,
and death are imminent. It is the toadies and the tuft hunters, the young and the
thoughtless who suppose that the men on their side are "patriotic angels" and
those on the other are "all fiends or idiots," who see every defeat as a tragedy.
Gentlemen are more detached.

The gentlemen among the Liberals did not conclude that the behavior of the
Conservatives showed them to be "conniving scoundrels." Though Mr. Gre-

sham made a passionate attack on the recommendation for disestablishment in the Queen's Speech, he told Lord Cantrip privately that Daubeny was probably only feeling out the ground, trying "to see if it is possible" to bring in disestablishment. Lord Cantrip disagreed about that but he was at one with Gresham in considering such a ploy for such a purpose permissible, even if Daubeny had been motivated by a desire to do something dramatic in order to stay in office. Both these Liberals believed also that Daubeny's party included the usual assortment of more and less honorable, patriotic, thoughtful, self-seeking men, who had a few simple ideas about their duties, not many arguments at their disposal, and no great anxiety to take on the "responsibility of real work."

The truth about how the Conservatives came to accept disestablishment is neither obvious nor simple. Every one of them, Trollope tells us, did "most certainly within his own bosom cry 'Ichabod' when the fatal news reached his ears." At first they could hardly believe that their leader would play Brutus to their Church, "the very Holy of Holies," and whispered among themselves mutinously that "their Brutus, in spite of his great qualities had ever been mysterious, unintelligible, dangerous, and given to feats of conjuring . . ." But on the other hand, they also considered it their duty to support their party, and when the two duties seemed to clash, they were made extremely uncomfortable. Most would have preferred "to go home" and console themselves with declaring "morning and evening with a clear conscience that the country was going to the dogs." To stand apart, "hiding his face beneath his toga" and dreaming of Rome in her splendor would have been easier. But they recognized, and rightly that a "party cannot afford to hide its face in its toga," and "has to be practical," and that therefore members of Parliament are obliged to stay and commit themselves one way or the other, however unpleasant they may find it to make the choice. Though when disestablishment was first mentioned to them, it had seemed unthinkable, the proceedings had compelled them to think about it longer and they came to see that perhaps disestablishment was no more at odds with long held Conservative convictions than other measures which they had endorsed in the past. After all, Catholic emancipation and the repeal of the Corn Laws, measures that had once been anathema to Conservatives, had been introduced by a Conservative government. Twenty years before household suffrage had arrived, even the most ardent reformers would not have dared to advocate it, and yet the Conservatives "had swallowed the dose without serious disruption of their ranks." Some did it, Trollope says, with "faces so singularly distorted" as to arouse "true pity"; some managed it with indifference, and others with affected joy. But somehow or other they "learned to acknowledge the folly of clinging to their own convictions . . ."

Such a change of mind is considered decent and reasonable by gentlemen like Gresham and Cantrip. Instead of being outraged by the Conservative turnabout, they recognized that they themselves might do the same. That awareness, however, also prevented them from jumping to conclusions about whether Daubeny would carry his party. Just as from the fact that "a man rides at some outrageous fence, and by the wonderful activity and obedient zeal of his horse is carried over it in safety," one must not conclude that his horse will carry him over a house, Gresham said, so there was no telling whether the Conservatives would on this occasion give up deeply held convictions.

Nor did judicious Liberals consider it to be a bad thing that the Conservatives should introduce disestablishment. The wise old Duke of St. Bungay
explained that Daubeny had undertaken the job "because he can do it and we
can't. He will get from our side much support, and we should get none from
his." When Phineas Finn objected passionately, "There is something to me sick-
ening in their dishonesty," the Duke told him, "The country has the advantage;
and I don't know that they are dishonest. Ought we to come to a deadlock in
legislation in order that the parties might fight out their battle till one had killed
the other?" The same indifference is expressed by Gresham when he says to
Lord Cantrip, "You know and I know, that the thing has to be done. Would it
not be better if he can do it with less animosity than we should rouse against us?
If the blow would come softer from his hands than from ours, with less of a
feeling of injury to those who dearly love the Church, should we not be glad
that he should undertake the task?" And this is a reasonable way to think, Trollope shows us, because all human affairs are mutable. Opinions constantly
change and it is no bad thing that they do in a world full of change. Men who
"ten years since regarded almost with abhorrence and certainly with distrust the
idea of disruption between Church and State in England" advanced to enthusiasm on its behalf and learned to say "it is only a question of time," without even
remembering how devoted they had been to the established Church a dozen
years ago. In saying this, Trollope is not disparaging public opinion for being
volatile, but congratulating his countrymen on having found a decent way of
accommodating to the human condition. They had learned to accept without
anguish so great an innovation as disestablishment, he explains, by "reconciling
themselves to it after that slow, silent, argumentative fashion in which convictions force themselves among us."

The same general attitude governs the way in which gentlemen assess the
effects of accomplished innovations. The reforms designed to do away with
corruption, the extension of the franchise, and the redistribution of boroughs
are all acknowledged by Trollope and by his gentlemen to have been desirable.
But once that was done, the millennium that the demagogues had promised was
still on the horizon. All new measures, like budgets and babies, Trollope says,
"are always little loves when first born. But as their infancy passes away . . . the
details are less pleasing than was the whole in the hands of the nurse." The old
system had had some good points which now were lost; men who might have
been especially useful in Parliament found it impossible to get in now, and some
of the new people who easily gained admission were at least as bad as the worst
of the old. Despite the great public outcry about reform, once it had been
achieved, the electorate was not after all delighted to be enfranchised. The
Duke of Omnium declared firmly that he would do nothing to influence the
choice in his borough and the electors felt obliged to demonstrate their independence by choosing an outsider. But having done so once, they were relieved
when the outsider resigned and they could welcome back the Duke's son without being at all concerned about whether he stood as a Conservative or Liberal.

The relation between how things are and how they are moved to what appears to be a better state of affairs, we are constantly reminded, is far from
simple. Shortly after the reform, there was a trial for corruption, in which,
because the prosecution was so faint-hearted, the accused was acquitted, even

though everyone was certain that he had been guilty of bribery. The young Phineas Finn was outraged, but Lord Cantrip and Mr. Monk saw the matter differently. Cantrip assured Phineas that "No member of Parliament will ever be punished for bribery as a crime. We are very far from that as yet. I should have thought a conviction to be a great misfortune . . . it would have created ill blood, and our own hands in this matter are not a bit cleaner than those of our adversaries. We can't afford to pull their houses to pieces before we have put our own in order. The thing will be done: but it must, I fear, be done slowly as is the case with all reforms from within." And the radical Mr. Monk agreed that no disgrace was attached to their verdict even though everybody knew that the accused had been bribed because "in political matters it is very hard for a man in office to be purer than his neighbours." When Phineas objected "What must we think of such a condition of things," Monk answered, "That it's capable of improvement. I do not know that we can think anything else."

The moral is that enacting a statute is only a small part of the story about a change in public arrangements. It takes time before the public learns to sub-scribe to the new conditions. While bribery in elections may not be desirable, to try to wipe it out overnight brings other evils. For one thing, it is hardly being just to make an example of one man for what is still being widely practiced, and the alternative, charging half the Parliament with corruption, would hardly en-sure the peacefulness of public life which is the aim of eliminating corruption. Once the bribery had become a public issue, it was right to bring the culprit to trial and thus to give notice that a new set of standards had come into force. But as the foundation for the new standards had not yet set, it was a good thing that the prosecution had been lax and the defendant acquitted. There would come a time when that would no longer be desirable—but it had not yet arrived.

The whole is a picture in which reforms are begun and carried through in highly indirect and unpredictable ways and there is no simple explanation of how they happened. Those who tell us that reforms are made when the powers that be yield to a demand for reform forget to answer the hard question: what constitutes such a demand? Are speeches by the romantic bootmaker, Ontario Moggs, to his mates drinking in the Cheshire Cheese, evidence of such a de-mand? At times, Trollope suggests, such speeches made by such men might be, though probably in a circuitous fashion. The excitement that generates a reform may grow out of a dissatisfaction with some aspect of the existing state of affairs which is expressed "by this mouthpiece and that" until there is "a strong throb through the country making men feel that safety was to be had by Reform and could not be had without Reform." At other times, the dissatisfaction may sim-mer quietly for many years, and in the course of the simmering there may come, quietly and slowly, a radical alteration in men's opinions. But it may also happen that the excitement grows "from the self-instituted leaders of popular politics down, by means of the press, to the ranks of the working men . . ."

In many cases more than one of these modes of arousing the country ac-counts for an innovation, and there is something to be said for all. When reform grows out of a widespread unselfconscious dissatisfaction, it is more likely that the change is desired by the country at large, and not just by a small group because it serves their interests. If there is a slow transformation of opinion, the change when it comes may be less disruptive. But it may also be the case that there exists an anomaly which ought not to be tolerated by people aspiring to be decent and just, and that men who occupy themselves with reflecting on public arrangements ought to bring such a matter to the attention of the public.

The ironic tone of voice in which Trollope relates the events leading to an innovation indicates something more profound and difficult than the falsity or unreality of the opinions and events that fashion political change. The irony points rather to the disparity between our absorption in the here and now, the importance and reality that the events of today have for us, and the evanescence of all human things. By his irony Trollope reminds us as well that even the exaggerations, nonsense, and falsehoods play a salutary part in illuminating a truth which could never have been discovered directly. The result is an intricate picture of how a variety of considerations and judgments shape events in an unforeseeable way. As Trollope and his gentlemen see things, Parliament is not what Bagehot described—"an inquiring and discussing machine" with a constituency of "classes" possessing given "interests." Instead the events in Parliament are choices made by individuals with distinct personalities, responding to one another in many different ways and creating their destination in the course of arriving. They are not troubled by a conflict between "principle" and "expediency" because there are no fixed goals which exist in isolation from contingent responses and interpretations, and no heaven-sent principles forbidding the adoption of what is "expedient" here and now. There are only considerations of different qualities and importance, which come to bear on events in different ways through many agencies.

But this suggests a crucial question which brings us back to the image of a game. If there are no fixed objectives and the scene is constantly shifting, what keeps chaos at bay? The answer is given in Trollope's emphasis on the resemblance of the parliamentary struggle to a game or tournament. There are adversaries, prizes to be won and defeats to be endured, and everyone takes sides. But the participants are not bent on defeating their opponents by any means whatever, with any weapons they can discover or contrive. They are undoubtedly serious about winning, but in the manner of players in a game. They are not bent on achieving victory by any stratagems at hand; they are out to win by conducting themselves in accordance with certain rules. Only some skills and tactics may be used in the battle. For underlying all the conflicts is an agreement on the obligation to subscribe to certain procedures, and this is what preserves order and gives a determinate shape to what goes on in Parliament. In this way the making of innovations is like a game.

But there is an important difference. The charm of a real game lies in its being isolated from the real world, and some of the charm is lost when players turn "professional" and let the concerns of the outside world intrude on the green. The peculiar virtue of the rules and rituals of politics is the opposite— that they make the outcome of the game correspond to a reality outside the playing field. What happens in Parliament reflects fairly accurately, though not always to the same degree, the opinion of the country because the parliamentary battle is neither a game nor a struggle for power. It is a set of procedures by means of which changes in the country at large are reflected in the activities of a relatively small number. How this congruence comes about is not easily discovered or explained. But we can recognize that over the years there imperceptibly grew up certain practices which have made it possible to introduce innovations in an orderly fashion without imposing a stifling simplicity.

In a sense, the whole thing is haphazard. Men may join one party or another for no reason they could defend. As the battle proceeds, the participants may be led further and further away from the original issue, until at last a measure is opposed by one man simply because it is advocated by another, and members of Parliament swarm into lobbies, blindly following the dictation of their leaders rather than their own informed judgments. What is said in Parliament does not precisely express what each or perhaps any of the speakers thinks. Nevertheless, the speakers genuinely help to expose and illuminate what many in the country believe to be true. And this happens because of the character of human judgments. For no man has only one idea or inclination but many, possibly conflicting, ones. No question has only one aspect, and there is always more than one question to consider. Therefore a new emphasis, whatever the motives or intentions that produced it, may bring some to appreciate and accept what they had before considered impossible or distasteful. The persuasion that goes on both inside and outside Parliament proceeds by enlarging the country's perception of the range of choices, though in a highly indirect and intricate fashion.

The words in a parliamentary debate bear the same relation to what is really relevant to the issue in hand as an enlarged microscopic slide of a cell does to the body from which it is taken. There is a real relation to a real thing, but it is out of proportion and many of the features which seem striking on the slide are insignificant in real life. But just as those who understand the character of a slide make such allowances without even being aware of doing it, so in the great joust between Daubeny and Gresham, those who were familiar with parliamentary practice were not misled. They were made aware, perhaps in a roundabout fashion, of aspects of the question before them that they had never before considered. An unpredictable number of variations came into play. Yet the great mass of convictions, prejudices, hopes, and fears did not fall into chaos, because at every point most people respected established procedures. Each participant was in earnest, but not always about the same matter, and yet each in his own way contributed to an outcome which was acceptable to the nation. Whether it was the best possible outcome, it was impossible to say, but it seemed to do, at least for a while.

In recognizing this to be the way things are done, the gentleman walks a knife edge between crass indifference and a nice sense of proportion, between cynicism and detachment. He takes seriously the responsibility of using well whatever power he wields, but he also appreciates the truth in the Duchess's remark that "The country goes on its own way, either for better or for worse, whichever of them are in." The kind of detachment required is illustrated in an exchange between the old Duke of St. Bungay and the younger Duke of Omnium, who is prime minister. They are arranging the new cabinet and the prime minister says, "The thing itself is so momentous that one ought to have aid from heaven." St. Bungay replies, "Aid from heaven you may have by saying your prayers . . . But an angel won't come to tell you who ought to be Chancellor of the Exchequer." As this fails to soothe the prime minister, the old Duke tries to produce better comfort by reminding him of what "dear old Lord Brock" used to say—that "it was much easier to find a good Sec'y of State than a good coachman." But the young Duke regarded a joke on "so solemn a subject" as blasphemy. Omnium's earnestness, Trollope makes it clear, was a shortcoming because it prevented him from being robust enough to weather the fortunes of politics. The old Duke was better at recognizing both the gravity and the triviality of everything they did. That awareness did not distract him from taking seriously and acting decisively on what he perceived to be his duty here and now, but it enabled him to shrug off both the fear and reality of failure.

In short, what distinguishes the attitude of the gentleman is his readiness to acknowledge the disparity between the urgency of what has to be done today and its unimportance in the future. That gives him the appearance of being against innovation. But the truth is that he sees and even enjoys the grim fact that today's joke may be tomorrow's revolution and vice versa.

The same attitude to disagreements and to changes of opinion that Trollope's gentlemen display in politics makes it possible for children to differ with their parents without thinking or saying, as Nicholas Petrovich told his mother, "We belong to different generations." What happens instead is well illustrated in the worst disagreement between the generations that appears in Trollope's novels, the Duke of Omnium's refusal to let his daughter marry Frank Tregear. It is easy enough to construct this into an example of a severe "generation gap." Even the Duke's friend, Lady Cantrip, says that the times have changed and parents can no longer hope to command their children's choices as they once did. Lady Mary is described as someone who is very clear about her "rights": "Being a child of rich parents she had a right to money. Being a woman she had a right to a husband. Having been born free she had a right to choose for herself. Having had a man's love given to her, she had a right to keep it." The Duke is adamant, and his very proper contemporary, to whom he sent Lady Mary, might be seen as a formidable duenna, instructed to persecute her charge into submission. On this reading of the events, the capitulation of the Duke might be interpreted as an inability to withstand the demands of a new generation who have no use for his prejudices and are able to rebel effectively.

But this conclusion is like the vulgar view of why the Conservatives supported disestablishment. The details that Trollope gives tell a rather different story about a man of remarkable integrity, who in middle age learned to question his own prejudices. The Duke had been blessed with a son and a daughter who had inherited their father's firmness and their mother's ebullience. In his persecution of his children we see the Duke struggling with conflicting ideas and emotions, painfully but doggedly destroying his own certainties, exploring implications of his convictions, and coming to know better what his respect for himself and for others entailed.

On the one hand, he believed that inferiority of birth should not be a barrier to success, as traditionally it had not been in England. If a man could "raise himself by his own intellect to become prime minister, no one will think of his father or grandfather"—that was the Duke's guiding conviction. And his natural disposition was in many ways in tune with these beliefs. He had never preferred to work with aristocrats; "he would as soon sit in counsel with Mr. Monk, whose father had risen from a mechanic to be a merchant, as with any nobleman who could count ancestors against himself." And the peer he sat next to in the House of Lords, "whose grandmother had been a washerwoman and whose father an innkeeper, was to him every whit as good a peer as himself." Throughout his life in politics, it had been the Duke's object as a Liberal to make it easier for the son of a tradesman to become a lord and to bring the Duke and the workingman nearer by "the spread of education and the increase of general well-being." Not birth, but personal quality was what mattered. And he had accordingly taught his children that how much rank or money a man possessed might make life more or less easy for him, but could neither distinguish nor disgrace him as a man. What mattered was whether he had learned "those lessons without which no man can live as a gentleman."

But in another part of his heart and mind, the Duke had sealed off a different set of convictions and sentiments that had to do with preserving the aristocracy. He saw it as a class that had been bred to safeguard certain qualities and to give selfless public service, and to destroy it would change the character of the life in England that he loved and admired. To be born of a long line of peers meant that one had inherited the best blood in the country. Of course, there were some worthless peers, such as the unprincipled Lord Grex. But he was an anomaly from "the blue blood and rank." And it was a duty of those born into such a rank to protect it against dilution by bad blood. A nobleman was no freer to marry than a king; he had a public duty to marry someone suitable to enter his class. Though following his inclinations might lead to a happier marriage, he was not free to satisfy his inclinations. For what would have happened to Rome if the daughters of old Romans had married Greek slaves whenever they happened to be appealing? The great threat to an aristocracy came from adventurers, engaged in the meanest of enterprises and seeking to live without working by marrying a rich wife, and the only way to guard the aristocracy against such adventurers was to keep marriages within the ranks. One might very well enjoy or prefer the company of others, but in marriage it was essential to observe the propriety in things, for "only by adherence to that propriety on the part of individuals can the general welfare be maintained." The Duke's own marriage had been faultless in propriety and he expected his children to do the same. It was a matter of honor that they did so, because any other conduct would sacrifice public duty to self-indulgence, and if allowed, "all restraint would be lost and there would be an end to those rules as to birth and position by which he thought his world was kept straight."

The Duke held these two incompatible convictions without noticing any discrepancy until his daughter proposed to marry a gentleman of no rank and no means. But that was not all that made the Duke fear the worst. Frank Tregear was an ambitious man, out to make his way in the world, and his poverty and his ambition made it plausible that he was an adventurer impudent enough to select his victim from the highest family of all. He suffered besides from a further, and to the Duke, more disturbing disadvantage—his great physical beauty gave him a strong resemblance to a man whom the Duke could not recall without pain.

There was a strain of unhappiness in the Duke's life. He had learned to love his wife just as he discovered that she loved Burgo Fitzgerald, whom her guardians had prevented her from marrying. She had come to reconcile herself to her marriage, had indeed been a thoroughly devoted wife, but the Duke knew that she never loved him as she had that other man. Yet the Duke knew as well, as his wife also came to believe, that a marriage with Burgo Fitzgerald would have been a disaster for her, that he would have gambled away her money as he had his own and not brought her any happiness. Nevertheless, she remained wistful about the beautiful dream that she had lost, and the Duke understood her feelings. Matters were made worse by the fact that not only had Lady Mary's engagement to Tregear been made secretly with her mother's connivance, but the revelation to the Duke came shortly after the sudden death of the Duchess, when the Duke felt that his world had collapsed and he could not bear to acknowledge any faults in his wife. This history encouraged the Duke to think that Lady Mary's love for Tregear was the story of his wife and Burgo Fitzgerald all over again. His wife's history made it clear, he believed, that young people should not be given what they wanted just "because they have declared themselves to be in love." But there was something more involved. If he now admitted that it was not necessary to sacrifice inclination to propriety, would that not be a confession that his own marriage had been a mistake?

Of all these undertones to his rejection of Tregear, the Duke was unaware. He felt certain that it was his duty to prevent Lady Mary from wedding Tregear and to stand firm even while he saw his daughter suffering, and he himself suffered. The austerity that under his wife's influence the Duke had lost revived under this challenge: "the higher the duties," he told himself, "the keener the pangs."

And nevertheless, from the beginning, the Duke had doubts about his stand. He kept turning over the question whether, after all, things might not have been better if his Duchess had been allowed to have her way: "might she not have been alive now, and perhaps happier than she had ever been with him?" Had he remained unmarried and devoted himself wholly to politics, would not the "troubles of the world have been lighter on him?" After all, he had been no more than a "respectable husband." Moreover, as he reviewed the manner in which his marriage was arranged, he found that "the idea when picked to pieces is not a nice idea." Though he ordered that his daughter should be exposed to eligible young men, the procedure was repulsive to him.

His responses to Tregear's applications followed a pattern familiar to those who knew him. First he was astonished and angered; but in time he came to be impressed by Tregear's quiet firmness. What struck him at first as impudence, he later interpreted as boldness and finally as manliness. When his own candidate for Lady Mary's husband criticized Tregear's conduct, the Duke defended Tregear. Though he was outraged when Tregear justified his claim to be worthy of Lady Mary by appealing to all those beliefs about the equality of gentlemen and the irrelevance of rank and money that he himself had always professed, the Duke saw that "he had to deal with a man—with one whom he could not put off from him into the gutter, and there leave as buried in the mud."

With regard to his daughter, it was slowly borne in upon the Duke that she had not thoughtlessly become infatuated with a feckless Apollo, that she had inherited much from her father, was clear about the character of the man whom she loved, and that, whereas her mother had suddenly agreed to elope with Burgo and then within a week agreed to marry another man, Lady Mary's determination to marry Tregear would not be affected by opposition. In his conversations with his daughter, the Duke seemed to be immovable. When Lady Mary said that Tregear was a gentleman, the Duke replied that every clerk in all public offices considered himself a gentleman. When she said, "I do not know any other way of dividing people," he told her that she had no call to divide people but only to do as she was told. When Lady Cantrip remonstrated with him, he insisted that his daughter "must be made to obey like others." But all the time he kept asking himself whether he was being cruel and dishonest. He came close to obsession in his obstinacy, but was saved by his capacity genuinely to question himself. It took time, but he came to see that his judgment had been distorted by incoherent prejudices—that the resemblances to Lady Glencora's situation were superficial and that this was not a case of a princess and an adventurer, but of true love for a man of excellent character. Though when Lady Cantrip had said to him early on that he was making a mistake, he refused to listen, by the time that Mrs. Finn told him that his propriety was destroying his daughter's life, he accepted her reprimand meekly. And so he came finally to confess: "Now I will accept as courage what I before regarded as arrogance." The Duke capitulated because he came to see that by his own lights he had been wrong.

His son's proposal to marry the granddaughter of an American laborer was even more trying, as the blood of all the future Dukes of Omnium would flow from that marriage. But here, too, the Duke learned to recognize in both the girl and the father, strangers though they were, just the sort of self-sufficiency and modesty, as well as respect for propriety, by which he himself lived. He learned to remember his own belief that if the aristocracy were filled with peers such as Lord Grex, whose daughter he had hoped Silverbridge would marry, not only would the order "go to the wall" but "in the cause of humanity it had better do so." As Isabel Boncassen was distinguished by the qualities that the Duke considered to belong to the aristocracy, with his usual candor, he plainly acknowledged his error.

What we see then in the Duke's capitulation to his children is the story of a man for whom every question, which he had taken to be closed, had been opened. He had conscientiously struggled not to betray himself or to be unjust, and however tangled his judgment became at times, those were the considerations that dominated his thinking.

It should be noticed that even while his children were firmly refusing to be moved by their father's opposition, they thoroughly respected and loved him. When the younger son broke the rules of his college in Oxford to attend a race with Silverbridge, and was sent down, the elder brother went to plead for him with the Master of the college. What concerned Silverbridge was the pain that the affair would cause their father: "If you know how this would,—would—would break his heart," he said, and the tears in his eyes brought tears to the Master too—"That a young man should pray for himself would be nothing to him . . . A father asking for his son might be resisted. But the brother asking for the brother on behalf of the father was almost irresistible." The Master did not yield because the position of a son of the Duke of Omnium was "exalted beyond benevolence," but he assured Silverbridge that "your father, if he were here would know that I could not interfere."

No one who understood the Duke and his family had any doubt about the son's regard for his father. It took a vulgar scoundrel like Major Tifto, Silverbridge's colleague in sin on the turf, to suppose that because the Duke had differed with his son, they were on bad terms. When Tifto announced that "There have been no end of quarrels," Tregear, the man who might not be expected to feel friendly toward the Duke, answered firmly: "There has been no quarrel at all . . . nothing on earth would make Silverbridge quarrel with his father, and I think it would break the Duke's heart to quarrel with his son."

Nor was the difference over marriage the only one that divided the Duke from his children. How unlike the sons were from their father is made plain in Trollope's account of a "family breakfast," when Silverbridge and his brother had decided to "give the governor a turn" by which they meant that they "would drag themselves out of bed in time to breakfast with him." Whereas the Duke considered it wicked "to eat anything but toasted bacon before lunch," they were used to an elaborate feast. When the salmon and kidneys were brought in, the Duke commented on the change in the breakfast arrangements, and the sons explained sheepishly that they were "awfully hungry of a morning." That provoked a little sermon from the Duke to the effect that "eating is an occupation from which a man takes the more pleasure the less he considers it" and that "a rural labourer who sits on the ditch-side with his bread and cheese and an onion has more enjoyment out of it than any Lucullus," which culminated in an ardent speech about the kind of happiness brought by the "grind" of parliamentary life. Lord Gerald tried to break the flow with a mention of "books," while stuffing himself with kidneys; Silverbridge defended the comfort of having "a second horse out hunting"; and after they finished eating they quickly retired to some distant part of the house where they could smoke without being noticed by the Duke.

The differences between the Duke and Silverbridge went beyond the breakfast table. Not only had Silverbridge also been sent down from Oxford. He spent many hours at the disreputable club, the Beargarden; worse still, he devoted himself to racing, of which the Duke strongly disapproved; when finally he did enter politics, he stood as a Conservative instead of as a Liberal, which the Duke considered to be the natural party of his family; Frank Tregear was his closest friend and had through him become an intimate of the family. Silverbridge had done all this not to annoy but partly because he had a very different temperament from the Duke's and partly because he was feeling his way in the world. The Duke made his dissent on all these subjects perfectly clear; Silverbridge disliked causing him pain, but he also was determined to go his own way; and the Duke, even though he disapproved, did not try to prevent him.

In short, Trollope portrays a relationship in which there is considerable disagreement and sometimes open conflict, and nevertheless respect, understanding, and harmony as well as love. Father and son are not two opposed forces fated to collide. Their relations are far more intricate and constantly changing as the son grows older and the father thinks again. They are continually reinterpreting and responding to one another's conduct. Each, like the Liberals and the Conservatives, is a choir of many voices, comprehending a multitude of hopes, dreams, fears, disappointments, loves, convictions, prejudices, information, habits, inclinations, and judgments, which keep shifting and have no fixed anchor. It is not the case that one is holding fast while the other tries to break away and move forward along the road that lies ahead. For there is no one road and no given goal—only a multitude of paths, some already well-worn, others yet to be made. Therefore when a difference arises, it is not a simple clash between two opposing ideals or conventions. A great variety of ideas and sentiments enters into the stand taken by each, and the adjustment can come about in any number of ways and take many different forms.

There is no question of conformity or repression. What makes for the coherence in the Duke, as in his children, and what they have in common is an allegiance to a certain conception of what constitutes honesty, decency, honor—in short, a conception of the integrity of a gentleman. Like the rules and procedures of Parliament, it prescribes certain conditions to be observed when speaking or acting, without dictating what should be said or done. In deferring to their parents, even in recognizing their right on some questions to command obedience, the children are not conforming to a code which the elders are trying to impose on them because in the gentleman's world there is no code, nor any one pattern or ideal, which requires conformity. What is demanded is not the performance of this or that but something much more abstract—a *manner* of behaving. The difference is like that between the ballet dancer's skill and the performance required by the choreography of a ballet. Just as a ballet dancer may perform a great many different movements in different moods and roles and still be recognized as a ballet dancer, so is agreement on what constitutes the behavior of a gentleman compatible with wide differences on how to live or what to do on any particular occasion. Of course shallow, unimaginative people may identify being a gentleman with wearing certain clothes, using certain phrases, making certain gestures, or attending certain events, just as the vulgar may think that a ballet dancer must always wear white net and pirouette on her toes. But those who have a genuine understanding, though it may not be a self-conscious one, will not be surprised by enormous variations in the behavior of gentlemen nor find it difficult to discern within those variations the distinction between a gentleman and a cad.

Though the Duke was pained by his son's decision to enter Parliament as a Conservative, when Silverbridge decided to change back, the Duke gave him good reasons for remaining a Conservative. What mattered to the Duke far more than that Silverbridge should belong to his own party was that his son should be a dedicated and useful member of parliament, which required him to understand that changing party every time the leader displeased him was being self-indulgent and silly, as well as that there are other reasons for changing one's party which are serious and valid. In the same way, though the Duke did not approve of racing and never himself had had anything to do with it, he chastised Silverbridge not for his interest in racing but for making an intimate of a man like Major Tifto, a reprimand which Silverbridge easily acknowledged to be just. Though the Duke was austere and his sons pleasure-loving, though his sermons at the breakfast table were hardly music to their ears, they recognized that the Duke was not insisting that they live as he did, but was concerned to make sure that they did not exaggerate the importance of eating kidneys and salmon or forget the virtues of living more abstemiously. They understood and respected his motives and took his words to heart without trying to imitate him.

What Trollope shows us in the story of the conflicts between the Duke and his children is how people of different temperaments and tastes learn to accommodate to one another. Instead of two generations necessarily driven into battle with one another, he shows us that not only the young but also their elders are constantly learning what it means to behave with the integrity of a gentleman. There are times of unhappiness but they are to be borne as part of the human condition. And though other fathers in his circumstances might have managed to cause less pain to everyone concerned, the Duke's opposition to the marriage had its redeeming features. Like the battles in Parliament, it indirectly achieved what might not have been done otherwise. It helped the young to become clearer about what mattered to them and to test the seriousness of their love. In the course of the difficulties, Tregear learned to admire the Duke, Lady Mary and he were reassured of the strength and depth of their feelings for one another, Isabel Boncassen came to understand better the difference between the conventional and profound convictions of the people among whom she was coming to live. If in other families, the conflicts might have a different outcome, in Trollope's world it is not because of any "gap" between the generations, but because the people at odds with one another are more unreasonable or do not have in common the gentleman's respect for integrity and individuality. Gentlemen may differ greatly and in many ways and yet live together amicably, but they do not accommodate to one another automatically. Just how they come to do so cannot be prescribed or predicted. It may happen imperceptibly as did the change of opinions about disestablishment. But there is neither fixity nor much danger of violent breaks in the relations between young and old, because the agreement that is wanted and given is at a highly abstract level, and compatible therefore with an infinite variety in concrete performances. As he knows this instinctively, a gentleman is immune to the vulgar error of elevating every disagreement or attempt at innovation into a battle between the forces of good and evil. He assumes that a difference in judgment or taste can be indulged without making a revolution.

ROBERT SKIDELSKY

Keynes and His Parents

MAYNARD KEYNES'S BREAK with the values of his parents needs to be put into its proper cultural setting, as part of a wider reaction against Victorianism.

The Victorians were activists. Their allegiance was given to making money, saving souls, and improving the world. Theirs was a religious age, but it was not the kind of religion which encouraged withdrawal from the world. Rather, it spurred men to pile up money and achievements for the greater glory of God and the security of their immortal souls. Morality was a matter of right conduct: acting rightly was deemed more important than thinking rightly or feeling rightly. In the standard utilitarian ethics of the time, actions were supposed to be judged by consequences. In practice, Victorian morality was largely conventional, a matter of good form, rather than ratiocination.

The high achievements of the Victorian age were purchased at a price. One casualty was the arts. In Matthew Arnold's view, the Victorians sacrificed culture to machinery; the cultivation of what is "beautiful, graceful and becoming" to the "machinery of business, chapels, tea-meetings and addresses . . ." The other loss was in the area of personal development, and personal relationships. Both were sacrificed to the extreme consciousness of sin, which repressed both sexuality and affection, and to the doctrine of work, which condemned what was not *useful* as a waste of time and energy. If there was any single principle of Victorian life it was the sacrifice of the present to the future. It was a society geared to saving, both economically and psychologically.

It was to a group of Cambridge undergraduates, of whom Keynes was one, brought up in this tradition, that G. E. Moore's *Principia Ethica* came, in 1903, as a revelation. What is of greatest interest to philosophers in this book is Moore's argument that "good" is indefinable. But what chiefly interested his young Cambridge friends was his distinction between good as a means and good as an end. Moore argued that the life of action, with its associated virtues, has no intrinsic value. It is valuable only as a means to the good, and, moreover, a pretty incalculable one, since "we can never be sure that any action will produce the greatest value possible." Ethics had been largely concerned with commending certain actions, to the neglect of what was intrinsically valuable. The things, says Moore, which are good in themselves are not virtuous actions, but certain states of mind which are sought for their own sake. These were "the pleasures of human intercourse and the enjoyment of beautiful objects." By making this central distinction between means and ends, and by wrongly accus-

71

ing ethics of having concentrated on the former at the expense of the latter, Moore in effect devalued the whole Victorian scheme of life—conventional morality, the life of action, dedication to public causes. Over thirty years later, Keynes called the *Principia Ethica* "the beginning of a new renaissance, the opening of a new heaven on earth" whose effect "dominated, and perhaps still dominates, everything else."

Moore's influence can be seen in the work of two leading members of Bloomsbury, Lytton Strachey and Clive Bell. Strachey's *Eminent Victorians*, published in 1918, is the dramatization of the conflict between good actions and good states of mind. His four eminent Victorians were all relentless activists, always wanting, like Florence Nightingale, to be "doing something." Their values were worldly; they were ambitious for honor and power, or wanted to do good. Strachey sets out to show how such lives of action are incompatible with what is intrinsically good, and also how action is quite likely to be futile, even destructive. Cardinal Manning tramples on Newman, the unworldly hero of the first essay; Florence Nightingale, in "doing good," drives Sidney Herbert to his death. The consequences of Arnold's actions turn out to be quite contrary to his intentions: "The earnest enthusiast who strove to make his pupils Christian gentlemen . . . thus proved to be the founder of the worship of athletics and the worship of good form." The one character for whom Strachey feels sympathy is General Gordon, whose actions were dotty. His state of mind was not as bad as the others'.

Clive Bell asks the question: what is meant by civilization? Civilization, he says, in a book with that title, published in 1928, is not a belief in private property, chastity, patriotism, or God, since all these beliefs exist in savage societies, and many societies regarded as civilized did not have them. Nor does it consist in being fittest for survival, democratic, or technologically advanced. Civilization is the direct means to good states of mind. Its defining characteristic is respect for art and thought. Civilized people dislike the "life of action." Some activities, it is true, may be means to the good. But since life is already full of immediate means to good, civilized persons are less concerned to promote indirect means. Action is a disease for those who cannot find satisfaction in love, friendship, conversation, creation, or contemplation of beauty, pursuit of truth and knowledge, gratification of the senses. It is the vice of those "inapt for civilized pleasures . . ." A civilized society, Bell feels, is one which contains groups of highly civilized men and women, living off the labor of others, and large enough to influence the whole tone of life. He was far from feeling that England met these requirements. In fact, English civilization was so "grossly Philistine" that any English boy "born with a fine sensibility, a peculiar feeling for art, or an absolutely first-rate intelligence" was bound to find himself "at loggerheads with the world in which he is to live," bound to become "an outlaw."

Now, the point about Keynes was that he was *never* an outlaw. He jettisoned much of what we think of as Victorianism, but not, on the whole, the values of his family, school, and university. The seeming contradiction is easily explained. Keynes's background was by no means typical of middle-class Victorian England. His family milieu was much more scholarly than was normal. At Eton, and at King's College, Cambridge, he stepped into an intellectual tradition: in fact, Moore's *Principia Ethica*, while rejecting Victorian morality, embodied much of what was best in the Cambridge tradition. Thus Keynes was brought up in a society sufficiently civilized not to force him into the rebellion which Clive Bell thought inevitable for anyone of his temperament. In their own lives, Keynes and his Cambridge circle broadened that civilization to include other "goods." They had no cause to repudiate it.

Keynes's parents, John Neville and Florence Ada Keynes, emerge from Sir Roy Harrod's biography as rather shadowy figures. John Neville was a fellow of Pembroke College, Cambridge, a logician and economist. He seems to have been a kind, modest, considerate, retiring man, honorable and punctilious, with a fondness for ceremonial and a weakness for Royalty. Florence Ada was the more forceful, active character. One of the first graduates of Newnham, the new women's college, she was heavily involved in good works, particularly as a member of the Charity Organisation Society. Through this, she became active in local politics, ending up as Mayor of Cambridge. "When is [your mother] not busy?" John Neville once asked Maynard, writing on another occasion, "What a devoted woman she is! If there is anything in heredity, her children certainly ought to have a sense of duty." Their marriage was, by his account, ideally happy.

In one crucial respect, they were also ideal parents for someone of Maynard Keynes's exceptional gifts. Very early on (he was born in 1883) they appeared to recognize that their eldest son had the makings of a genius. According to Maynard's school reports, he was showing "talent" at arithmetic at six, "power" at seven. At nine he was "decidedly the brightest boy in his division" at St. Faith's preparatory school; at eleven, the senior wrangler who taught him reported him doing "really brilliant" work in mathematics. His classics, too, were "full of promise." (He was to win an open scholarship in both to King's College, Cambridge.) His parents, particularly his father, provided the strongest possible support, intellectual and moral, for Maynard's mental development. Not only was he encouraged to take part in adult conversations with such visitors as W. E. Johnson, Alfred Marshall, and Henry Sidgwick, but John Neville appointed himself, in effect, his director of studies.

As Maynard's mentor, his father probably found an increasingly satisfying intellectual outlet. His second, and last, book, *The Scope and Method of Political Economy*, appeared when he was thirty-seven, and Maynard seven. Thereafter, although he became a university administrator of legendary good sense, he wrote nothing of importance. Perhaps he felt that, with nothing original to say himself, his time was best spent encouraging his son's originality. Father and son worked together in John Neville's study, in a relationship which recalls that of James Mill and John Stuart Mill. There was another motive. Although Maynard's parents were comfortably off, they were not wealthy. They wanted Maynard to go to Eton; but this depended on his getting a scholarship; and his educational program was geared to that end. Maynard duly became a King's Scholar at Eton in the autumn of 1897. Among the many advantages which his background gave him, conspicuous financial advantage was not one. He was a "scholarship" boy.

This strenuous intellectual regime was, on the whole, perfectly suited to Maynard's quick, active, incisive mind. But there were signs of stress. Up to the age of sixteen or so he was subject to frequent, and rather mysterious, illnesses.

They were so habitual, in fact, that they were known in the family as his "periodicals." He was also subject to stammering. In 1896 his father wrote in his diary, "Maynard's holiday task was some four or five hundred lines of Homer and as there has certainly been an increase in stammering lately—indicating a need for entire rest—I wrote to ask that he might be excused this." His headmaster, Goodchild, agreed, replying "[Maynard] seemed so bright all round that I did not connect the increased hesitation in speaking with his work." Maynard's mysterious fevers and "liver attacks" may well have been "migraine," which, like his stammering, suggests that he was under considerable strain.

As an Eton "Colleger," Maynard found himself in a highly stimulating, competitive intellectual environment. Weekly letters of encouragement and exhortation, which included detailed advice on examination strategy, poured in from his father. But undoubtedly the main stimulus was provided by the school itself. To a remarkable extent, Eton had managed to escape the Arnoldian blight; at College, the scholars' house, Maynard sharpened his wits against those of some of the cleverest boys in the country. Athletics reigned, but they did not reign supreme. Intellectual accomplishment was highly valued; and there was enough privacy, and sufficient numbers of able and dedicated masters, to make the most of a boy's intellectual talents. In this atmosphere, there was little enough reason for Maynard to rebel, as did so many outstanding boys at more philistine boarding schools. In fact, his was a triumphant progress, punctuated only by illness. He won forty-nine prizes, and became a member of "Pop." What struck his tutor, Gurney Lubbock, was the entire absence in him of the "mercenary, mark-getting feeling which so often spoils excellent scholars." For him work was "worth doing for its own sake."

I have indicated one of the great strengths of Maynard's upbringing—the encouragement of his intellectual growth. But there were at least two important weaknesses. The first was a certain coldness in family relationships, the product of a bourgeois suspicion of emotional experience. The conventions of Maynard's upbringing did seem to exclude the expression of feelings. Remarkable in the dense correspondence between Maynard and his parents is the absence of any clue to the emotions of the letter-writers. The only exceptions are his parents' expressions of pride in his accomplishments and worry about his state of health. There is no sense, for example, that either Maynard or his parents missed each other in his years of boarding. Even as an adult, when any youthful embarrassment at the expression of such sentiments may have been expected to fade, Maynard never discusses in his letters to his father or mother his feelings about himself, or his friends, or about them. Making every allowance for the conventions of the time, this does suggest a rather constricted relationship. Maynard's younger brother, Sir Geoffrey Keynes, uses the word "neutral" to describe his home, and perhaps this quality permeated the home environment. (Maynard was not close to Geoffrey, four years his junior, though he was more intimate with his sister Margaret.) The evidence suggests that they were a "happy" family—but perhaps happiness was achieved only by transferring out of the family anything awkward or sensitive.

From a certain point of view, family life was indeed ideal. There was much tolerance: Maynard, in particular, seems to have established a remarkably independent life-style from a quite early age, successfully claiming the un-Puritan right to sleep late in the mornings (and to get breakfast served long after the others). Family members were linked together by a large number of hobbies and activities. There was a collectively produced family newspaper, which ran intermittently, under different names, for many years. There were long family summer holidays, visits to the grandparents at Bedford (Florence Ada's father was an eminent Congregational divine, author of a standard life of Bunyan), occasional trips abroad. Maynard's father managed to involve the others in his passion for stamp-collecting, chess, and golf. In fact, golf, which he took up, together with university administration, when he abandoned serious scholarship, seems to have been the one thing which caused John Neville real agonies of mind. He struggled with his recalcitrant swing in much the same spirit as Gladstone wrestled with sin, and apparently equally unavailingly. After his earliest years, it was his relationship with his father which was central to Maynard's childhood.

Maynard did not, on the whole, break through these emotional barriers at Eton. A clue to why this may have been so is provided by his confession to Lytton Strachey in 1906 that "I have always suffered and I suppose always will from an unalterable obsession that I am . . . physically repulsive . . . The idea is so fixed and constant that I don't think anything—certainly no argument—could ever shake it." That this was the most powerful barrier to the open expression of feeling can readily be imagined, especially in a school, and even university, world dominated by a supercilious physical aristocracy. At Eton, Maynard was romantically attracted to the older Daniel Macmillan; but otherwise his friendships were with other amusing, intellectual boys of his own age. His public demeanor was high-minded, even priggish; his feelings were veiled by clever and amused gossip.

Although the Keynes family paid great respect to thought, art was at a severe discount, retaining, in Noel Annan's words, its status as the "temptress which they had to control by inadequate theories." On their marriage in 1882, Maynard's parents moved into a bleak, double-fronted house at 6 Harvey Road, part of a new "development" for married dons. Here Maynard grew up. "The furnishings," writes Sir Geoffrey Keynes, "were undistinguished, but comfortable. The pictures were conventional specimens of period taste . . . Our home surroundings afforded no aesthetic stimulus." The literature, too, was conventional, with popular writers like Anthony Hope in the ascendant. There was no music. The theater was one of John Neville's great hobbies, and visits to plays in London were the special treat of Maynard's schooldays. But what they saw were conventional comedies, musicals, and melodramas, with titles like "The Rose of Passion." We find no mention of Ibsen, nor even of Pinero and Wilde. In this respect, the Keynes family merely mirrored Cambridge's parochialism. Maynard's own aesthetic emotions remained largely dormant, the exceptions being a certain dandyish delight in smart clothes and a passion for putting fine bindings on the book prizes which he received in such abundance. His buying of secondhand books, which started when he was at Eton, is more properly considered as an example of the collecting urge, a family trait which he shared with Geoffrey.

Keynes was liberated from this constricted world of high-minded academic and civic values by his postschool experiences in Cambridge and London. One should not make exaggerated claims. His new interests, tastes, and feelings were, in a sense, simply part of growing up. He came in 1902 to King's College, Cambridge, intellectually precocious, but emotionally undeveloped. Relieved from the pressure of continuous examinations, he could develop other sides of his personality. Nor should it be imagined that Keynes "dropped out." He worked hard enough to become twelfth wrangler in the mathematics tripos, a result which Harrod calls "respectable, but not triumphant." He became president of the Cambridge Union. In fact, his extraordinary energy and quickness enabled him to do many things well. Nevertheless, there occurred a permanent shift in values. Intellect retained its high place. He found it a "much more comfortable passion" than some others he had started to experience. By the end of 1905 he was finding economics "increasingly satisfactory," and commented, "I think I am rather good at it. I want to manage a railway or organise a Trust or at least swindle the investing public. It is so easy and fascinating to master the principles of these things." However, his order of priorities had changed. To Strachey he wrote in 1906 "I don't wonder Aristotle put this intellectual activity first. Still, I don't agree with him. Love first, Philosophy second, Poetics third, and Politics fourth." And over thirty years later he recalled that "our prime objects in life were love, the creation and enjoyment of aesthetic experience and the pursuit of knowledge. Of these love came a long way first." This was not the language of his parents, much less of the Victorian age as a whole. Neither was it characteristic of his generation. About the same time, the twenty-two-year-old C. P. Trevelyan was writing to his parents, "I should never mar my prospects of doing good to the people for the sake of any love for woman." This was the authentic note of upper-class Victorianism.

One needs to place this "transvaluation of values" in its proper setting. Sir Roy Harrod has rightly emphasized that Maynard's new departure depended on "the security and good order of the British Empire . . . Within the framework of a secure society thus kept in being, it was possible and desirable to make new experiments and to set one's eyes fixedly upon certain ideals, too long neglected." We can be more precise. The Edwardian era was an interlude of prosperous calm between the economic troubles of the eighteen-eighties and eighteen-nineties and the First World War. As Keynes wrote after the war "The projects and politics of militarism and imperialism, of racial and cultural rivalries, of monopolies, restriction, and exclusion, which were to play serpent to this paradise, were little more than the amusements of [the] daily newspaper, and appeared to exercise almost no influence at all on the ordinary course of social and economic life . . ." And if England was a paradise, Cambridge was a paradise within a paradise, even more remote from the world of practical affairs. The other important factor is the general breakdown of Victorian morality. "I know I believe in nothing . . . but I do not less believe in morality," wrote Leslie Stephen. But the Victorian moral code could not long survive the loss of its religious supports. This was the setting in which a leisured class could experiment in new styles of living. Both its situation and its morality were transitional. The Bloomsbury group, as Roger Fry claimed, were the last of the Victorians. They were also the first sexual and aesthetic radicals.

In the formation of Keynes's personal "ethic," three names stand out: G. E. Moore, Lytton Strachey, and Duncan Grant. The first two he got to know in an exclusive and secret Cambridge discussion society, the "Apostles," to which he was elected in his second term at Cambridge. According to the mid-nineteenth-century Apostle Henry Sidgwick, the Society was animated by "the spirit of the pursuit of truth with absolute devotion and unreserve by a group of intimate friends." In Keynes's day, the dominating influence was G. E. Moore, and discussion revolved to a great extent round those ethical and aesthetic questions which made up the subject matter of the *Principia Ethica.*

We have already referred to Moore's distinction between good actions and good states of mind, and, in summary fashion, to his ideal of personal affection and aesthetic enjoyments. But an equally important part of his appeal lay in what Keynes and his friends called Moore's "method," by which they meant his technique for ranking states of mind in order of value. Its centerpiece was his theory of "organic unities." Moore held that the good was a complex whole which did not equal the sum of the value of its parts. A whole formed of one good part and one indifferent or bad part might have far greater value than the good part itself possessed. For example, the most valuable aesthetic enjoyments were made up of an appropriate emotion, a cognition of beautiful qualities, and the true belief that the object of appreciation possessed those qualities. But which was more valuable: an inadequate appreciation of a superior object, or a true appreciation of an inferior object? It is easy to see what scope for intellectual games such questions provided. Keynes later gave examples of the games he and his friends played: "If A was in love with B under a misapprehension as to B's qualities, was this better or worse than not being in love at all? If A was in love with B because A's spectacles were not strong enough to see B's complexion, did this altogether, or partly, destroy the value of A's state of mind?" The point about Moore's ideal and method was that they gave young intellectual Puritans an approach to the feelings: emotions themselves became the subject matter of intellectual and moral analysis. It may seem a remarkably indirect way of coming to terms with basic things; but many basic things were excluded by the Victorian scheme of life. It was "not done" for middle-class Victorian males to attach high, much less supreme, value to intimacy and beauty. Clever young people, brought up in moral Victorian homes, could only approach these, initially, by indirect paths. That is why Moore's highly abstruse "method" was seen as a liberation. What is, perhaps, more surprising is that early Edwardian Cambridge remained completely untouched by parallel movements of revolt against the nineteenth century, in Britain and abroad. (It could not be expected to know about Freud, whose work was as yet untranslated.) For example, Keynes wrote to Strachey after having seen Shaw's *John Bull's Other Island,* "Is it monomania—this colossal moral superiority that we feel? I get the feeling that most of the rest never see anything at all—too stupid or too wicked." Although Moore's revolution in ethics can be seen as part of a wider movement, it was a very homegrown affair, tailor-made to the needs of repressed young Cambridge intellectuals, whose striving for greater intimacy and joy in life had to be justified by a new moral philosophy.

Moore's ideal had a lasting influence on Keynes. But after the initial sense of liberation, his "method" proved too restrictive. By 1904-1905, Maynard was looking for a more direct expression of sexual emotion, one which would, at the same time, free the intellect for analyzing more substantial questions than whether A's defective vision lessened the value of his state of mind. Basically, he was fed up with endlessly intellectualizing the problem of forbidden love. He complained that Moore's "method" had made him too "idealistic," without realizing that this was the effect, not of Moore, but of his moral upbringing. In his quest for psychological liberation, Strachey was his companion and confidant. To Strachey he wrote on November 6, 1905, "I foresee no remedy without a new method. There *must* be a new method: something that will bring ease, that will allow a half and halfdom when there are ten, and the whole hog when there are two." On November 15, 1905, he wrote to Strachey, more realistically, "Of course, everyone would be a hedonist if he could, in practice. Certainly you and I would. The disease is that we can't. Will we have to give up the Grand Life?" But the remedy was to come not through a new method, but through the move to London. Strachey was strongly encouraging. "It would surely be mad," he wrote, "to be a Cambridge economist. Come to London, go to the Treasury, and set up house with me. The parties we'd give!" Keynes, who felt reasonably sure of getting employment in Cambridge if he wanted it, took the plunge, sat for the Civil Service Examination, and went to the India Office. It was in London, between 1906 and 1908, that he discovered a satisfying personal identity. By doing so, he freed himself to return to Cambridge—and home. But only partly: he never left London entirely, and Bloomsbury was to become his second family, giving him the things which his own family, and Cambridge, could not.

It was Maynard's friendship with the painter Duncan Grant, whom he met in London in 1906, which made the arts an integral part of his life. Duncan was the cousin and (at the time) the lover of Lytton Strachey. He had studied painting at the Westminster School of Art and in Paris under Jacques Emile Blanche. Duncan Grant recalled the holiday he and Maynard spent in the Orkneys in the autumn of 1908:

> Naturally I took my paint box, brushes, etc., and he his writing books, pens, etc. I don't think either of us doubted that we should be each employed in doing regular work of our own. Maynard with his writing board was a good subject, so when he was immersed in the *Theory of Probability* . . . I was immersed in trying to figure out the shape of his face. The result of this, I think, was that Maynard gradually accepted the fact that painting had its difficulties, without me having to point it out, that the painter had a serious job in hand. I may be quite wrong but I think that from this time on, he became very much aware of the part the arts might play in life. I am thinking ahead now, of the great part he played in the formation of the Arts Council and after his marriage to Lydia Lopokova of his passionate interest in the Ballet and the Theatre.

In these ways, Maynard continued, added to, and rearranged, the values he had grown up with. His upbringing, at home and school, was never sufficiently philistine to make him a rebel or "outlaw" in Clive Bell's sense. Yet it left out sufficient of what Keynes came to regard as valuable to make him a reformer. We are left with a final question. What influence did his "ethic" have on his work as an economist? There are a number of suggestive leads which are worth following up.

Moore's distinction between "good as means" and "good as end" was clearly relevant. Economics was a "science of means." It was valuable only as a means to the good. This meant that it must above all be practical, relevant, useful. Keynes's complaint against economics in the *General Theory* was that it had lost its "practical influence." Having no practical use was a luxury reserved for those things which were intrinsically valuable, not those whose only value was to promote good results. He determined to remedy this. A second influence stemmed from the nature of Moore's ideal itself. Political goals such as justice or equality had no place in Moore's utopia and Keynes's economics were not geared to achieving them—he was never a socialist. He saw economics, rather, as a means to make life beautiful, intelligent, loving. Wasted resources, he wrote in the depth of the Great Depression, could have been used to make Britain's cities "the greatest works of man in the world," rather than being degraded slums which shut out art and culture. The third influence is more speculative. If the kernel of Keynesian theory be translated into Mooreite language, it amounts to this: that saving or abstinence, which is undoubtedly good as a means under some circumstances, had come to be mistaken as good in itself. As Keynes himself put it in the *Economic Consequences of the Peace*, through saving, "the cake increased; but to what end was not clearly contemplated . . . the virtue of the cake was that it was never to be consumed." Keynes believed that the time had come to consume the cake. Standing in the way was the utilitarian psychology of Puritanism which, as Moore wrote, tended to hold that "what is here and now never has any value in itself." *Principia Ethica* set out, among other things, to destroy this belief in moral philosophy. Keynes set out to destroy it in economics. In succeeding in doing so, he fulfilled his parents' expectations, and helped undermine their world.

NOEL ANNAN

"Our Age": Reflections on Three Generations in England

Do GENERATIONS EXIST? Maurice Bowra, the greatest Oxford don and wit of his times, had no doubt that they did. If you asked him how old someone was, he was as likely as not to reply, "Our age." This meant anyone who came of age or graduated from university between the end of the First World War and the end of the Second. To him they were all the same generation. It is possible to be even more precise. The age to which Maurice Bowra and I belonged—he was eighteen years my senior—began in England at the end of 1910 in the month when the Post-Impressionist Exhibition opened, and it ended in 1952 when the last of the veterans of the Second World War had taken their degrees. Such precision is intended to provoke. Are there such things as generations and how, if at all, can they be characterized?

Many professional historians would dismiss the concept with contempt. The Sixième Section of the Ecole des Hautes Etudes, which has dominated historical research since the war, appears to find no place for individuals in the study of the demography, geographic changes, and social movements in the past. Since babies are born through any period and the fluctuation in the birth-rate provides no justification for separating any particular cohort in the age group from its predecessors, the word generation itself has no meaning. Cataclysmic events, such as the Counter-Reformation and the French Revolution, denote periods rather than generations. In a period as well documented as the Victorian age, research ever since G. M. Young's inspired essay[1] has reemphasized how at the height of what he called the Victorian noontime, or W. L. Burn, the Age of Equipoise, the fifties in the last century were a period of "deep-seated folding, straining and faulting: old strata and new shifting against each other into fantastic and precarious poises."[2] At the very time when national euphoria was at its height, the churches were struck by the ferment of religious doubt, socialism was beginning to challenge liberalism, the proclamation of imperialism coincided with the growth of the terrorism which was to lead to an independent Irish state, and the languid sentences of Matthew Arnold began to melt men's allegiance to the Romantic Movement. When historians describe men and their affairs they do so in terms of the historical process rather than in terms of a static generation suspended for a moment in time.

There is, of course, one piece of evidence that generations exist. People have always thought that they did. In one of the most famous lines in Homer, Glaucus reminds Diomedes, "As the generation of the leaves such are the gener-

81

ations of men"; and the Psalmist never ceased to remind men they belonged to a generation. Of course, the reply may be that people once believed in the existence of witches; but the sense of belonging to a particular peer group who, widely varying in opinions, nevertheless share common assumptions about their own society and its relation to other parts of the world, about estimable goals and despicable means, about desirable ways to live and ignoble pursuits in life, is not an entire delusion. No doubt it is partly a delusion. No doubt people who believe that their generation stands for this or that delude themselves. How can such egoists represent more than a fraction of their age group? Their class, their position in society, their influence, their power to realize their aims, all dictate the standpoint from which they address us. Those who so often make claims to interpret their generation come from a very small section of society. They are usually drawn from the professional classes. They may be lawyers or doctors or academics; the higher civil servants or editors or journalists; the purveyors of ideas through paperbacks and the media; or the accredited spokesmen for interest and pressure groups. A century ago in England one would have to have added clergymen. Today one would have to add the leading trade unionists. Suppose one asked of those whom Bowra called "our age," a sample of the gentry or of businessmen or of those in the labor movement; of those who worked in light as distinct from heavy industry, or who worked in the North of England and in Scotland rather than in South East England; each group would tell a different tale—would interpret their generation in a different way—might indeed not see it as the same generation whether in length of time or character. Perhaps the deepest difference in sensibility would be between the vast majority of those who left school at fourteen and those who received full-time secondary education in England. The claim of those who pronounce what a generation stands for is therefore always suspect and likely to be a piece of special pleading.

And yet there are times when the most articulate among a generation of young men become convinced that they are quite distinct from their forebears and so influence the next few cohorts of adolescents that they give the impression of belonging to a new age. Young men felt this in Europe after the French Revolution and in Russia during the 1840s. So they did again in England at the height of the Oxford Movement, and the surge of Romanticism, and the founding of Philosophic Radicalism. Certainly this sensation of breaking with the past seized numbers of the young in the twenties and thirties of this century living under the shadow of a war to end war, the Russian Revolution and modernism in the arts. But before we ask who "our age" really were, what was it that they were revolting against and why did they see themselves so self-consciously as men and women who thought and behaved differently from their fathers and mothers?

The society in which "our age" came into existence was not yet a mass society; large sections of the population had not yet been incorporated into British society. Before 1918 women still had not the vote, and universal male suffrage was still (incredibly) new; the ruling class acknowledged the existence of the mass of people, but large numbers of them were merely objects of which they took account, "hands" to be laid off or taken on. The welfare state was in its infancy. Yet despite the vigorous political and intellectual disputes of the times the strength of the consensus in society was enormous. The consensus that existed was not stamped by a sense of citizenship. It was molded from an amalgam of national self-consciousness and a religious code of behavior; from being North Country or Irish and knowing that to be "respectable" meant adhering to a certain way of life usually expressed through a church's creed. Where nationalism and religion conflicted with the ruling class, as it did in Ireland, the consensus was there to be most violently broken and rejected.

The consensus was also buttressed by the strength of authority, less strong than in high Victorian times, in that syndicalist strikes fought with much bitterness were a commonplace of the adolescence of "our age." But in all parts of life—the parent in the home, the teacher in the school, the employer and the elder generation—all were vested with a charisma that would be regarded with astonishment by the young today. With this respect for authority went a corresponding fear of nonconformity. The rulers at the center of society demanded and obtained conformity to their way of life as an ideal. They were able to do so because most thinking men agreed broadly what pattern social relationships should take and what ends in life were desirable. People were willing to acknowledge the way of life of the ruling class as a norm to which those rising in society should be willing to accept. The customs and conventions of those in the profession or job or class which they were entering were to be imitated and admired by all but a few sturdy radicals. Perhaps it is not going too far to say that a man and his family came to be regarded as citizens by the degree to which they were able to conform to the accepted mode of the clan and part of the country to which they belonged. Only those in the years before 1914 who could show some signs of assimilating to the ruling class's way of life were regarded as fully within the social pale, hence the importance of servants, leisure pursuits, or correct clothes for different occasions. Talleyrand's famous dictum that no one who did not move in society before the Revolution could know the true douceur de vivre was often repeated after the war by those who idolized the balls in the great London houses of the rich aristocracy, the procession of the London season with its landmarks of Ascot and Goodwood, the Glorious Twelfth of August when grouse shooting began, the country house parties and low personal taxation. Deviance was clandestine. Even those who stood a little apart from and enlivened late Victorian and Edwardian society, such as the Souls graced by Margot Tennant and George Curzon, or the clever young epigrammatists whose supreme example was Wilde, did not pick a quarrel with that society; indeed with a few notable exceptions they conformed in their dress, their decorum, and in the way they expressed their opinions.

The immense difference between the Victorian and Edwardian age and the generation which succeeded it lies in the fact that before 1914 intellectuals counted for little. It was not that men of intellect were divorced from political life: Gladstone was a formidable scholar and theologian, and the most unlikely ministers such as Salisbury often had distinguished themselves in university examinations. In retrospect, Victorian life seems peopled with sages, scientists, editors, philosophers, economists, learned men, and, of course, theologians. But their direct influence on affairs was limited. The ruling class and administrators, the politicians and the servants of the state, absorbed them effortlessly, dominated social life and determined the consensus. What is striking is how feebly they were challenged, or, rather, how willing the middle classes were to defer to the landed nobility and gentry even after they had won political status, and how solid and conservative the working classes were despite terrible periods of hardship and suffering when the terms of trade shifted and a whole area such as Lancashire would feel the pinch of hunger. Such a confident society, for all its expressions of doubt about Higher Things, was sustained by an ethos which went back into the eighteenth century and certainly evolved in recognizable form by the battle of Waterloo. Wellington certainly embodied it. What was this ethos and why did it eventually come to be undermined and despised?

The old ethos has been caricatured for so long and sometimes so amusingly that it is difficult to comprehend that there was anything fine in it—until one recollects that Churchill gave it allegiance (though some disputed that) and was to invoke its finest characteristics in 1940. It portrayed the role of an Englishman as being one who ruled his life under the guidance, no longer of God, but of an overpowering sense of civic duty and diligence. He must be above all courageous but not a bully; he must discipline himself to reject both easy solutions or merely profitable employment; he must serve the institution to which he belonged, his ministry, his regiment, his school or college or his calling in a professional manner and put it before his private life and the call of his family. Service entailed an acknowledgement that there were others less fortunate in the community or in imperial territories which it was now Britain's duty to rule. But it did not mean compliance with the ephemeral and inevitably ignorant wishes of those whom one served. On the contrary: the wise public servant was one who did not yield to the self-interested pleas, often a mask for the duplicity of politicians, demagogues, and agitators. One studied the classics and read Plutarch to find examples. Lycurgus as well as Pericles, Julius Caesar rather than Pompey or Brutus were models, and one should beware of politicians such as Cleon or Cataline.

But despite the fact that a man owed a professional duty to his calling, he was above all else obliged to be a gentleman; and that was defined in terms of adherence to certain codes and customs, to certain clothes and accent, to a certain way of life which, if it could hardly be defined in detail, was nevertheless so coherent and implicit that a detail if unobserved would be taken as evidence that there was something ungentlemanly about the deviant. The key to the code was good manners—unceremonious, relaxed, designed to put people at their ease.

The gentleman disguised his abilities as much as he disguised his emotions. His abilities were brought to a fine pitch simply by engaging in gentlemanly pursuits. An officer acquired his eye for country by riding to hounds and his power to command men who would follow him anywhere by excelling as a sportsman or by playing games fearlessly. Too great intellectualization of a man's professional calling was dangerous, for it would be an error to reduce what is valuable in tradition and custom to dry principles or to promote technology which should be the handmaid to sound performance and should not dictate the acceptance of what might well turn out to be harebrained schemes. People who had theories therefore needed to be watched! Men should be judged by their conduct rather than by their ideas, in particular by the way they treated other human beings. Mark Anthony was an example of self-indulgence and of that weakness of character which tempts a man to desert duty for pleasure. It was proper to regard women as romantic objects but wise to treat them judiciously, and the young were all the better for being put in their place until they were no longer callow. The supreme virtue was loyalty, and loyalty to institutions must be put before loyalty to people, if only because the supreme loyalty which did not need to be spoken of was to king and country.

Such were the ideals which were admired by, for instance, the entourage of the new king, George V. They were interpreted more austerely by him than by his predecessor Edward VII: George V did not like dubious company or pursue women. But there was not all that difference, other than exuberance, between the son and the father. There was, of course, as always, a fast set in Society and there was also a set which laid much store by worldly success and were not ashamed of ambition. Churchill, F. E. Smith, Max Aitken, later Beaverbrook, and above all the jumped-up Welsh solicitor, Lloyd George, were regarded as buccaneers all too ready to lay athwart the vessels of weaker men and plunder them for their own advantage. No one could deny that Churchill was born a gentleman, but the upper classes doubted whether he was one: he was too ambitious, too vehement, too ready to change parties for his own advantage, too given to self-advertisement, too intoxicated by words and frivolous schemes. Such criticism overlooked the historical sense and breadth of Churchill's vision, of his fine patriotism and genuine comprehension of England's interests as a Great Power. But when, after the war, in 1922 Baldwin finally decided to bring down Lloyd George's coalition government, people interpreted his decision as a recall to integrity and scrupulousness and as a protest against the debasement of honor in public life. Lloyd George was held to have been shameless in his conduct of affairs, vindictive in the pursuit of enemies and venal in attracting friends.

The mention of Lloyd George should remind us of another modulation which must be made about the country's ethos. Yes, the British gentlemanly code was mocked or hated by other nations who detested the effortless assumption of superiority by the British. But Britain differed from other European countries in a marked respect. By European standards England was a liberal country, the home of political and religious freedom. There was no bitter division within its ruling classes as in France between Catholics and anticlericals or equivocal loyalty to parliamentary institutions as in many countries. There were no violent right wing movements as in Germany and Italy. Like every western state at this time there were expressions of anti-Semitism; but when Hilaire Belloc and Cecil Chesterton tried to make it into a political cause, they were drummed out of political life. In writing of Weizmann, Isaiah Berlin declares that for him, for Namier and for many intelligent Jews from Eastern Europe, England represented a stable democracy, humane tolerance, respect for individual rights and legal equality. If England was philistine it was not fanatical. Proconsuls in India and Africa might grumble about politicians, but parliamentary give and take and the acceptance that one's opponents belonged to the same club produced that solidity and empirical approach to problems which foreigners envied. Civil liberty stood in the center of the ethos.

Many gentlemen were admirable scholars, men who had joined the Indian civil service at a time when scholarship in England, even in science, could be pursued by amateurs. But they were not disaffected intellectuals. The welfare economist Pigou, or the historian G. M. Trevelyan, who thought of himself before 1914 as a radical, or trade unionists such as Ben Tillett or Burns were not, as the handful of English Marxists bitterly pointed out, at all inclined to challenge the assumptions of the ruling ethos. When I read poetry aloud to Trevelyan in his blind old age, I noticed how heavily scored with sardonic exclamations were his volumes of Hardy's poems. To him Hardy was a sad pessimist, far less bracing and manly than Meredith. As for Wilde and the posturings of the aesthetes, liberals might demur at the harshness of his sentence and protest against the suppression of his plays and novels, but they did not identify with Decadence or moanings at the bar. Their belief in progress, and in the eventual acceptance by other states of parliamentary democracy, was too strong.

Echoes of these beliefs with many modulations can be heard in the writings of Henry James, Conrad and, of course, Kipling; but the finest creative writers are nearly always questioning, refining and modulating rather than confirming codes. If one searches for an expression of the old pre-1914 ethos in its cruder, and therefore infinitely more assimilable, form, one must go to the writers of mediocrity but of great popularity, to Sapper, Dornford Yates and Buchan, the creators of what Richard Usborne called clubland heroes.[3] These writers convey more vividly than any analysis what it was in this ethos in its debased form that aroused the hostility of the new generation. Their yarns were popular not solely because of the skill of the authors as storytellers, but because the heroes mirrored so faithfully, yet with greater clarity than real human beings could, how the ethos expressed itself through the lives of ordinary middle-class citizens of the business and professional worlds. The official guardians of the upper- and middle-class culture of the times—the headmasters and housemasters at public schools, clergymen and judges—and its interpreters—the editors of some serious and many middlebrow periodicals or of the leading newspapers—often reacted to events in a manner not at all dissimilar from the way the clubland heroes judged matters.

What then shook the faith of "our age" in this ethos? Their faith was shaken by the self-destruction of Europe of the belle époque in what was for some years to come to be known as the Great War. For a century England had not known what a continental war was: the Crimean War, colonial wars, and the Boer War were all interludes which after humiliating beginnings turned in the end into heart-warming victories. Nor had England known a citizen war as France, Germany, or the United States had. The experience of a citizen war was all the more strange. The numbers who fought, the slaughter and the agony of the First World War, was unparalleled in men's memories. For the casual observer the First World War appears to be on a smaller scale for the British than the Second: for the civilian population food rationing and privation were not so strict and air bombing was really only a dangerous nuisance. The armies were locked together on the western front and hardly moved more than a few dozen miles one way or the other for four years. But in the Second World War the civilian population was often more conscious of the war than the soldiers, there were the vast displacements of populations, the massacre of the Jews, the devastation of cities by bombing, the annexation of whole provinces by troops. The Second World War was genuinely worldwide. At one point the armies fought as far east as the Caucasus, and a quite separate war was fought in the Pacific.

But for the British the shock of the First World War was infinitely greater. The butchery was so appalling. All over the country stand dumb testimonies to the sense of the annihilation of a generation. If you enjoy church-crawling in England—stopping on a drive to look at the churches in villages through which you are passing to note the mixture of medieval styles and the way in which, usually in Victorian times, the church was restored, to read the family names on the tombs in the chancel and transepts, and the lapidary inscriptions commemorating those long dead—you will invariably find a memorial to men killed in the war of 1914-18, long lists of names even in tiny villages often bearing the pathetically trite words, "Their name liveth for evermore," sometimes flanked by a tablet to the officer son of the squire who never returned to live at the "big house" and whose family have long since disappeared. Every village has such a memorial, but you may well search in vain for a similar inscription to those who were killed in the Second World War. The trauma induced by the horror of the western front took years to wear off, if indeed it ever did. There had always been a strong pacifist movement in England, the only European country before 1914 to have one; it went back to the days of John Bright and it manifested itself in the resignations of ministers from the Liberal cabinet when war was declared, in the antiwar stand taken by Ramsay Macdonald, the leader of the still small Labour party, and in the conscientious objectors who were to be found in the intelligentsia. This movement became immensely stronger after 1918. But what occurred after that date was far more significant than pacifism. It was the rejection of the ideals and the way of life which had sustained the armies in the field and derision of the heroic qualities which their soldiers had shown.

The reaction did not set in at once. For a year or so there was a gleam of hope. The League of Nations was to end international anarchy; the United States, the honest broker for a just peace, would help to police the world; and the cameraderie of the trenches would permeate industrial and business relations and replace class warfare. None of these hopes survived. Keynes denounced the peace treaty in a reasoned polemic of extraordinary power, exposing both the folly of statesmen who understood so little of economics that they had imposed upon Germany debts of ludicrous magnitude which would beggar not only Germany but Europe, and their viciousness in betraying the principles of the Fourteen Points which were at least an attempt to establish that the victors would not conclude the war, as they had, by squalid exchanges of territory and punitive treatment such as would make another war likely. America refused to sign the treaty and retired into isolationism. The class struggle grew more intense and culminated in the general strike in 1926. On the one hand, gloom, bitterness, spiritual as well as financial deflation descended like a pall. On the other, protest took the form of frenzied gaiety and satire of the past. An ominous reaction set in against the ethos of the past and began to steal over the scene.

Yet once again one has to record how strong the old ethos proved to be. The miserable decline of the Third Republic in France or the subversion of the Weimar Republic, the collapse of parliamentary regimes throughout Europe, found no parallel in Britain. In the United States the Depression transformed the American ethos. The acceptance of the fact that the business of America was business, and that the businessman and banker, checked from time to time by congressional action such as the passage of antitrust acts, should be the arbiters of the country's destiny, was demolished by Roosevelt and never in that crude form returned. With the business community and practically every newspaper against him, Americans voted Roosevelt in as president four times, and he transformed the obligations of government to its citizens. In Britain no such transformation can be observed in the thirties. British power might have decayed, unemployment and the slump might bewilder people, but the ethos of the ruling class remained virtually unchanged; and when a king collided with it, he was forced to abdicate.

Nevertheless, during the interwar years the redoubt was being sapped and undermined by a generation which had begun to tunnel before the war. The young man who became the third Lord Esher and was the son of a clandestine homosexual, the intimate of Edward VII and George V, and a power behind the scenes in the War Office, expressed his sense of boredom with his class in a way which was not infrequent in his circle. He married an American wife. Intelligent men among the upper classes frequently did. They found English girls infinitely less vivacious, openminded, and witty and more manacled by snobbery and etiquette, and this young man was intelligent, highly amusing, and sagacious. I heard him once declare that no one who came of age after the First World War could fully understand how stuffy, philistine, and conventional life before 1914 was expected to be and, indeed, for most people was.

But with only rare examples was the revolt to come from within the aristocracy. The provenance of the revolt of "our age" was upper middle class, and it was a revolt of the intelligentsia. Nor is this strange. It is the intelligentsia who give things names. By describing and analyzing, often by protesting and demonstrating, they create a sense of purpose, they identify the causes of social ills and moral corruption, and make even the rulers conscious that people at large want change. The rulers may ignore them. In a despotism they suppress them as best they may: not very effectively in Czarist nineteenth-century Russia, far more effectively in Stalin's Russia, in today's Russia gradually less effectively. When all qualifications have been made, it is difficult for anyone but the intelligentsia, the formers of opinion and its brokers, to define a generation—and it is hardly surprising if they define it largely in terms of ideas and tastes and their own behavior. To do so is misleading or false only if their terms of reference are so narrow that they identify the mood of the nation with the expression of a clique. During the interwar years the old ruling class contrived to ignore the intelligentsia and dismiss their antics with tolerant and amused contempt. The patronage of Baldwin, Chamberlain, Simon, Macdonald, and Snowden was impervious to the new postwar spirit. And so one gets the impression no longer of a society moving imperceptibly and serenely with the tide of the times, but of a new generation pressing for change as the older generation resist. As the old generation fades or slips from the scene, the new generation enters upon their inheritance and puts into effect their ideas which they believe will transform society for the better—and just as they are so doing they hear the distasteful sound of a new generation, their successors, abusing them and sneering at their so-called improvements which, so the interlopers declare, are nothing more than soft soap and palliatives and do not touch the real malaises which affect society and which can never be cured unless these so-called reformers are swept away and replaced by those who understand just how radical change has to be to save civilization. But before we rehearse this melancholy tale, let us turn the searchlight upon the generation which Maurice Bowra called "our age" and see who they were and what they were doing.

The Post-Impressionist Exhibition in November, 1910, was the first battle-field of modernism in England. Like the first night of Victor Hugo's *Hernani*, it created a sensation, and notoriety, obloquy, and hatred descended on the head of its organizer Roger Fry and through him, by association, the Bloomsbury group. The works of Cézanne, Matisse, Picasso, and the rest were greeted not only with laughter but with rage as a swindle at the expense of those who had paid to see them. Every movement in art has parents even when it denies them most vigorously; but although today we are accustomed to tracing the origins of modernism back to the Middle Ages and beyond, the breach with the age-old tradition of the visual arts was enormous.

So it was in poetry. The Symbolists and their paler contemporaries the Aesthetes in England spoke the same language as their predecessors, the language of mysticism, beauty, of hermetic idealism and of music in language. But all over Europe the new generation of poets emerging were as conscious as the Post-Impressionists of using a new language. In the same year as the Post-Impressionist Exhibition, Yeats published *The Green Helmet* and Rilke published his novel *Malte Laurids Brigge*. Vorticism and Wyndham Lewis's *Blast* or Harley Granville Barker's productions in the theater were other instances before 1914 of the modernist revolution announcing its arrival. A chasm also opened in serious music. In 1911 Diaghilev's ballet opened in London. The designs of Bakst and Benois, the choreography of Fokine and Stravinsky's music, though it was some time before London heard it, were incomparably exciting. Stravinsky in his early years had debts to pay to Debussy, but in one sense his music was unique. That admirable conductor of ballet, Constant Lambert, noted how in *Le Sacre* the relation between the melodic line and its harmonic setting were, unlike the music of the past, in a state of enmity: the relation, he said, seemed to resemble "more that between the unfortunate yokel in the dock and the cynical barrister prosecuting him."

The Bloomsbury group did not belong to "our age." That they became leaders of opinion of the new generation can hardly be denied, but they did not, like so many of our age, leap into fame in their twenties. They were nearing or in their thirties when they first became notorious by sponsoring the two Post-Impressionist exhibitions. Only one of them, E. M. Forster, had published anything of significance before the war. But each of his four novels was an attack upon his country's ethos. With his indictment of the public schools which turned out boys with "well-developed bodies, fairly developed minds and undeveloped hearts" and his criticism of the Englishman's idealization of Italy and Greece, of the English businessman's mentality, of English women dominated by will even more than were their husbands, of the hypocrisies he finds in the liberalism of his time and its disastrous flirtation with imperialism, Forster was to become a more durable hero of the new generation than the other great demolition expert in Bloomsbury, Lytton Strachey. But *Eminent Victorians* had the more immediate appeal. Appearing in 1919 it ridiculed those Victorian values which were still so widely praised. The essay on Gordon pilloried Evangelicalism and Britain's imperial role; that on Arnold the public schools; and the converts to Roman Catholicism, Newman and Manning, were chosen in order to deflate the version of Christianity which in recent years had been making a number of powerful converts. Finally Strachey struck through Florence Nightingale at the movement which salved the conscience of comfortable middle-class England—humanitarianism—depicting the lady with the lamp as a ruthless egoist, an eagle, not a dove, who in pursuit of her schemes would destroy any man or woman, friend as well as foe, who got in her way. Bloomsbury befriended T. S. Eliot, and, as far as he would let them—which was not far— D. H. Lawrence, against whose persecution at the hands of the Home Office on account of his German-born wife and his paintings and novels they protested. Somewhere on their flank was the formidable figure of Bertrand Russell, another pacifist who had been in prison for his convictions, now emerging not only as the man who had effected a revolution in logic but a critic of marital relations and child education.

The sexual and educational revolt was perhaps ultimately the most telling of all the criticism of the past. In 1917 there appeared a novel which a young officer had written in seven and a half weeks about his public school. The school story is a peculiarly English genre. Enormous numbers of yarns existed about boarding schools, some of them fantasy, as Orwell recognized when he wrote about such magazines as *The Gem* and *The Magnet*, most of them about imaginary schools which conformed to a stereotype such as John Finnemore's Teddy Lester series. But some of them followed the example of the first and most famous of the genre, *Tom Brown's Schooldays*, and purported to describe the life led by boys in an actual public school, such as Rugby or in Vachell's *The Hill*, Harrow. Kipling's *Stalky and Co.* was a strange off-beat example of this type of school story. At first sight it appears to be subtly subversive of the public school spirit. The good herd schoolboy who accepts the world of prefects and games is satirized and exposed to ridicule at the hands of the cynical Stalky and his allies. The heavyhanded moralists among the housemasters who praise house spirit are opposed to the realists among the masters who accept that boys crib and bully each other. Real education is not what the boys learn in the classroom but what they teach others in ways which their schoolmasters cannot use. But Kipling was in fact in no way subversive. His book vindicated the public school system. It is precisely the absence of fairness, the compulsion upon boys to recognize the brutal facts of life and not to permit themselves to be blinded by resentment or emotion, which commends the public school to Kipling. Those who had learned to endure the horrors of existence in a public school and seen through the falsities of its official code would know how to command and to rule the Empire, defeating not only its foreign enemies, but the bureaucrats in Whitehall and the pacifist radicals in Parliament whom Kipling despised.

But the young officer, Alec Waugh, who wrote *The Loom of Youth*, did not come to this comforting conclusion. His was the first work of fiction to question the public school system in its entirety. It questioned the obsession with games, the building of character, the distrust of the intellect and of dangerous ideas, all of which characterized the vast majority of the public schools at that time. His book was the first wave of the storm of novels and memoirs which, for the next twenty-five years, were to pour through the presses ridiculing, exposing, and denouncing the tribal rites of the public schools. These rites centered upon compulsory games and their worship: the school language which often had to be learned by new boys within a week of arrival; the minutiae of dress which had to be meticulously observed; the bullying and above all the caning of boys by prefects; the narrowness of the curriculum. But what beyond all else outraged the Old Guard was Waugh's exposure of the romantic homosexuality which flourished in the public schools where adolescent boys never met girls and often had the greatest difficulty in learning how to get on with them during their short holidays, the girls—themselves also the product of boarding schools—being only slightly less gauche than the boys.

Homosexuality was the supreme taboo of the old regime. Everyone (except for millions of the king's loyal middle-class subjects) knew it flourished in London and in Paris, Berlin, and Vienna; everyone accepted that it was the one vice which led to instant expulsion from public school; everyone allowed discreet reference to it in literature recognizable only to the cognoscenti, such as when the charming and wicked cousin of the hero in Howard Sturgis's *Belchamber* refers to there having been a great slaughter of the innocents at Eton from which he as a boy narrowly escapes. To join the cult of homosexuality in the interwar years was one of the two main ways of proclaiming oneself a revolté. English upper- and middle-class homosexuality had none of the relaxed spirit of Paris, Berlin, or Vienna. The Lesbian salons of the Princesse de Polignac or of Natalie Barnes and Romaine Brooks had no counterpart in London. The disgrace of Lord Arthur Somerset and later of Wilde made heterosexuality the key test of respectability. What better way therefore to declare one's contempt for the official mores of society than to take a whirl among homosexuals? Homosexuality had all the thrill of being illicit (as taking drugs has today) and all the pleasure of being certain to outrage the older generation. There were so many forms which it could take in England. It could be epitomized in the minds of boys as the romantic friendships of schooldays, redolent with allusions to ancient Greece, of the love of Harmodius for Aristogiton or of the Theban lovers. (The classics, as Victorian schoolmasters well understood, were full of subversive notions.) Or it could be a species of High Church fantasy. Or it could be a genuine repudiation of the boredom and revulsion which numbed so many intelligent men when confronted by the conventional girl of the time. But in the twenties the aim of homosexual undergraduates was above all to shock. It was not only the painted and powdered undergraduate queens at Oxford, so wonderfully evoked by Evelyn Waugh, who, though tiny in number, made an impression by the strength of their personality. London Society learned to accept the goings-on of Miles Malpractice, Anthony Blanche, and the rest: the popular stage's leading writers and performers, Ivor Novello and Noel Coward, were foundation members.[4]

The term Bloomsbury began to be extended beyond the original group to those who followed and admired them, to a younger set of Raymond Mortimer, David Garnett, Gerald Brenan, Harold and Vita Nicolson, Edward Sackville-West, Joe Ackerley, Roger Senhouse, and to a handful of dons such as George

Rylands at King's College, Cambridge. The new criticism developed at Cambridge by Tillyard and I. A. Richards was another development of some significance. It broke with all previous models of the despised subject of English literature by requiring its students to ask what poems meant and why they were enjoyable and moving. What a work of art meant, what its creator intended it to be, were questions which were far more important for those who were interpreting and defending modernism than the evaluation of works of art. "It is now accepted," wrote Raymond Mortimer about Duncan Grant's paintings, "that the principal function of a picture is not to give information about the visible world but to express the imagination of the painter and to infect the spectator with his emotion." Bloomsbury was suspicious of pontificating critics: the world was full at that time of haughty denunciations of Eliot, Joyce, Lawrence, of poetry which did not rhyme, of novels without a plot: if there was one thing as bad as a philistine it was a fogey.

There was in addition another subversive group in the making quite distinct from Bloomsbury and operating in a different manner. These were the Oxford wits.[5] The Oxford wits were never a self-conscious group as Bloomsbury was. The term is a convenient way of referring to a number of young men, some exceedingly clever, who were animated by a ridiculing spirit which led them to encounter life with a certain abandon even if they came to different conclusions about its meaning. Some of them had virtually no influence. But in the amusement they generated by fantasy, high spirits, mockery and gaiety they repudiated the culture of their elders. Maurice Bowra had no desire whatsoever to reform his university or change its character; but he was a critic of the Establishment, the lover of freedom especially for the young, the enemy of drabness in national as well as Oxford politics. Pleasure, vitality, and spontaneity were his delight; caginess, philistinism, pretentiousness, cowardice, and pomposity his targets. Through his dazzling talk and his freedom from the inhibitions with which most of us conceal our naked feelings about the private and public lives of friends, acquaintances, and enemies, he liberated successive years of clever Oxford undergraduates. His younger friend among the dons, Isaiah Berlin, another renowned talker, was very different from him: he related people to general ideas, and general ideas had for long been regarded in English life as somewhat suspect, the mark of a light, perhaps even frivolous, mind, less worthy of attention than sound textual scholarship. Different from both and exceedingly different from each other were the two literary figures Cyril Connolly and Evelyn Waugh; and Waugh's Roman Catholic interpretation of the world was quite unlike that of his contemporary Graham Greene and still more unlike that of his predecessor in the older generation, G. K. Chesterton.

Indeed I hesitate even to coin the term "Oxford wits." To herd together men and women of very different temperaments and, ultimately, of beliefs, is to perpetrate an error which runs through books such as Colin Wilson's *The Outsider* and its successor over twenty years later, Martin Green's *Children of the Sun*. That error is to apply terms drawn from anthropology or psychoanalysis to groups of people, declare that these people fit inexorably into these categories, and then assert that these "explain" events within society. The shorthand terms which literary critics use to impose some sort of intelligible order upon the wild variety of creativity sometimes serve a purpose, as when they refer in the nineteenth century to the Lake Poets, the Spasmodics, or the Pre-Raphaelites. But such names are more often nothing more than the portmanteau terms describing a group of contemporaries who come together for a few years and then go their own ways. What could be more natural than to speak of the Roman Catholic vision of life and to cite Greene and Waugh as among its most potent expositors? Yet how different they were from other Catholics of the time, such as Douglas Woodruff, Frank Longford, Muriel Spark, and how different from each other! Greene, the socialist, in creating Scobie and a dozen other characters exemplifies the men and women who are destroyed by their human virtues, pity, gratitude, decency, tolerance; and yet even in the act of falling into mortal sin may be redeemed by God's grace. Waugh, a genuine reactionary, explains why the Church alone can explain the horror of the world and the fact that it is inhabited by Vile Bodies and declares that any attempt to better conditions in the world is valueless. So far from praising hedonism, Waugh believes that all men's pleasures are sinful and that liberalism and socialism are as great errors today as they were thought to be by the Vatican in the days of Pio Nono.

Nevertheless, during the twenties the high spirits of the Oxford wits and the way in which in their private lives as young men they put such evident stress on freedom from the conventions of the past were of some importance. There was one great difference between Bloomsbury and the Oxford wits. Bloomsbury invented a way of life for the intelligentsia: the townhouse or apartment in an unfashionable part of London; the minute country cottage, at that time unheated and often without electricity and even without indoor sanitation; contempt of formal dress and the conventions of fashion; an unwillingness to make more than an occasional raid into Society and then at once to satirize it; a dedication to live life "rationally" without rows, scenes, excess, disagreeable passion. It was an almost conscious creation of a new class. The Oxford wits, however, were worldly. They were agreeable to moving in the Great World to get what they could squeeze out of conventional society, to enliven those upper-class circles who by no means belonged to the intelligentsia, but who were amused by their audacity. They were often exhibitionists, reveling in belonging to as well as shocking the upper and middle classes, and in suggesting new roles and goals for them. Bent on pleasure and breadth of experience, they did not simply lampoon the stuffy and conventional; they invaded their parties and haunts. Bloomsbury was unworldly and hermetic; the Oxford wits, true to the tradition of their university, were undismayed by any charge of snobbery.

Such were the characteristics of the minute avant-garde who ranged themselves against the still philistine and conventional ruling and managerial classes of the time. No one could possibly maintain that this avant-garde was "representative" of their contemporaries in the twenties and thirties. No one could possibly regard Oxford and Cambridge as a mirror of northern England, where the major part of the population then lived. The musings of Bloomsbury and the antics of the Oxford wits and the Bright Young Things, or in the thirties the polemics of university Marxists, produced as little impact as a fly alighting on a brick. Indeed the avant-garde were not even representative of Oxford and Cambridge. The ancient universities themselves in the twenties had hardly changed since prewar days. The undergraduates were still absorbed by sport and games and many of them did the minimum of work, took pass degrees and regarded their college as a finishing school. The dons were on the whole Conservatives or old-style Liberals, few indeed supporters of Labour. In the acid test of the general strike which was seen at the time, and indeed must be seen now, as an action which could not only have brought down the government but thrown the country into the economic chaos which it faced in 1931 and the political chaos which overcame Germany in the early thirties, undergraduates flocked to man the government's emergency services. Even fewer undergraduates than dons were on the side of the strikers, the most notable being Hugh Gaitskell. Nor were students at London or the provincial universities all that different. Their aim was to get a qualification for a job.

As I have said, there is nothing absurd in judging that a handful of young intellectuals and wits in London, Oxford, and Cambridge were to have an influence out of all proportion to their numbers. "The Revolution of the Dons" in the nineteenth century—the revival in teaching through tutorials and the explicit attempt to influence and enlighten undergraduates beyond the confines of their official studies—had a perceptible effect in building a tradition of service which was at the heart both of the home civil and the colonial services, and which also confirmed the two ancient universities in their primacy.[6] It is justifiable to focus upon Oxford and Cambridge because in the first half of the twentieth century they, in particular, transmitted cultural values to those in the generation who would eventually influence the generations preceding and succeeding theirs.

But the mention of the general strike must bring to mind the movement in ideas which was to have a profounder influence on the culture and assumptions of the British than anything yet mentioned. This, of course, was socialism in all its forms. What form was it to take? From 1910 to 1926 it looked as if the kind of parliamentary socialism favored by the Labour Party would be overwhelmed by syndicalist policies advocated by the trade unions. But the defeat of the general strike killed syndicalism within the trade union movement for forty years. The new trade union bosses, Citrine, Bevin, and Deakin, saw to it that there would be no further collision with central government, let alone a Labour government. The trade unions developed their own type of internal conservatism (David Low, the celebrated cartoonist, always represented the Trades Union Congress as a vast carthorse). It was therefore all the more bewildering to "our age" forty years later, with their generation ruling the country to be faced with a revival of syndicalism. Not that a Labour government with a working majority appeared at all likely. The devastating rejection of the party in 1931 and again in 1935 reemphasized how conservative Britain remained. Between 1864 and 1964 governments to the right of center held power for nearly 70 years.

The speed at which the Labour party displaced the Liberal party as the alternative to government by the Conservatives was more apparent than real. It seemed to happen within fifteen years or so and between the general elections of 1910 and 1924; yet in fact it was nearer forty years between the general elections of 1906 and 1945 and after two world wars before the Labour party could form a government on its own. Between those wars the Fabianism of the Webbs, the Christian Socialism of Tawney, the guild-socialism of G. D. H. Cole, and the radical socialism of Laski were in a sense less important as a dissolvent of deference to the Establishment than the cockiness of the young J. B. Priestley and the challenge of the North of England to London and the South East. Priestley, a Yorkshireman, embodied far more than the university Marxists of the thirties the rebelliousness against the incompetent Victorian capitalists of the once great industrial cities in the north and in Scotland. Yet it took a long time for socialist ideas to permeate either the industrial classes, still more the rural counties. This was not odd: for grim as the thirties were for numbers of traditional industries in the north or in Scotland and Wales, cities such as Leicester and the light industry of the South hardly noticed the depression, which for them was a period in which prices fell, the pound recovered its value, and rearmament and greater public spending after 1936 began slowly to bring about improvement. The year 1938, so depressing in America, was a year of prosperity in Britain.

The Marxism of the thirties is usually held to be a decisive cultural change from the hedonism and pessimism of the twenties. In retrospect it appears much less important than it did then. It was a six-year effervescence before the war, and its leading exponents were again the public school products of Oxford and Cambridge, earnest and severe, with a handful preserving a sense of humor. But as a revolutionary movement British Marxism was laughable when compared to the Marxist parties which were fighting, splitting, collapsing all over Western Europe, genuine mass movements fueled by ideologists.

In fact, the main stimulus behind British left wing politics was sympathy for the unemployed and condemnation of the inefficiency of capitalism rather than the antifascism of the new members of the intelligentsia. The general strike was a test of sympathy for the desperately poor, and for those such as the miners most obnoxiously oppressed by capitalism. It was an appeal to reject the notion that the interests of the state, of the ruling class, and of the system must always be put before those who did the hardiest and dirtiest industrial work on which the state depended. British socialism was indeed an extraordinary hodgepodge of ideas, a mixture of pacificism, state intervention, syndicalism, belief in good causes, support for poor people and for internationalism, hatred of privilege and a challenge to capitalist inefficiency and arrogance. Undoubtedly it was in favor of equality; but then it also claimed to be in favor of individual liberty, relying on the doctrine of "positive freedom" developed in England in the 1870s by the Oxford philosopher T. H. Green as a means to square the circle and reconcile these two conflicting good ends in life. Nothing better exemplifies the confusion and exuberant mishmash of ideas which animated socialist intellectuals than the *New Statesman* in the thirties and forties, when it was edited by Kingsley Martin. This week it could be pacifist, the next week strident in its demands to stand up to fascism, while simultaneously denouncing rearmament as a capitalist plot to turn machine guns on the working-class movement. Vegetarianism, birth control, sexual freedom, and every progressive movement was somehow connected to socialism and made to appear an integral part of it. No one with any shred of intellectual integrity or honesty, it might be supposed, could follow Kingsley Martin week in week out; but Martin was an influential editor precisely because he was so much part of the left that he could reflect exactly that desire to have every cake and eat them all while declaring that it was a monstrous lie put about by reactionaries that they had been eaten.

The *New Statesman* in those years recorded the two most voluble voices of the times. The first half of the periodical resounded with the clear con-

tradictions of the political left; the second and literary half reproduced the tone
of Bloomsbury in the voice of the Oxford wits. The activities of Victor Gollancz
were also influential in founding the Left Wing Book Club, which poured out
squibs, polemics, diatribes and propaganda, much of it Marxist, against the
Establishment. It is arguable that Michael Foot's *Guilty Men*, which pinned the
disasters of the period upon the Tory leaders, was one of the most influential
political pamphlets since the days of Junius. Just how influential was to become
apparent in 1945. To the astonishment of the United States, the Communist
East, and the exhausted and humiliated client states of America in Western
Europe, Churchill and his Tory party were resoundingly defeated at the polls in
the hour of victory. Certainly some of those who had been sapping the culture
of the old regime had hopes that some of their ideals would be realized. Quite a
number were, however, disappointed. The fellow-travelers were crushed by
the old bosses of the new Labour government; intellectuals such as Richard
Crossman, lacking in loyalty to the leadership and unstable in their brilliant
analyses of policy, were snubbed and excluded; the trade union movement,
indeed the whole nation, accepted under the savage and ungenerous terms of
the American loan in 1946 even more severe food rationing and import controls
than had ever been necessary during the war. Former heretics of the thirties,
such as Cripps, who had called for a Popular Front against fascism and alliance
with the communists, or young Marxists such as Denis Healey, did not allow
the euphoria of the wartime alliance with the Soviet Union to make them forget
the Nazi-Soviet pact of 1939 and the double role which Communist parties
throughout Europe had played during the war. The first majority Labour government was a great reforming administration, notably extending the welfare
state and bringing about long-awaited socialist measures such as the national-
ization of the coal mines and the withdrawal from India. Yet in its style—in the
highly disciplined treatment of the parliamentary and national party meted out
by Attlee, Bevin, and the trade union establishment—it was run by a generation
which was anterior to "our age."

It is the fate of most generations that, at the very time when they grow up
and move from youth into middle age and power, they are either rent from
within or hear the ominous sound of their successors hunting them down. It is
also the fate of those few creative beings in a generation who do not see their
ideas totally ignored, to see them taken up and applied, and in that process
vulgarized, misunderstood, and distorted. So it appears to them, although in
part at least it is the impersonal forces of history which batter and warp them.

For a time "our age" still continued to dominate the universities in the postwar period. Lord David Cecil's literary taste charmed not only Oxford but
London, and Cyril Connolly's *Horizon* reflected the ascendency of the hedonism
of the Oxford wits. Just as the demobilized officers at Oxford and Cambridge in
1919 had behaved as public school men imbued with team and regimental spirit,
prototypes of the prewar world, the veterans returning to the universities after
1945 were recognizably the same as those who had completed their higher education before the war. But there were three significant changes. It began to be
apparent that some writers who had been thought to be representative of the
culture of hedonism and the private virtues were its most savage critics. Not

only Waugh's fierce Augustinian theology, but the melancholy of Henry Green, and the satire of Angus Wilson ate like acid into the copperplate of the society they described. The old sentimental socialism was represented as being in reality a system which benefited not the manual worker but a new and repellent genus in the species of the lower middle class. Fellow-travelers still made a noise in Parliament, but in the country Marxism was regarded as identical with Stalinism and despised. In Cambridge there was a powerful reaction against the pamphleteering version of the history of the thirties put about by Michael Foot. The target now was socialism, and the most stimulating political theory of the time was the conservative critique of social democracy developed by Michael Oakeshott and Herbert Butterfield. The one declared that *both* political parties were infected by the mania of believing that governmental action, based on "rational" analyses of social problems could improve society; the other that the study of history imparted no lessons, followed no course, and was subject to no "interpretation" whether Whig or Marxist, because the study of the past, if undertaken scrupulously and for its own sake, could reveal nothing of interest or relevance about the present.

Only an observer within Oxford or Cambridge probably could have seen that in 1952 a new generation of undergraduates displaced the old. "Our age" had been amateurs and many were to remain amateurs all their lives. When Dick Crossman at last became a minister in 1964 he had no idea how a ministry worked, how central government related to local government, how Whitehall (the civil service) and Westminster (the cabinet and Parliament) related to each other. He had been writing books and pamphlets about politics for years, but it was the politics of the amateur. Eden and Macmillan were old, seasoned politicians, but when it came to the one issue which was of vital importance to their country, its economy, they were amateurs; their successor as a Conservative prime minister, Alec Home, even made a fatal joke that he had to use matchsticks to calculate. The ideal of "our age" as depicted, for instance, by T. H. White was that of Renaissance man, painting or hunting in the morning, making love or learning to fly in the afternoon, playing music or conversing in the evening: the Aristotelian *Eleutheros* doing all things but servant of none.

The new generation of undergraduates differed. Their ideal was to be a professional. They were uninterested in mocking authority, they were dominated by grammar school rather than public school boys, their intellectual level was higher, they came consciously to read subjects in order to qualify as university teachers, to act or produce plays, not as a diversion, but to make a career in the theater, cinema, and television, to produce ephemeral magazines or edit the campus newspaper not to "discover" new talent but to master the technique of lay-out and promote circulation in order to enter Fleet Street. The homosexual cult disappeared overnight. New language schools set up in the cities of Oxford and Cambridge produced a comforting supply of European girls, and even the number of girls' colleges began to increase. But yet more significant was the gradual eclipse of Oxford and Cambridge as the pivot of university education. The provincial universities, "Redbrick," were at last beginnng to grow, and Lucky Jim began to teach in them. In 1956 Edward Shils could still lament that Oxbridge continued to cow Redbrick and that British culture was still metropolitan. Yet within a decade opinionmakers were to be found in the provincial

universities rather than within Oxbridge. The new generation looked for inspiration to the outsiders, to Oakeshott and Butterfield and Popper, who criticized the conceit and complacency of "our age"; and the outsider who made the
greatest impression and whose pupils began to get jobs in the new universities
was F. R. Leavis.[7]

Leavis was admired for many reasons, and he deserved to be admired for the
high professionalism which he applied to the criticism of poetry and the novel.
If his success owed something to the unscrupulousness of his polemics, it owed
more to the fact that he palpably spoke for—and his critical methods directly
helped—the grammar school boys from modest families who were now coming
to the university on government grants in ever-increasing number. Gone was
the need for such a boy or girl to stand dazed before the profusion of literature,
to be told that without Greek and Latin it was hard to make much of English, to
have his first attempt to make literary judgments crushed by the observation
that he was not acquainted with French, German, or Italian literature and that,
until he had read the Elizabethan canon, what sense could he make of the metaphysical poets. In the place of the plucking and smelling of sweet flowers, in the
place even of his Cambridge colleagues, who like him were helping to invent a
new and rigorous literary criticism, but who insisted that there could be many
good kinds of literature, Leavis offered the certainty that salvation lay in understanding why a small number of poets and novelists were infinitely superior to
the rest, and most of the rest not worth time. Whereas Bloomsbury and the
Oxford wits had praised *creation* and were willing to overlook how poor much of
the creativity by contemporary writers which they praised was, the new style
was to praise *criticism* and to rate the judgment of others as the most profitable
(and most pleasurable) of activities. The narrowing of the framework of reference, the intensity of feeling, the moral fervor of Leavis's criticism and his un-
sparing attacks on establishments of every kind fell like music upon the ears of a
class of student whose counterpart in the interwar years had for the most part
concluded that they had to conform to public school manners. Now they felt
more competent to question the assumptions of the public school avant-garde
revolté and to rebel in their own idiom and against the rebels of the past.

The Angry Young Men of the time were angry with the kind of society
which the generation of twenties' and thirties' intellectuals seemed to accept
without question. They detested its blandness, its public school echoes, its lack
of seriousness, its acceptance of the second-rate in public life and the complacency of assuming that the private life alone mattered. But their revolt was
not a mere throwback to the puritanism of the nineteenth century. It represented a genuine shift in class culture. Kitchen sink theater was a manifesto that
the new national medium, television, was going to entertain mass audiences
who were bored and bewildered by dramas representing upper-class characters
in upper-class situations and dilemmas. Twenty years later the Angry Young
Men of the fifties were to peer somewhat appalled at what their energies had
released.

One piece of legislation illustrates what was occurring. "Our age" had always mocked and groaned at the laws relating to obscenity and censorship of
the theater. Roy Jenkins, one of the last representatives of "our age," despite the
fact that he was in Opposition, got his bill to reform the law of obscenity passed

in Parliament. That in itself was an indication of how far "our age" had begun to take over the political as well as cultural direction of the country. For had the Conservative government been solidly behind the old pre-1914 ethos, Jenkins could never have got his bill through Parliament. The truth was that in the Conservative party were dozens of liberals, careful like the most successful of them, R. A. Butler, not to go too far ahead of opinion in the party, but nevertheless sympathetic to changing the law in favor of more personal liberty. It was, after all, a Conservative who set up a committee under John Wolfenden to look into the laws relating to prostitution and homosexuality.

Roy Jenkins' Obscenity Act was almost immediately tested when the director of public prosecutions was so unwise as to advise the crown to bring an action against Penguin Books. Taking advantage of the new act, Penguin was publishing the unexpurgated version of *Lady Chatterley's Lover*, the very kind of serious work of fiction which the act was designed to protect. The prosecution failed and the Old Guard fell back discomfited. But in one sense the opponents of Jenkins' bill and critics of Penguin such as Leavis, that champion of Lawrence, were to be vindicated. They had prophesied that the act would be used to give cover to indisputable pornography; and so it proved to be. Within fifteen years the appetite of at least a sizable part of the British public for pornographic movies, books, objects, and parties was unmistakable; and so was the sense of outrage by another part who were horrified by pornography, by the realities of working-class speech, rich in four-letter words, by violence in action as well as in speech on television, and by unbridled innuendo. Some of "our age" regarded these developments with amused detachment; others resembled Virginia Woolf confronted with *Ulysses*—they blanched. By the seventies totally new conventions in what could be publicly said, portrayed, and discussed on media which would reach a mass audience had come into existence.

The thirteen years of Conservative rule from 1951 to 1964 indicate how far the revolt of "our age" in the twenties and thirties was a revolt about manners, style of life, and freedom for the individual. As late as the thirties a subaltern in the Brigade of Guards could be told that to spend the summer vacation on the French Riviera and not on the grouse moors of Scotland or Yorkshire was hardly the done thing. Pluralism now began to be a reality; people accepted that there was no single norm of spending one's days to which reputable men all aspired.

With the acceptance that in an affluent society it was natural for people to choose to spend their money each in his own way came another shift in traditional party alignments. The humiliation of Suez reversed the roles of the parties on the issue of the empire. Conservatives now could hardly wait to get rid of these odious expensive dependencies seething with nationalist revolt. Whereas they had hooted Mountbatten for selling out on India, their spokesman now toured Africa speaking of the winds of change. Conservatives suddenly became aware that clinging to empire meant unlimited black immigration to England. Per contra the Labour party equally suddenly discovered a Third World and Britain's obligations to it. Praise for the Commonwealth and overseas aid replaced denunciations of imperialism. That there should be no appeasement of world Communism was, of course, the agreed policy of both parties. But appeasement on another front was a cardinal tenet in Macmillan's political theory.

Macmillan, to all appearances a member of the Old Guard, was in fact by date as well as by inclination one of the oldest members of "our age." To him the greatest error the Conservative Party before the war ever made was to identify itself in the eyes of the nation as the opponent of the trade unions. At all costs the trade unions must be appeased and full employment maintained, and it was in his regime that the trade unions made such a notable advance in bargaining power so that when in the sixties a Labour government came to power and the leadership of the unions shifted to the left the new government found it all the more difficult to resist the unions' claims. The change in Conservatism was marked by the coming of a word which suggested that "our age" was imposing a new consensus upon the nation. The word was "Butskellism," with the implied sneer that R. A. Butler and Hugh Gaitskell saw little to divide them. The most influential book on socialist policy, written by Tony Crosland, contained much from which the new Conservatives would not dissent. Keynesianism was the accepted policy of both parties; what Keynes would have thought is another matter.

This movement towards an ordered pluralism was suddenly to change. The sixties, as is well known, saw the break-up of Britain's cultural consensus. Until then the ideals of middle-class culture, so felicitously expressed by Matthew Arnold, had created a continuum of taste and opinion, able to change and absorb the avant-garde within its own urbane principles. But in the sixties it became the fashion to drive wedges. Of course the most publicized difference was between the generations. This was not new. Old Bloomsbury in the first decade of the century made as decisive a break with the manners of the older generation as did any group in the sixties. But in the interwar years "our age" welcomed those of older generations whom they found sympathetic. Young socialists sat at the feet of the Webbs or Tawney or Laski. The Oxford wits mingled with intellectuals of an earlier generation at Lady Ottoline Morrell's country house at Garsington. There had never been a time in the universities when dons were so accessible and made such personal friendships with undergraduates. The break between the generations, when it came in the sixties, was therefore all the more traumatic, particularly in the universities.

But it was not only a break between the generations. It was a break between north and south, between Scotland and England, between Whitehall, that is, the central civil service and the local authorities, between Westminster and Whitehall, between pragmatists and idealogues. Superficially it resembled the revolt in the thirties of the Marxists among "our age" in that it was both inflationary in the expectation of what political power could achieve and deflationary towards those in power who failed to give effect to these expectations. But there was one important difference. The old rhetoric of a worker's government replacing a corrupt capitalist regime impotent by the failure of its economic policies and bewildered in its inability to find solutions for ending the Depression, had vanished. The new attack was launched against all who were in authority in whatever institution—against hospital boards, local government councillors, vice-chancellors and professors as well as management. How was the attack launched? It was launched by the new generation using a new weapon and new tactics. What was the new weapon?

Astonishing as it may seem to Americans, it was sociology—sociology learned not from Talcott Parsons but from Glazer, Lipset, Bell, Riesman, and

Lazarsfeld. In the sixties it seemed that every university set up a department of sociology, even though the supply of trained graduates was incapable of meeting the demand. A new Social Science Research Council was established; government departments commissioned research into social problems on a scale hitherto unknown. The standard of sociological research was far lower in Britain than in America; the number of sociologists graduating in the fifties was tiny. The new lecturers in the polytechnics and universities, all of whom set up or expanded vestigial departments, were therefore for the most part not of high calibre any more than were the members of innumerable research teams who without too great difficulty arrived at conclusions of an agreeably progressive kind in their enquiries. By the end of the sixties those in authority heard a new and disagreeable question. The question was phrased with simplicity: "Why are you such a shit?" Here is a social problem, so the argument ran, which has been "thoroughly researched." Our research team has provided an unanswerable solution. The solution requires the expenditure of a few millions, a trifle compared with the cost of the latest defence weapon or prestige aircraft, the employment of numbers of bureaucrats and the establishment of supervisory or advisory boards who will tell the minister what should be done as the scheme evolves. What, then, prevents authority immediately fulfilling this program? The economy? You must be joking—this social evil is so dire that any man or woman of good will must wish to eliminate it at once. You still say it is impossible? Then it is clear that you yourself are the stumbling block impeding the way of progress. Why are you such a shit?

The new left employed this tactic with skill. In the thirties the left pilloried the stock figures of fat top-hatted directors and Colonel Blimp, and made generalized denunciations of capitalism. The new left replaced that kind of First World War frontal attack by a series of probes and lightning raids by tanks and the mechanical weapons of quantitative research. They had read the military handbooks of the new Marxism: Althusser, Marcuse, and the rest. As usual, British student militants were regarded by their German or Parisian counterparts as extraordinarily ignorant of neo-Marxist theory. But the Europeans did not realize that in Britain a theory of worker's control was already to hand and was far easier to put into practice than a version of Marxism which would come up against the frustrations of gaining power through parliamentary elections or would express itself through the formation of terrorist groups. In Britain the left had only to look back to their past for ways of bringing management in public concerns or in private enterprise under control. Under what kind of control? Under syndicalist control.

During the sixties, despite appearances to the contrary, power steadily drained away from the Trades Union Congress and the trade union officials down the line and into the hands of the shop-stewards, the local branch bosses in the individual factories and businesses, who often refused to obey instructions from the headquarters of their union and negotiated with the management of the factory a multitude of benefits in the form of better working conditions, restrictive practices, and wage gains for their members. Throughout the sixties the real wages of organized labor in many key industries rose, and the real salaries of management fell. In the seventies the differentials between skilled workers and unskilled labor were equally eroded, and skilled labor took its revenge in unofficial strikes. Behind these changes a theory developed. It was the theory that trade unionists and citizen groups should rule. They should rule, not in the sense of taking over totally from management, but in the sense of operating a veto on anything which management proposed and they opposed. Management should submit their plans to them, should "consult," and the workers' representatives should "participate" in discussions designed to see whether these plans could be improved.

In the seventies this happened at the highest level. Harold Wilson's second government had been formed in the wake of a resounding defeat by the miners' union of central government under Heath as prime minister. The new Labour government began to pass the papers of cabinet committees to the headquarters of the Trade Union Congress for their "comments" before submitting them to cabinet. Nothing of the like had ever been seen in Whitehall before. To pass confidential policy papers to an organization outside government, an avowed and self-interested pressure group, astounded the mandarins of the civil service. To Wilson it appeared the only way of obtaining government by consent; and to see just how far the ideals of "our age," its belief in the importance of personal relations, its distrust of power and the worship of success, its hatred of hard-faced capitalism, and its concern for social improvement were transmuted into political practice, one ought to take a glimpse at the kind of government which Harold Wilson ran.

Wilson broke with the practice of government which went back for generations. Until Harold Wilson became prime minister, it was a platitude in the teaching of politics in universities, or of "civics" as it was once called in the schools, that the Cabinet, the executive with the civil service as its adjunct, ruled so long as it could command a parliamentary majority; the House of Commons, as the legislature, existed to check the executive; the judiciary was independent of both. Ultimately all pressure groups and other bodies, while free to exert such influence as they could muster, were subordinate to the will of Parliament—which meant the sovereignty not so much of Parliament as of the cabinet buttressed by the majority vote of the political party which had won the last general election—the vote being maintained by the Whips and the vast patronage which a modern prime minister exercises. Harold Wilson, very much a man of "our age," a young Oxford don before the war who became a civil servant during it and emerged as a member of Parliament and president of the Board of Trade in Attlee's government, was to change the well-worn stereotype of prime minister and to run a government in which the prime minister did indeed become no more than a *primus inter pares*.

Wilson believed in democracy *within* the cabinet. Policymaking by endless discussion was the way in which the left had always conducted its affairs, and nominally he was a man of the left. Or, if you prefer it, he was a man at once so genuinely kind and unwilling to wound any of his colleagues and yet so insanely suspicious of them, accusing them behind their backs to his kitchen cabinet of cronies at No. 10 Downing Street, of conspiracies, double-dealing, leaking to the press, limelight stealing, and plotting his replacement, that he formed no alliances, trusted no inner group, and, by giving in to this minister one day and to that the next, drained away the enormous power a prime minister had for years exerted in Britain. Since he never trusted his chancellor of the exchequer, whether Callaghan, Jenkins, or Healey, and would not slap down the ministers of the spending ministries, the power of the chancellor who had become responsible not merely for the control of the monetary supply and taxation but for the economy as a whole with the full power of the Treasury behind him—which traditionally had unchallenged control over all the spending ministries in Whitehall—was weakened to a degree hitherto unknown. Cabinet now resembled the meetings of Labour party committees. Votes were regularly taken, speeches of inordinate length were made by ministers arguing their special interests, ministers made pacts with each other of reciprocal support to defeat Treasury control, and the prime minister, who had fought the 1964 election on the slogan that years of inefficient, inexpert, gentlemanly Tory rule by oafs who could not understand the new technological world were to end and would be succeeded by a new age ruled by technocratic government imbued with the techniques of the third (electronic) industrial revolution, was to be revealed as someone who did not have the ability to put any of these ideas into practice.

There had always been a strain of technocracy among Labour intellectuals, particularly among some of the former young Marxists of the thirties; after all, had not the Webbs taught that socialism was a more efficient way of organizing society than inefficient capitalism? But the strain was very thin. There were indeed many attempts made to plan the economy through vast superministries, to plan cities and the countryside, to rationalize industry. But as project after project ran into opposition and withered as the economy sickened, faith in the efficacy of technocracy, which some of the bolder spirits of "our age" had envisaged, began to evaporate. "Our age" had always maintained that it was stupidity which led to wars and want. Unemployment could be cured by better thinking. Part of Keynes's appeal lay in his delight in exposing the folly of his detractors and the inefficiency of their remedies; and indeed the very *efficiency* with which Britain organized herself in the Second World War, her ability to combine civilian discipline (queues, rationing) with grumbling, ribaldry, and liberty, spun the illusion that it would be possible to recreate such conditions in time of peace.

The opposition to Wilsonian technocracy came both from the left and from the right. New technology which produced overmanning was condemned by the unions; and the tiny groups of the extreme left, the International Socialists, the Workers Revolutionary party, and the International Marxist Group, burrowed away not only in the unions but in the Labour constituency parties and in the national headquarters of the party itself. To them technocracy was another version of capitalist Conservatism in which hard-faced businessmen merged firms, creating vast impersonal corporations or sacked workers instead of workers sacking them. Yet when the Conservatives came into power in 1970 their own version of technocracy ran into the sands. They could not face the unemployment such schemes created and they were defeated time and again by the pressure groups as well as the trade unions. In any case some of the City mergers smelt bad. Either they were palpable examples of asset stripping in which sound little businesses were sold off and their employees dismissed in order that the real estate which they owned could be turned by property developers into office buildings gaining higher rents; or the economies in manpower and efficiency which the mergers purported to effect were never made, as in the case of the British-owned car industry. The Conservative conscience was troubled by their record in the past. Too many Conservatives felt that Heath was mad to have taken on the one union, the miners' union, which had been badly treated by their party in the past. Too many representatives of "our age," sentimentalists though they may have been, agreed with that sturdy early twentieth-century radical, the historian A. J. P. Taylor, who exulted that the descendants of those miners who nearly fifty years ago had been driven back by the lash of hunger to the pits, had first in 1972 and again in 1974 defeated the descendants of those Tories who had backed the cruel coal owners in 1926. For in fact many of the Conservatives of "our age" had no stomach for a fight. Deeply perturbed as many of the British were that a duly elected government could be not only brought to its knees but defeated in a general election after a reverse at the hands of the unions, Conservatives realized that they could no longer rely on mass public support for sound government any more than they could for sound currency. The years 1926 and 1931 had passed irrevocably; and the general tolerance, the demand for greater equality, the general dislike for class distinctions and barriers which were so prevalent among the leaders of "our age" had made resistance to militant unionism difficult. One looked in vain for the emergence of Bulldog Drummond's "Black Gang" of monocled sportsmen of the upper middle classes who spent their leisure hours in the post-World War I years kidnapping Communist agitators, fellow-travelers and Russian agents and incarcerating them on a remote Scottish island where they were mercilessly drilled by a retired sergeant-major. Everyone knew that if there was a general strike now the students would be on the side of the strikers. Everyone saw how quickly official Conservatism smacked down odd-ball vigilante groups under retired generals or war heroes who played with the idea of setting up some countervailing force to the "flying pickets" which the miners had used to threaten the closure of all power stations. The truth was that the governing class of "our age" from whatever section of the community it came was for the most part imbued with the same principles of hedonism, relaxation, and tolerance as its intelligentsia. Few longed for the life of telegrams and anger. Those who worked long hours and over weekends did so because they enjoyed their work; but numbers arranged their lives so as to mix with their business the maximum of pleasure and distraction, if possible on an expense account. Imperceptibly the old right wing ascendancy had vanished, and in its place was a liberal front which was uneasily looking over its shoulder as it was harried by a new generation of trade union syndicalists who were out to gain power and, like the priest at Nemi in James Frazer's *The Golden Bough*, to kill their predecessor.

No generation in a free society, as I have said, is monolithic. "Our age" included a bewildering spectrum of political and cultural colors. As they grew older, some, as is natural, adhering to their old beliefs, appeared to move to the right; others tried to swim with the tide and, undignified in their efforts to be with it, toiled after the latest fashions of protest and disenchantment with the present.

Yet on one topic there was astonishing agreement between its sages. Whether it was Evelyn Waugh and Leavis, or Cyril Connolly and Graham Greene, or Orwell and Stephen Spender, all were agreed that the life of the industrialist and businessman was contemptible and degrading. Every sage who influenced "our age," Eliot, Forster, Lawrence, Tawney, or Herbert Read portrayed the world of commerce, advertising, speculation, automation, management, and enterprise as hateful. Leavis longed to return to the age of the wheelwright and the blacksmith. It must be admitted that among them was one conspicous exception whose influence upon the thinking of "our age" was immense. Keynes had no fear of business or of speculation; he lost two fortunes and died having amassed a third. But his legendary irony at the expense of bankers and businessmen and his very calling, a don at Cambridge, reinforced the prestige of the life of the intellectual. So too did the prestige of the postwar scientists who, justly taking wing on the esteem in which the wartime boffins were held for their work in radar, code-cracking, aeronautics, artificial harbors, and antibiotics, demanded new laboratories and resources to conduct fundamental research and win Nobel prizes. So too did the sociologists and economists. From being a cottage industry, higher education had become a major calling by the seventies.

A new life-style had evolved. Prestige followed those who pontificated, analyzed, recommended, and advised other men how to conduct their business. There was a shift in Britain out of business into the new bureaucracies of higher education, broadcasting, journalism, research organizations, social welfare, planning, and into the multitude of boards, commissions, committees, regulating agencies designed to restrain evil and promote virtue. The professions had always been "respectable" and "trade" disreputable in Victorian times. The City counted for more than industry as it always had. Certainly since limited liability in mid-Victorian times enabled the entrepreneur to protect himself against the worst disasters which followed an error of judgment or economic misfortune owing to a change in the terms of trade, it was always more profitable to manipulate capital than to produce a product. Certainly the line between investors and industrialists grew longer with ever more middle men and service agencies. In the postwar years of the fifties, other ways of making money without incurring the odium of managing—and hence exploiting—large numbers of one's fellow men directly became fashionable. Merchant banking, property development, business consultancies, research business all appealed to those who operated with comparatively small staffs. And in industry itself by the seventies it was more reputable to be a trade unionist or shop-steward fighting for the right of workers whose pay and conditions of work stood always in need of improvement, than to be a middle manager who, owing to the reluctance of industry to recruit graduates, sometimes through lack of skills, appeared to be standing in the way of efficient production and whose differential in salary has been eroded by government pay policy.

Now, nothing could be more natural than for the intelligentsia to despise and pillory middle-class moneymaking and the capitalist system. Such opposition to the acceptance of the forces of the market place, such denunciations of capitalist society, its values, and all its works, were a commonplace in Europe and found many echoes in America among citizen groups. In France for years the intelligentsia had been *marxisant* and the student revolt in 1968 was even for a few days thought to pose a threat to government. Yet the appeal to the slogan *Enrichissez-vous* had lost little of its appeal. No sooner had disaffected bourgeois youth emerged from their turbulent universities than they settled down to a sedate bourgeois existence. The Communist-dominated trade union movement was the most conservative in Europe. Nor was Western Germany all that different. They might be more nervous; they might have more devastating critics of Western democracy in Böll or Grass; *Der Spiegel* might be more alert and bold in exposing reactionary measures; the Baader-Meinhof gang more terrifying than any other single manifestation other than their analogues in Italy. But the German trade unions declined to ask for vast wage increases and the country still put its faith for a better life in hard work and discipline.

Yet in Britain the message of the sages in whom so many of "our age" believed, that we should turn our back on the life of grasping go-getting, has been all too effective. The reforms of the last twenty years have created a vast new well-intentioned bureaucracy in central and local government financed during a decline in productivity from an ailing industry which has been given a short respite to recover while oil gushes for the next decade from the North Sea. Unlike other European countries, the British have listened to their sages. "Our age" has deliberately tried to practice what their sages preached.

"Never forget about the Greeks," said Cavafy, the great Alexandrine poet, in 1917 to E. M. Forster, a sage who had immense influence in England upon "our age." "Never forget that we are bankrupt. Pray that you—you English with your capacity for adventure—never lose your capital, otherwise you will resemble us, restless, shifty, liars . . ." Cavafy knew that art is manured by money. So too did Forster; and in his novel *Howards End* he makes it clear that the Schlegels, that intelligent and attractive family who love Beethoven and ideas and want to help the poor, exist on capital which has been earned indirectly by the boorish, selfish, insensitive, gradgrinding Wilcoxes of the business community. But Forster never left his readers in any doubt which family he preferred. In Britain we are all Schlegels now.

History is not drawn in a straight line. When Wilson, foreseeing a new economic crisis of his own as well as the Tories' making, resigned, Callaghan restored discipline in the cabinet, curbed Marxist infiltration in the Labour party and won wage restraint from the Trade Union Congress. But Callaghan has built his career on identifying the Labour party with the trade union movement. Did he not defeat Wilson in cabinet in 1969 on the issue of the bill which would bring trade unions (as they are in every other western country) firmly within the law of contract? He believes, with those trade union leaders who do not want to smash social democracy, that the trade unions must be brought into the board room if the dream of industrial peace is ever to be realized. Humane treatment of the labor force, the abolition of the gulf between the conditions of work and leisure under which a wage earner exists and those which management enjoy, fair play rather than efficiency, devolution of power from Parliament to Scottish and Welsh assemblies, from management to committees, from public authorities to consumer councils, have turned out to be the program which "our age," under pressure from the third generation which "our age" educated, has evolved to express its ideals.

In some ways the ideals of "our age" have produced a humane and highly agreeable society. Intelligent foreigners often prefer to live here because they feel less oppressed by the inhumanities of the capitalist rat race or the drabness of a communist dragooned state. But can a modern technocratic state ignore the realities of the market? Can the demands of trade unionists for genuine cooperation with management with the intention of eliminating "we" and "they" ever be met, or will they prove to be demands for destroying the managerial structure as we know it? How far can individual liberty be reconciled with equality, for it can never be really reconciled as so many of the weaker-headed and warmer-hearted youth of the twenties and thirties thought they could be. Or will individual freedom, high standards in art, high culture in education disappear, and a state emerge which ensures low standards of living but equality of treatment? A few intelligent people of "our age" now praise what remains of the virtues of the pre-1914 culture which have survived their attack; and, traveling in the United States or West Germany, sigh with delight at living in a consumer society instead of in one in which the producer treats the consumer with contempt. The British are an interesting people, but they are not exciting, which is a political benefit if an intellectual loss. So the betting is that they will bumble along and may well produce a way of life which will not be as depressing as pessimists predict, nor so satisfying as optimists suppose.

The three generations which I have been attempting to sketch have been beset by a problem which, despite changes in society, still haunts Britain. Ask any foreign observer what he believes is at the root of Britain's trouble, and he will almost invariably answer: class distinctions. This is very painful for "our age." It has to be admitted that some of them—the novelist Elizabeth Bowen is a case in point—sank into a sour resentment of the welfare state and denounced leveling down. But those, whether of left or right, who recognized the malaise, believed that political reforms might diminish it. Like prostitution, which a more credulous generation believed would disappear when poverty was no longer widespread, class distinctions seem to evade all the regulations and laws made to ameliorate them. Other countries accept far wider differences of income and do far less for their immigrant population then we do in Britain. The old-style snobbery of the pre-1914 days is dead; the aristocracy and even café society keep the lowest of profiles; celebrities do not win the undying affection which the musical comedy artists evoked in days gone by. And yet there is something in the way which the British treat each other—their desire for privacy, their love of possessions, their clubbable qualities (involving choosing some but excluding others)—which grates; and it galls their society.

What does one mean by class distinctions? Before the war there used to be a fixture in the cricket calendar, a match played at Lords between "Gentlemen and Players." The gentlemen played cricket all summer long as amateurs; the players were professionals paid a wage. That kind of class distinction has dwindled and survives more as a figment of propaganda than a true divisive force. "Our age," like their predecessors, spoke a recognizable upper-class English; that accent will become as obsolete as eighteenth-century diction as the grandchildren of "our age" increasingly adopt a neutral form of speech. Today class is less identifiable with birth than with loyalty to your own group, profession, fellow workers: where should such loyalty end and what obligations are owing to those outside your group? What obligation do you and your group owe to other groups which lack the power to enforce their claims to decent treatment? Professors and schoolteachers who belong to "our age" feel shame at the notion of striking and breaking faith with their students and the children in the classroom: not so their successors. The slice of the population who reject their interest group's orders to use syndicalist action against the public at large who rely on that interest group's services is diminishing.

Indeed caste favoritism is more noticeable today than class solidarity. Certain jobs or occupations are becoming the preserve of certain groups whether they are Jews, Etonians, Scotsmen or, in Leeds, Pakistanis. The rearguard action fought by the railway or the printers' unions against the reduction of the labor force or the introduction of new technology is as much a fight to maintain safe and exclusive entry for their children into these industries as the protection of their own jobs. Management is drawn from all classes but it still seems to assume in the eyes of foreigners a specific flavor of a class structure differentiated, not only by being salaried rather than paid in wages, but by its leisure pursuits and hobbies. Whether class or caste, foreigners tear away the bandages and point to the wound.

Can trade unionism cauterize this wound? One of the themes of this sketch has been the rising power of trade unionism, as unforeseen by "our age" as the rise in nationalism, indeed of tribalism, throughout the world was unforeseen by its sages. Trade unionism with its weapons of the strike, disruption, and picketing is a countervailing force not merely against the employers, who are weakly organized and at odds with each other, but against Westminster and Whitehall whose plans for "economic recovery" can be thrown into confusion by the upheavals in inflated prices and increased imports and in the money supply which trade union pressure can produce. There are among their leaders those like Tom Jackson, who believe that, if, in the board room directors of concerns came fifty percent from management and shareholders and fifty percent from the trade unions in the business, industrial harmony would prevail; for the interests of both sides would be legitimately served. Other trade unionists demand more stringent syndicalism. They want the trade union movement to dominate the boards of public as well as private corporations and of such quangos as universities. Then come the trade unionists of the extreme left who will play no part on any managerial board. To them, the present political structure must be scrapped, what privileged people call individual freedom suppressed, and galloping inflation positively encouraged as one of the many means which can be employed to bring down the western way of life; they have their own versions of Euro-Communism. Within the movement there are many divisions: small craft unions fighting to preserve differentials for skilled work against those trade unions among them the largest which represent unskilled and lower status workers, and both menaced from time to time by unions with immense political muscle, such as the miners or power workers, who can tie up the whole life of the nation. In the year 2000 when "our age" are in their tombs, and the new generation of the sixties many of whose ablest have dropped out of management and distrust the notion of leadership take their place, a distinctly interesting development may take place. But nothing suggests that the class divisions in society are diminishing as fast as they have in other countries. That great division in the school system has deepened rather than narrowed since secondary education became comprehensive and the maintained grammar schools disappeared. Private education still remains one of the greatest divisive forces in the country, yet, for many of the intelligentsia as well as the upper and middle classes, the cultural loss which its extinction would mean seems so appalling that it cannot be contemplated—certainly not by "our age."

"Our age" took legitimate pride in having won their war and in not having been occupied by the Nazi invaders as nearly all other European states were. In so doing it avoided the hideous self-inflicted wounds which violent political upheaval and the polarization of social forces, the accompaniment of military defeat and revolution, bring. In Britain all "revolutions" since 1642 have been peaceful. "Our age" can reflect that they have increased individual freedom and self-respect among classes and groups who hitherto felt themselves constrained and despised and diminished by snobbery and social and cultural taboos. And yet Britain still has to answer the question: how is she to reconcile her class differences without the humiliation of defeat in war or the torment and bitterness which follow the destruction of the social contract?

REFERENCES

[1] G. M. Young, *Portrait of an Age* (1936). A new edition in 1977 edited by G. Kitson Clark annotates the delphic allusions in this classic work.

[2] G. M. Young, *Daylight and Champaign* (1948), p. 161.

[3] The worst of these three authors, Sapper, provides the best examples of the ethos in its debased form, but not so much in the Bulldog Drummond series which brought him fame as in his collections of short stories depicting the war and postwar periods, such as *Shorty Bill*, *The Dinner Club*, *The Man in Ratcatcher*, *Jim Brent*, and *Out of the Blue*.

[4] It should not be forgotten that heterosexual relations also began to change before 1914 among the younger middle classes. Rupert Brooke and the Olivier girls, the informal clothes and the camping holidays, had their infinitely more impressive parallel in Rebecca West's liaison with H. G. Wells. The accident of Brooke's early death in war has caused him to be remembered for the opposite of what he was—a Fabian, a neo-pagan, dissatisfied with the society in which he lived.

[5] The names that come most readily to mind are Maurice Bowra, Isaiah Berlin, A. J. Ayer, John Betjeman, Evelyn Waugh, Cyril Connolly, Anthony Powell, Kenneth Clark, Henry Yorke, John Sutro, Harold Acton, Brian Howard, Alan Pryce-Jones, Robert Byron, Graham Greene, Patrick Kinross, Hugh Gaitskell, Robert Boothby, and Christopher Sykes.

[6] Sheldon Rothblatt, *The Revolution of the Dons* (1968).

[7] There were before the war numbers of other detractors of the descendants of Bloomsbury and the Oxford wits—Wyndham Lewis, Roy Campbell, Edgell Rickworth, Geoffrey Grigson, and, of course, Eliot himself. But the politics of the thirties led some into unprofitable fields, Leavis with integrity and wisdom kept free of political entanglements.

CARL E. SCHORSKE

Generational Tension and Cultural Change: Reflections on the Case of Vienna

DOUBTLESS GREEK MYTH-MAKERS AND MODERN PSYCHOANALYSTS touched an eternal verity when they documented the troubles which beset the relations of fathers and sons. Eternal verities, however, do not express themselves uniformly in historical life. In Sophocles' Thebes, an Oedipal situation produced a political crisis; in Hamlet's state of Denmark, an Oedipal tension coincided with political rottenness. Among the intellectuals of Freud's Vienna, Oedipal tension first received reenforcement from a political crisis, then became generalized as a cultural phenomenon and finally was swept away by the expressionist culture-makers of the early twentieth century.

The object of my concern here is not with the nature and validity of generational theory, but with the historical understanding of the emergence of twentieth-century higher culture in Vienna. To what extent did those who hammered out a new set of cultural values identify themselves as a generation? When was generational self-definition connected with the substance of cultural innovation, when detached from it? The exploration of such questions, however tentative, may offer some clues to the stages by which the cultural innovators of the twentieth century asserted their independence both of the immediate past and, in a larger sense, of history as such. For a sense of distancing, a break from all that has preceded, characterized the consciousness of the Austrian "moderns" from their first appearance.

To connect this cultural change with that of generational identity, I shall follow the trail that the historical actors themselves marked out with a simple blaze: the term *die Jungen*. Whenever *die Jungen* appear, we shall pause to investigate, to see whether new modes of meaning-making are issuing from the matrix of nineteenth-century culture under the sign of youth, of generational solidarity.

I

Austrian liberal politics provided the context for the first appearance of *die Jungen*. It was the unhappy fate of the Austro-German liberals in 1867 to establish constitutional government only as a consequence of national defeat. Prussia's victories, first over Austria in 1866, then over France in 1871, destroyed all possibility of a democratic Greater Germany with Austrian participation. With their long-cherished and juridical objectives largely realized in the constitutional reform of 1867, the classical liberals placed Austrian patriotism above German nationalism. The drama of Bismarck's unification of Germany, however, fanned the flames of national feeling, creating among many Austro-Germans bitter resentment against their government for its cosmopolitan indifferentism and its anti-Prussian posture.

In 1870, the parliamentary liberals divided on the national issue, with party cleavage taking the form of a generational one. "He who placed his Austrianism above his Germanism was 'old,' " the historian Richard Charmatz wrote. "He who felt that he had come into the world as a German . . . was 'young.' " At the polls, the Old Liberals prevailed, but in the universities, *die Jungen* found powerful resonance. The universities became in the 1870s and 1880s the storm center of German nationalism, with student organizations and demonstrators engaging in almost constant conflict with university authorities. Old social divisions contained to some degree the spreading nationalist anger. The traditional, more aristocratic student formations—the so-called corps—remained loyal to the Austrian state. The more open *Burschenschaften* and the newly founded German national clubs, whose members were middle class and often Jewish, became the centers of nationalist political and cultural ferment.

Youthful indignation with the Old Liberals over the national question was compounded by the increasingly pressing social question. The so-called "Citizens' Ministry" of the Liberals, while destroying the remnants of medieval craft organization in the name of economic freedom, took no measures to cope with the social suffering attendant on rapid industrial development. In 1870, socialist leaders of demonstrations for universal suffrage and the right to organize were tried for treason and sentenced to prison. The economic crash of 1873 occasioned new economic deprivation for which ascendant liberalism, both political and economic, was widely held responsible. It also led to the disclosure of scandals of speculation in which the liberal political elite was widely involved. Since civic rectitude and economic prosperity had been central to the liberals' claim to rule, corruption and depression struck to the heart of their legitimation.

The failures in four different areas then—national unity, social justice, economic prosperity and public morality—converged in the early seventies to produce a deep crisis of confidence in liberalism before it had had the chance to stabilize its newly won power. University youth, in anger and frustration at the comprehensiveness of liberalism's failure, sought not only a new politics, but also new philosophic and cultural premises to replace the juridical rationalism of their fathers. The political side of this quest brought the student movement into alliance with the nationalistic new right. Its leader, the disaffected liberal Georg von Schönerer, found an intellectual foothold in the strongest Vienna student organization. The students found a cultural rationale for their new politics in Richard Wagner and the early Friedrich Nietzsche. Critical of the rational state and the scientific spirit, both thinkers exalted archaic Greek culture as models for the regeneration of German society. Wagner added to the glorification of the *polis* the special allure of Germanic myth, thus enriching his archaic communitarian vision with a national-populist appeal for the young German militants. Both thinkers affirmed instinct, vindicating its claims against "bourgeois" reason and the analytic spirit. Activated in the public sphere, instinct seemed to offer a new fraternal bonding that could transform a state based on competition and rationalized egotism into a true folk community. Liberated in the individual sphere, instinct would restore the life of feeling to a psyche suffering from an excess of intellect and rational desiccation. The new Dionysian culture, as William McGrath, the pioneering scholar of the subject, has called it,[1] thus had both a social-communitarian aspect and a depth-psychological one. Both elements challenged and eroded the authority of liberalism as a sociocultural system.

Biographical and literary evidence suggests that the emergence of the new Dionysian culture produced in its political phase both a sense of generational identity in university youth and a tension between fathers and sons. The critic Hermann Bahr recalls returning to his home in Linz from his freshman year at Vienna and announcing to his father, "Liberalism is finished. A new age is dawning. Make way for us!" "What," asked his stunned father, "have they done with you in Vienna?" Soon, the son reports, it turned out that other fathers in Linz—"old liberals like him"—gathered with the elder Bahr to recount similar experiences with "sons who had brought [the word] from Vienna that liberalism was over. And the fathers sat together, unable to grasp it, to see all youth defecting . . ."[2] McGrath has shown similar tensions invading the families of the *Gymnasium* students who were to provide the intellectual leadership of populist nationalism in the university.[3] Reflecting on his youthful experience in maturity, one of these erstwhile antiliberals reminds us that youthful rebellion could be not only heady but traumatic: "Torn loose from everything existing around me, separated from my beloved father . . . , robbed of any support, I stood on a surface which shook volcanically . . . Years passed in which I had the feeling of being a lost swimmer struggling against the waves of the ocean. Thus I had to experience within myself the entire dismemberment, the monstrous spiritual and moral distress and struggle of an individualistic time."[4]

From a purely historical perspective, the power of community-formation exhibited by a peer group in times of sociocultural crisis would seem to provide fortification and support to its participants. From a psychological perspective, however, the drastic reshuffling of the self required by the break from obsolescent inherited values perhaps generates the strong communal bonding associated with such movements—especially of students—as an answer to the individual's loss of familial anchorage and support. Certainly in the case of the crisis of fin de siècle Austria, Oedipal conflict surfaced as generational tension only in the context of the incapacity of the liberals in ascendancy to realize more than their constitutional goals. The quests for wholeness in the community and for instinctual gratification for the individual were ideologically cognate to the psychological needs of children of a legalistic culture caught in the dissolution of their own heritage.

The term *die Jungen* did not long attend the radical national movement. With the establishment of a full-fledged German National Party by Georg von Schönerer in 1885, the movement "grew up," and students lost their determining role in it. Although student nationalism continued as a strong political factor in Austria until 1914, it lost all autonomy. In contrast to the youth movement in Germany, which exploited the space allowed it by the social system but held aloof from politics, Austrian university nationalists were politicals, articulated into the radical right. The Wagnerian culture which the generational revolt had spawned survived among them only in flattened form as political ideology, while the creative potentialities of that culture were developed in the non-political spheres of art and philosophy.

The critical factor in sundering the cultural impulse in *die Jungen* from the political one was the rise of anti-Semitism. A traditional current in the conservative student organizations, anti-Semitism began at the end of the 1870s to spread through the newer clubs that were the principal carriers of the nationalist movement. Young Jews who had participated in the crusade for German folkish "regeneration"—often in leading positions—found themselves extruded and excluded as the nationalism of the new right showed its atavistic side. Theodor Herzl, Sigmund Freud, Gustav Mahler, the later Socialist leader Victor Adler, and the historian Henrich Friedjung were among those who underwent the traumatic experience of the corruption of their German cause and the blighting of their hopes by anti-Semitism. As each perforce withdrew from German folkish politics, he carried with him to the sphere of his life's work some portion of the Dionysian culture. For all these men the rise of anti-Semitism was not the first trauma, but the second of their short lives: as the liberal culture of their fathers had failed them in the seventies, so the nationalist culture of their brothers turned on them in the eighties. Having quested for a new, holistic cultural community as Germans, they found themselves threatened and abandoned to a new isolation as Jews. Many gentile antiracists shared their fate, and joined them as they sought to make new meaning in a world that had eroded their social faith.

II

Having fallen into disuse during the 1880s, the term *die Jungen* reappeared in the following decade on another terrain: that of the arts. The literary movement which became known as *Jung-Wien* or *Jung-Oesterreich* dissolved the linkage of culture with politics that had characterized *die Jungen* of the seventies. German nationalism, the powerful catalyst of cultural renewal in the seventies, gave place to a conscious cosmopolitanism and a deliberate outreach to the artistic models and movements of other countries, especially France. Hermann Bahr, who more than any other tried to define the movement's character, had in 1883 gone to Berlin in pursuit of his nationalist dreams. Soon disillusioned with Bismarck's Germany, he went on to Paris, where he passed from political activism to aesthetic passivism. He returned to Vienna as a devotee of the French symbolists and decadents. Bahr's career represented concretely the wider evolution of the young bourgeois intelligentsia as it turned from communitarian politics gone sour to aesthetic culture.

Jung-Wien had no formal organization, nor did it center upon a major figure in the manner of the school of Stefan George in Germany. Not even a stylistic orientation gave coherence to the movement, for its writers ranged from the sociological naturalism of Arthur Schnitzler to the lyrical impressionism of young Hugo von Hofmannsthal. What gave the group its identity were two preoccupations: the nature of modernity and the life of the psyche.

The quest for "the modern" obviously implied a break from the past, but the young literati conceived this differently from the political Wagnerian culture-makers of the seventies. The young Wagnerians had rejected the immediate past, in the form of liberalism, but sought attachment to the remote past, both Greek and Germanic, to regenerate society in the present and to build for the future. They were still historically minded. *Jung-Wien* espoused the "modern" (a word used only in deprecation by Wagnerians) as a form of existence and a sensibility different from all that had gone before, one detached from history. Although they still used the repertorium of history as a source of images, they ceased to regard history as a meaningful succession of states from which the present derived its purpose and its place in human destiny. Modernity· meant "das Gleitende," said Hofmannsthal—the slipping or sliding away of the world. The literary figures who embodied the modern condition for these *Jungen* were playboys and/or aesthetes, men of sensuality or men of sensibility, socially functionless and existentially disengaged. In its psychological aspect, the modern malady was the dissolution of the ego. The seismographic consciousness of the fin de siècle character was assailed now by the forces of instinct within, now by the inchoate powers of the world without. The resultant condition portrayed in the literature was drift.[5] Ernst Mach's psychology, with its integration of stimulus and sensation into a single complex, provided the writers with an epistemological legitimation for their sense of loss of control. "The 'I' is unrescuable" became a virtual slogan for the literati.[6]

Jung-Wien showed little of the Wagnerians' anger at the culture of the fathers and their world—only sadness at the illusory nature of their elders' rational and moral premises. As Austrian society fell into the political impasse of national and social struggle in which none seemed able to win and none to control, the Promethean temper of the younger generation yielded to an Orphic one. The autumnal mood of impotence and pessimism, to be sure, only increased the sense of a break with the culture of the fathers. Generational identity focused now, however, not as in the seventies on the failure of the fathers to realize the full promise of the progressive liberal creed, but on the sons' incapacity to create community out of the pluralized elements into which the erstwhile social whole had become fragmented.

What remained was for modern man to find his own voice, to learn how to state his own truth, independent of the dead hand of the past. Hofmannsthal expressed the new distancing from the past in a lyric prologue to Schnitzler's *Anatol*. Though Schnitzler's play dealt with a modern sensualist, a role-player without social function or commitment, Hofmannsthal set his prologue in a rococo garden, to the modern Viennese a paradise lost of a gracious and well-ordered world. There the new Young Ones could fleetingly erect the scaffolding to play "the commedia of [their] spirit," the "agonies and episodes" of their precocious, sad existence. The ancient garden setting that gives meaning to the play-to-come is historical: formal, geometrically ordered, and dead. The drama is modern: an instinctual whirl. The traditional drama of society evoked in the setting of the prologue is dissolved in Schnitzler's play itself into a psychic scene of drifters.

In *The Road into the Open* (1907), the novel which he regarded as his greatest achievement, Schnitzler painted a more comprehensive group portrait of the young generation of educated Viennese trying to find a way in Austria's social centrifuge. A large cast of young adults, largely Jewish, illustrates the full range of options still open to them in postliberal politics and culture. Although the members of this generation espouse conflicting positions—socialism, Zionism, the army, and so forth—they form and sustain social and amorous relations with relative ease across the intellectual and ideological barriers which divide them, as though united by a tacit recognition of the partial and provisional character of all positions, all values, in their destructured world.

An Oedipal tension runs as a strong, subtly unifying subcurrent beneath the pluralized world of the young. Whatever the differences among them, the youthful characters have all espoused outlooks that set them off from their fathers. Yet Schnitzler treats the Oedipal tension, despite its omnipresence, in terms of cultural difference between generations, not as an eternal verity.

His older generation figures are committed to work, individual responsibility, and humane understanding. They lack all insight into the historical condition which distorts the lives and commitments of the young. Their values are at once admirable and anachronistic. One character of the younger generation, the writer Heinrich Bermann, an evident spokesman for Schnitzler's own melancholy perceptions of the modern condition, also manifests father-hatred at its most drastic. Heinrich's father was a Jewish liberal whose parliamentary and legal career was destroyed by anti-Semitism. The son's existential wisdom is coupled with a bitter rejection of his father for his rationalistic illusions. He accepts the contradictory character of the new social reality and treats all the options his contemporaries embrace as having only a subjective validity. "I do not stand above the parties," he says, "but rather side with all of them or against all of them. I have no divine justice [like the father's], but a dialectic one."[7] Heinrich's too comprehensive vision reduces him both to political passivity and to ineffectiveness as a literary artist. His ultimate conviction is that all the "roads into the open"—the myriad philosophic or political alternative approaches to the problems of modern Austrian society—"lead into the self."[8] Schnitzler thus transmutes the social problem he so realistically describes into a psychological one. Where the fathers had lived by naive faith as the underpinning of social action, the sons, suffering from loss of control over life and destiny, can approach public life only as private option; hence they often withdraw to the life of art and instinct. Richard Beer-Hofmann expressed *Jung-Wien's* sense of the collapse of cohesion in modern culture and society in a phrase: "Keiner kann keinem Gefährte hier sein" [None can here be companion to another]. The communitarian ethos of the political *Jungen* of the seventies, with its nationalism and its still-strong ties to history, had been swept away by the trauma of anti-Semitism, leaving only a sense of the incoherence of modern society and a turn inward in the search for meaning.

III

In the plastic arts, the cultural break from the past in the effort to define modernity came later than in letters, but was even more self-conscious. Within the *Künstlergenossenschaft*, Austria's principal artists' association, *die Jungen*—the name was used once more—began in 1895 to organize against prevailing academic constraints in favor of an open, experimental attitude toward painting and the applied arts. Like *Jung-Wien* in literature, the young rebels in art looked to the more advanced countries for models of modernity: to French impressionists and English Pre-Raphaelites, Belgian art nouveau and German *Jugendstil*. By 1897 the dissidents broke away to found a new organization called "the Secession."

No single aesthetic characterized the new movement. The artistic common ground of the participants was negative: their rejection of the classical realist tradition of the mid-century in their search for "modern man's true face." Thus in its inception, the movement was as much a phenomenon of dissolution as of new construction.

The ideology and rhetoric of the Secession, however, was rich in resonances from the radical political culture of the 1880s. A spokesman explained that the Secession drew its inspiration from the Roman *secessio plebis*, when the plebs, defiantly rejecting the misrule of the patricians, withdrew from the Republic. At the same time, the Secession proclaimed a regenerative intent, calling its journal *Ver Sacrum* (Sacred Spring). This title was drawn from a Roman ritual of consecration of youth in times of national danger. Whereas in Rome the fathers pledged their young to a divine mission in order to save society, in Vienna the young pledged themselves to redeeming art from the spirit of commerce and the dead hand of tradition which the fathers represented for them. The painter Gustav Klimt, spiritus rector of the Secession, expressed the Secession's aggressive accent on youth and its will to liberation in a poster for its first exhibition. He portrayed the figure of Theseus slaying the Minotaur to free the children of Athens.

On the new exhibition building of the Secession built in 1898, a veritable temple of the religion of art, was blazoned another provocative profession of modernity: "To the time its art; to art its freedom." Klimt contributed to the first issue of *Ver Sacrum* an allegorical drawing linking youth and modern truth: *Nuda veritas*, in the form of a nubile waif, holds up the mirror to modern man. Thus the Secession combined in its initial rhetoric elements from both previous movements of *die Jungen*: from the political-folkish *Jungen* of the seventies and eighties were drawn the themes of cultural regeneration and of revolt against corruption; from *Jung-Wien* of the early nineties, the antihistorical modernism. A tincture of Oedipal revolt suffused the whole.

Almost two decades separated the appearance of *die Jungen* as protagonists of a new political culture and the Secessionist rebellion in the quite different sphere of the visual arts in 1897. Can these be seen as parts of a single generational phenomenon? At the most literal level, that of the age cohort, there is clear commonality. In both *Jung-Wien* and Secession, most of the leading figures were born between 1860 and 1870.[9]

Although those most deeply engaged by the nationalist student movement were for the most part children of the 1850s,[10] those born in the early sixties, like Gustav Mahler, Hermann Bahr, and Theodor Herzl, also participated as students in the peak of the movement's Wagnerian intoxication in the early 1880s. It is not clear whether any of the artists of the Secession were involved in populist politics. But those who belatedly (in their thirties) became *die Jungen* in the visual arts were certainly influenced by the cultural ideas associated with the earlier revolt. Two principal formulators of the Secession's aims were direct carriers. As literary advisors to *Ver Sacrum*,[11] Hermann Bahr and Max Burck-

hard injected the spirit and rhetoric of populist politics into the crusade for a
new visual culture. Both had been active first in politics: Bahr, as we have seen,
as student nationalist in 1882-1883; Burckhard, as an important progressive legal reformer who had set up a system of administrative courts to handle griev-
ances against the decisions of bureaucrats. Whereas Bahr found political
inspiration in Wagner, Burckhard was a Nietzschean as well. Both men had
turned from politics to literature in the late 1880s. Bahr became a critical voice
of Austrian modernism in *Jung-Wien*, while Burckhard in 1891 achieved one of
the most prestigious positions in Austria, the directorship of the *Burgtheater*. In
this post, Burckhard enlarged the classical historicism of the *Burgtheater* playbill
with two new kinds of play: dialectic folk theater and the works of modern,
naturalistic dramatists such as Ibsen and Schnitzler. The first of these reflected
Burckhard's populism, the second his commitment to the avant-garde. With
Bahr, he brought to the Secession a politics of regeneration transposed into the
cultural sphere, to give a civic significance to the new art. The two men assured
that all the layers in the history of *die Jungen* were incorporated into the Secession's ideology. Only German nationalism was now noticeably missing from
their ideology. In a spirit not specifically German, but cosmopolitan and modern, the Secession would open Vienna to the arts of all Europe in order to find
forms appropriate to a modern Austria.

The burst of cultural communitarianism that gave a kind of parapolitical
stamp to the Secession's "springtime of art" in 1897 and 1898 quickly evapo-
rated. While folkish motifs appeared in some of the group's decorative arts—
book illustration, art for children, textiles, and so on—their principal stylistic
tendency was sophisticated and abstract. In painting, where the ideational content was strongest, Gustav Klimt set the tone, recapitulating in his own way the
concerns of the literary men: the dissolution of the ego, the power and meaning
of instinct—especially sexuality. In Klimt's drawings, one can see the energetic
curvilinear style borrowed from the German *Jugendstil* dissolve into the short-
fibered nervous contour of his tense and febrile female figures. His search for
sexual liberation brought forth lubricious playgirls who were as threatening as
they were seductive. (Nineteenth-century repressions died hard.) In his landscapes, the luminous color of French impressionism became transformed in the
last years of the waning century into a somber *plein-airisme* of the fog. As previous generations of painters studied anatomy, Klimt attended lectures in psy-
chopathology for inspiration.

Klimt's Orphic quest into the nether reaches of the psyche particularly
shocked contemporaries, for he had firmly established himself as a master of
what he now subverted: the solid historical naturalism that he had used with
such success in decorating the great public buildings of the Ringstrasse. In the
last of his major Ringstrasse commissions, a series of ceiling paintings for the
University of Vienna, Klimt expressed the new generation's postpolitical sense
of life. These paintings, representing the faculties of philosophy, medicine, and
jurisprudence, made the university a center of conflict over modern art as it had
been over nationalist politics. Klimt used some of the same philosophical materials as the student radicals before him, but for pessimistic metapsychological
purposes rather than militant political ones. Asked to produce pictures glorify-
ing the victory of light over darkness, he projected instead a Nietzschean vision

of philosophy in which Enlightenment rationality disappeared before the riddle of a universe of suffering, with only Zarathustra's midnight courage to transform chaos into beauty. A second painting representing medicine, inspired by Schopenhauer's pessimism, showed the procession of the suffering generations, Death in their midst, moving aimless in a viscous void. Finally, in a third panel symbolizing jurisprudence, three charming allegorical figures of civilized justice are only the deceptive surface of the law. Its deep reality is not their superficial order but punishment at the hands of naked, sunken-eyed femmes fatales. Perched in a deep yet spaceless world, they watch the victim of "justice" consumed by a womblike polyp. Law is unmasked as instinctual vengeance; judgment, as in the words of Blake, is in the loins. In the storm of protest unleashed by the painting, liberal university professors and anti-Semitic politicians found themselves for once at one, condemning from their different perspectives Klimt's subversive vision, so akin to Freud's.

By the years 1900-1903, the time of the public controversy over Klimt's university paintings, no one seems to have thought any longer in terms of generational conflict. The contestants defined what was at issue, rather, in moral and aesthetic terms. The pessimistic philosophic and psychological truths which Klimt purveyed had strong defenders, but not strong enough to make them acceptable in the public sphere. After a first defense, both Klimt and the Secession retreated, transferring their talents from formulating shocking truths to offering visions of sybaritic beauty. The Klimt group after 1904 turned increasingly to applied arts and portraiture, catering to the private patronage of the "advanced" elite. The regeneration of Austria through culture—the original aim they had so vigorously formulated—shrank to the definition of modern high style for the aestheticized life of the haut monde.

IV

As Vienna's fin de siècle pioneers of twentieth-century higher culture came to the end of their creative thrust, a new generation of innovators arose to proclaim harsher truths and values. Like their predecessors the first "moderns," the Expressionists—for under this label they may loosely be grouped—found each other across the barriers that separate the cultural specialties. The painters Kokoschka and Schiele, the poet Trakl and the novelist Musil, the composers Zemlinsky, Schoenberg, and Berg, the architect Loos, the philosopher Wittgenstein—if they did not all know each other personally, they supported the same periodicals and eagerly consumed one another's intellectual products, as the Wagnerians, *Jung-Wien*, and the Secession had done before them. There was, then, a sense of kinship as a generation. Yet they did not, as far as I can discover, call themselves *die Jungen*. Nor did they revolt in any specific way against the fathers and their works.

The Expressionists were, I should suggest, too free of specific social loyalties to define themselves in relation to history, to cultural structure and function in a temporal sequence. Not even "modern" had much utility as a concept for them, for the modern must derive its meaning in negative relation to that which, as history, precedes it. The Expressionists had taken up the task of overcoming history where the fin de siècle explorers had left it, and pressed forward on the *voyage intérieur* to the realm of raw, existential anxiety or anger, where all previous structures seemed phenomenological sham. Not the past, not modern life was the object of their apocalyptic vision, but human existence as such. They felt neither Austrian nor German, but human. When one of their magazines, *Der Ruf*, called for pulling down the boundary posts between Austria and Germany, it was not to reunite or "save" the Germanies, but to remove a meaningless symbol of statehood.

"Loneliness," wrote Oscar Kokoschka, "compels every man, like a primitive, to invent the [very] idea of society. But the knowledge that every society must remain a utopia forces one to take flight into loneliness." "Let us understand Expressionism as the living voice of man, who is to recreate his own universe." Ex nihilo: a large task! The only such order one could make was a heuristic one, posited by the individual in the face of tough enduring chaos. To discover the inherent destructiveness of that reality was the ground for affirming man's creative—if ultimately fated—power. Where the fin de siècle recovered the sexual instinct, eros, the Expressionists recovered thanatos. The metaphysical wrath of the Expressionists was perhaps too large to find focus in Oedipal revolt or generational resentment. Indeed, they often held their forebears in love and respect: Schoenberg worshipped Mahler; Schiele idolized Klimt; Loos had highest praise for Otto Wagner. They could perhaps accept their elders as role models because it was the elders who had dissolved the whole previous cultural inheritance, while the young began with modernity as premise to complete the elders' trajectory of alienation. Given the content of their ideas, generational resentment had little place. Robert Musil, in a legend for a future autobiography, suggests the distance of his peer group culture from an Oedipal self-definition. It reads: "My father was younger than I."

Where Musil and the Expressionist generation totally dismissed the Oedipal problem by subsuming it under a historical reality proclaimed dead, Freud proceeded in the opposite direction. He placed the Oedipal conflict at the center of all social existence. Freud's theory, the most widely diffused and visible legacy of the Viennese sociocultural upheaval to modern thought, occupies a special place in its own historical context. Out of his personal response to his experience as young revolté, Freud avoided self-identification with "the modern," even while, more like the Expressionists than the fin de siècle culture-makers, he confronts the chaos of history with the order of archetypes.

Freud worked out his theory of primal conflict between father and son in his extensive self-analysis between 1895 and 1899. In those years, the "increasing effects of anti-Semitism upon our emotional life," as Freud made clear in *The Interpretation of Dreams*, surfaced both in his dreams and in his waking recollections of his earlier deep commitments to politics, both as child and as university student. As one born in 1856, Freud had undergone all the experiences of political hope and frustration that shaped the generation of German-Jewish communitarian populists: from the glorious victory of liberalism in 1867 through the crisis of liberalism's national and social failure in the 1870s, the intoxication of the participation in the radical student movement, and the sudden transformation of its meaning by the rise of anti-Semitism. Like Schnitzler, Mahler, Klimt, and others, Freud pressed the experience of political defeat into the service of psychological exploration. But when all the others defined their predicament through the distinction between "historical" and "modern," Freud dissolved the whole cultural sphere into metahistory. Unlike the others, he kept the face of his father—its self-conscious Judaism, its principled liberalism, and its rationalism. Where his peers defined their tension with their fathers out of their demand for a new culture, Freud defined his paternal conflict not in revolt against the values his father professed, but in criticism of his failure to live by them fully. In recalling and recounting in the 1890s his dreams and memories of childhood, Freud indicts his father for lack of courage as a Jew and for failure to encourage his child in intellectual pursuits. When Freud finally made peace with his father in a dream crucial to the formulation of his Oedipal theory, he pictured his father as successful political leader and himself as servant through medical science. Integrating his conflict with his father with his own hostility to political authority, Freud coped with the second by establishing the primacy of the first. He thus elevated personal history, determined in the family, over general history, determined in the culture as a whole.[12] Oedipus for him carried all the dimensions of family relations and identity, but lost his capacity as *rex*. That is, Freud omitted the public significance of the myth in favor of its purely psychological significance.

Seen in terms of the experience of his intellectual peer group, Freud shared their trauma of dissolving liberalism, but subsumed the uniqueness of that experience under the eternal verity of father-son relations, rather than interpreting it as a historical crisis of the breakdown of rationalist culture. He found a form of thought for confronting the modern situation which eliminated the need for that *special* determination of the nature of modernity to which Schnitzler, Klimt, and his other peers devoted themselves. In so doing, he shared more with both the confident rationalism of the orthodox liberal fathers and the existential, archetypal world-view of the Expressionist sons than with his brothers, the ambiguity-ridden culture-makers of his own generation.

V

In the years 1866-1867, when both Austrian and North German liberalism were facing the crisis of redefining their relationship to state, nation, and society, the philosopher-historian Wilhelm Dilthey raised the theoretical question of the role of generations in cultural change. He was then at work on an earlier deep crisis of the German bourgeoisie, that of the French Revolution, which gave birth to German romanticism. Dilthey discovered that many of the strongest creative individuals among the romantics—Schlegel, Schleiermacher, Hegel, Hölderlin, Novalis, Tieck—were born within a single decade. Well aware that he was concerned with a small subgroup, Dilthey avoided a definition of generation applicable to the whole society. "[A] generation," he wrote, "is constituted of a restricted circle of individuals who are bound together into a homogeneous whole by their dependence on the same great events and transformations that appeared in their age of [maximum] receptivity, despite the variety of other subsequent factors."[13]

In the case of Vienna, the pioneers of twentieth-century high culture conform well to Dilthey's definition. The generational center of gravity of our culture-makers falls in the early 1860s; their formative context, the failure of

Austrian liberalism in the era of German unification and depression, in the 1870s. That the university became the center of political frustration for the scions of liberal families endowed the rebellion of *die Jungen* with an initial sharpness of age group definition and introduced Oedipal tension into the political antagonism. More significant for the future of liberalism as a value system was that *die Jungen* developed the Dionysian, populist counterculture as a support for their political criticisms and aspirations. This counterculture lent itself to anti-Semitism, in the same way that Jacobin rationalism spawned the reign of terror, with its grave intellectual consequences for Enlightenment culture. On the other hand, for those who recoiled in shock from the racist consequences of their nationalism, the Dionysian culture and the dissolution of the rationalist ego which accompanied it made possible the exploration of the psyche, the recovery of the nonrational dimension of man in all its richness and ambiguity. Thus *die Jungen* in literature in the nineties, and *die Jungen* who broke open new vistas in the visual arts at the century's turn were the twice traumatized. The consciousness of the break from history and the search for the special nature of modernity belonged to the experience of depoliticization. The subordination of the social to the psychological as the arena where meaning was to be found was the special contribution of Vienna's generation of *Jungen* to late liberal culture.

In the light of this trajectory of cultural change, we should not be surprised that the new young ones, the Expressionists, however vigorous—even violent—in their rejection of society and culture, showed less sense of generational identity or Oedipal hostility than the culture-makers of the fin de siècle. For this second wave of young revoltés only gave a final, drastic, archetypal formulation to the experience of social destructuring and psychological abandonment which their sensitive elders, in painful recoil from their own aborted regenerative crusade, had already proclaimed as the ground of being in their disintegrating liberal world.

REFERENCES

[1]William J. McGrath, *Dionysian Art and Populist Politics in Austria* (New Haven, Conn.: Yale University Press, 1974).

[2]Hermann Bahr, *Austriaca* (Berlin, 1911), p. 115.

[3]McGrath, *Dionysian Art*, pp. 17-32.

[4]Max Gruber, quoted in McGrath, *Dionysian Art*, p. 20.

[5]Carl E. Schorske, "Politics and the Psyche in *fin de siècle* Vienna, Schnitzler and Hofmannsthal," *American Historical Review*, 66 (1961): 930-947.

[6]Manfred Diersch, "Empiriokritizismus und Impressionismus," *Neue Beiträge zur Literaturwissenschaft*, 36 (1973): passim.

[7]Arthur Schnitzler, *Der Weg ins Freie*, vol. 3 of *Gesammelte Werke* (Berlin, 1922) p. 420.

[8]Ibid., p. 282.

[9]*Jung-Wien*: Heinrich Schnitzler, 1862; Hermann Bahr, 1863; Richard Beer-Hofmann, 1866; Hugo von Hofmannstahl, 1873; Peter Altenberg, 1859. *Secession*: (1) painters Gustav Klimt, 1862; Adolf Böhm, 1861; Wilhelm Bernatzik, 1853; Josef Engelhart, 1864; Carl Moll, 1861; Koloman Moser, 1868; Felizian Myrbach, 1853; Emil Orlik, 1870; and Alfred Roller, 1864; (2) architects Otto Wagner, 1840; Josef Olbrich, 1867; and Josef Hoffmann, 1870.

[10]Victor Adler was born in 1852; Heinrich Friedjung, 1851; Sigmund Freud, 1856; Theodor Herzl, 1860.

[11]See *Ver Sacrum*, 1 (1) (January, 1898): 1-3, 8-13.

[12]Carl E. Schorske, "Politics and Patricide in Freud's *Interpretation of Dreams*," *American Historical Review*, 78 (April, 1973): 328-347.

[13]Wilhelm Dilthey, *Gesammelte Schriften*, vol. 5 (Leipzig, 1924), p. 37, as cited in Hans Jaeger, "Generationen in der Geschichte," *Geschichte und Gesellschaft*, 3 (4): 432.

MORTON KELLER

Reflections on Politics and Generations in America

A JOURNAL IS TWENTY YEARS OLD and the theme of generations comes naturally to mind. There is special comfort for an historian in the fact that *Daedalus* celebrates this milestone not with another tour d'horizon of the perplexing present, but rather by exploring the concept of the generation. For this is a topic that leads inevitably to the central historical question of continuity and discontinuity over time.

Is the generational theme a valid and useful one? Unquestionably, the term itself poses difficult problems of definition. In one sense, biological generations are omnipresent, since all that lives is replaced in due course. But in another sense, the term has little social meaning, for there is no necessary link between the propagation of the species and the state of society.

Karl Mannheim and José Ortega y Gasset have argued that historical generations—that is, groups of contemporaries whose "historical coexistence" is determined by the major events of their time—are an important social reality. More recently, cohort analysis, defined by Norman Ryder as "the quantitative description of dated occurrences from the time a cohort is exposed to the risk of such occurrence," has been put forward as a more systematic way of dealing with the generational theme. It is not clear that a cohort, defined as "the aggregate of individuals (within some population definition) who experienced the same event within the same interval," has more precise meaning than a generation for purposes other than demographic analysis. Perhaps it is best to accept the imprecision inherent in the concept of the historical generation, to treat it as a formulation with both an objective and a subjective social existence similar, say, to that of class, and to explore its significance in an applied rather than a theoretical context.[1]

That significance is more apparent in some areas of human experience than others. Diffuse social institutions such as the family, the church, and the economy are not normally subject to the frequent and abrupt transitions implied by the generational theme. But certainly cultural history readily lends itself to treatment in terms of generations. And so does the history of politics.

The very nature of the political process—its intimate connection with transient events, its highly visible, structured institutional framework, its reliance on periodic elections—makes it a fit subject for generational analysis.[2] This is notably so in the case of American politics. Ours is a politics of pulse more than flow. It is a chronicle of movements, periods, eras—each lasting all of twenty or

thirty years. The isms of American political history—Federalism, Jef-
fersonianism, Jacksonianism, Populism, Progressivism—are conspicuous more
for their chronological limits than their ideological coherence. In this sense they
are quite unlike the major political categories of modern European history—
Liberalism, Socialism, Christian Democracy, Conservatism—which are far less
time-bound.

The reasons for this difference lie in the inmost character of American politics and the society in which it functions. The very structure of American government fosters a rhythmic public life. The Constitution prescribes periodic
and frequent elections; the federal system and winner-take-all presidential elections assure that our national parties are loose and varied coalitions, not coherent ideological entities.

There are still more profound causes of the strongly generational cast of
American politics. The lack of a deep past in the European or Asian sense and
the rapid pace of socioeconomic change from the beginnings of settlement are
distinctive features of American life. Ours has been a compressed national history, compressed in time and experience. Justice Oliver Wendell Holmes knew
both John Quincy Adams and Alger Hiss.

This quality of concentrated change reflects not only a relatively brief historical time-span but the character of American society itself. "Among democratic nations," Alexis de Tocqueville observed at a time when only the United
States came close to fitting that description, "each generation is a new people."
It is not difficult to see why this should be so. At least since the Revolution the
traditional props to social continuity—an established church, a hereditary elite,
fixed social status, ingrained habits of deference—have been conspicuously absent from America. Tocqueville movingly described the social consequences:
"Amongst democratic nations . . . the interest of man is confined to those in
close propinquity to himself. Aristocracy has made a chain of all the members of
the community, from the peasant to the king; democracy breaks that chain, and
severs every link of it . . . Thus not only does democracy make every man
forget his ancestors, but it hides his descendants and separates his contemporaries from him; it throws him back forever upon himself alone and threatens in
the end to confine him entirely within the solitude of his own heart."[3]

Yet throughout American history this dissociation of present from past and
future has coexisted with a notably stable and long-lasting political structure.
From the beginnings of settlement to the Revolution, the outward forms of
local, provincial, and imperial government of the colonies changed little. And
with the notable exception of the Civil War, the same has been true of our
national public life. Ours has been a dynamic and variable political history. But
the American Constitution, system of government, and political parties are
among the world's oldest.

Historians usually have dealt in one of two ways with this apparent paradox
of constant political ferment in a setting of strong institutional persistence. The
progressive-Marxist tradition of historiography ascribes America's political stability to the power of its elites, its political turmoil to popular struggles against
that elite hegemony. Those committed to a pluralist or consensual view of
American history find in the permanence of our public institutions evidence of
their popular underpinning and in political change evidence of the scope for
adaptation provided by the system.

Neither view takes sufficient account of the intragenerational similarity and intergenerational change that, it will be argued here, are a major part of American public life. These qualities exist independently of class (or ethnic, religious, or sectional) conflict, or pluralist consensus. Arthur M. Schlesinger perceived this generational impulse when he described the history of American politics as an alternating series of liberal and conservative periods, averaging out to about seventeen years each. He argued that relatively small shifts in public opinion were responsible for this variation, and that it occurred because the political tendency in power inevitably generated popular discontent sufficient to lead to its defeat. More recently, Samuel Huntington has suggested that the conflict of generations is one of the significant dynamic elements in the American political process.[4]

What follows is an attempt to put some evidentiary flesh on these theoretical bones, to take a look (of necessity a discursive and episodic look) at the place of generations in American political culture. Two themes will prevail: the similarities that bind the participants in each political generation and the differences that distinguish one generation from another. It may be that generations play in American politics a role not unlike that of classes in European political life. They are modes of political identification deeply rooted in underlying social reality. They serve both to reflect Tocqueville's insight into the dissociation of the American present from its past and future, and to act as forms of identity in the constant American struggle against that fearsome atomization. In this sense the generational theme casts light on the most characteristic feature of American public life: the coexistence of settled political institutions and an unsettled political culture. For generations are as much a way of repeating the past as of escaping from it.

Let me add that this is intended to complement rather than replace the familiar class, ethnocultural, pluralist, and consensual interpretations of American political history. I am exploring a theme, not propounding a theory. As William James once observed, the trouble with all social theories is that they leak at every joint.

From the earliest time of settlement, American political leaders were in doubt as to the security, even the legitimacy, of their station. And often with good reason. In 1635, less than thirty years after the founding of the colony, Virginia's governor John Harvey was "thrust out" of office and the colony with the warning that if he returned he would be whipped or shot. The lineaments of authority appeared to be in question in Plymouth Colony as well. Soon after its founding, Governor William Bradford found it necessary to assure anxious English backers that it was *not* true that women and children participated in— indeed, voted on—public affairs.[5]

John Winthrop came to Massachusetts Bay in 1630 knowing very well what a proper polity was: "God almighty in his most holy and wise providence has so disposed of the condition of mankind, as in all times, some must be rich some poor, some high and eminent in power and dignity; others mean and in subjection." But very quickly the peculiar conditions of American life led him to the gloomy conclusion that "here are some persons who never showed so much wickedness in England as they have done here." Fifty years later, William Penn was no less dissatisfied with the state of things in his colony. He begged the

Pennsylvanians in 1685, three years after the founding of the settlement: "For the love of God, me and the poor country, be not so *governmentish*, so noisy and open in your dissatisfactions."[6]

Factiousness and factionalism, riots and disturbances were conspicuous parts of colonial American public life. But for all its superficial resemblance to the acts of Hobsbawm's "primitive rebels" in early modern Europe, this turbulence differed fundamentally in character. For the most part it was profoundly conservative in purpose, aimed not so much at authority per se as at threats to a social order whose legitimacy lay in the fact that it was taking form from below rather than being imposed from above. Town mobs rioted against the spread of brothels (in Boston in 1734), against the handling of a smallpox epidemic (in Norfolk in 1768), against the new imperial policy of the Sugar and Stamp acts. In the Carolina backcountry, bands of solid farmers attacked outlaws and tax-gatherers not as rebels but as "regulators," the progenitors of the American vigilante tradition. As a later American phrase had it, they "took the law into their own hands." These were "lawful mobs" acting against "lawless law." Boston's mob refused to riot on the Sabbath.[7]

Those in authority relied on the traditional constraints of social deference, hierarchy and status, and inherited position. But the rapidity of change and the openness of life in colonial America eroded these inhibitions. Given this state of affairs, it is not surprising that intergenerational conflict quickly became a major and persistent theme of colonial politics. Newcomers (biological, social, economic, or migrational) constantly challenged their established predecessors. Thus political power in seventeenth-century Virginia recurrently shifted on generational lines. The "gentlemen and illuminati" who made up the first generation of Virginia political leadership gave way not to their chosen heirs and assigns but to a thrusting group of younger, more vigorous and adaptable planters. By the century's end these in turn were superseded by yet another rising elite. Snopeses were part of the American scene from earliest times.[8]

This generational dynamic in American politics was, if anything, heightened by the Revolution and the establishment of the new nation. Rising men everywhere rode the Revolution to power: of two hundred thirty-one occupants of executive positions in the colonies in 1773-1774, only twenty-two percent still were in office in 1776-1777. It is revealing that the rhetoric of the Revolutionaries (as in the case of Tom Paine) was filled with the image of intergenerational family strife. "Sons of Liberty" (English opponents of the Crown called themselves "Friends of Liberty") dwelt on the metaphor of ridding themselves of the king as "the father of his people." To see the Revolution in terms of an uprising of sons against father was natural, given the frequency of intergenerational conflict in colonial American life.[9]

The dispute in the 1780s between Antifederalists, who wanted the Confederation government to continue, and Federalists, who favored the new national government of the Constitution, was in part a generational clash. Antifederalist leaders Patrick Henry, Samuel Adams, George Mason, and George Clinton on the average were fifteen years older than their Federalist counterparts Alexander Hamilton, James Madison, John Jay, and Robert Morris. There were differences of experience and outlook as well. Antifederalists tended to have been more active in bringing about the Revolution, Federalists in fighting it. Antifederalists tended to be provincial, the Federalists to be cosmopolitan. Not for the first, or the last, time in American political history, inheritors challenged, and were resisted by, founders.[10]

The central theme of our national political history is the evolution of the two-party system. Have there been in fact Federalist-Whig-Republican and Jeffersonian-Jacksonian-Democratic party lines of descent? Do the two parties represent distinctly opposed economic interests? Have ethnic and religious distinctions been the most salient measures of party division? Or is party politics little more than the shadow play of Tweedledum and Tweedledee organizations, each serving in its own way a predominant American capitalism? These are the questions that underlie most of what has been written about politics in American culture.

A generational approach supplements rather than supplants this analysis. It helps us to see that in any given period parties and politicians have shared qualities transcending their ethnocultural, economic, ideological, or sectional differences. They are, in fact, part of a unitary political culture. At the same time, the theme of successive political generations may add to our understanding of the relationship of political to social change in American life. Together, this coherence within and distinction between political generations speaks to perhaps the major problem in American political history: how and why the political system (save once) has been able to sustain its institutional integrity in the face of the challenges posed by the explosive American way of life.

For all their ideological differences, the Federalists and the Jeffersonian Republicans, the major parties of the 1790-1815 period, had much in common. Jefferson's familiar declaration in his 1801 inaugural, "We are all Republicans; we are all Federalists," was truer than he meant it to be. Both parties reflected the elitist and deferential political culture of the late eighteenth century. And both contributed to the political transformation into the mass, democratic party politics of the early nineteenth century.

Support for the first two parties followed no clear sectional or class lines. Rather, it came from patchworks of adherents reflecting highly specific economic, religious, ethnic, and factional interests. Many Shaysites of western Massachusetts, ideal recruits to the Jefferson Republican cause, one might think, followed the lead of their Congregationalist clergy and supported the Federalists. So did prominent planters of Georgia and South Carolina; but so too did many backcountry Southern farmers, and old Antifederalists such as Patrick Henry, and up-and-coming young men such as John Marshall, who had their own reasons for opposing the regnant Jeffersonian Virginia dynasty. At the same time, the Jeffersonians had supporters in urban-mercantile circles in Delaware, New York, and Pennsylvania.

The structure and style of the two parties had as much in common as the variety of their constituencies. Both were "cadre" parties in the sense of being run by small and tight elites. And both contributed to the development of a more democratic politics through local conventions, a party press, ethnic appeals, and self-interested efforts to expand the electorate. "Reports say, that you was very civil to the young and handsome of the sex, that you flattered the old and ugly, and even embraced the toothless and decrepit, in order to obtain votes—when will you write a treatise on electioneering?" So wrote not some democratic-minded Jeffersonian, but rather Philip Schuyler to his fellow New York Federalist friend William Cooper (the father of James Fenimore) after a successful upstate campaign in 1792.[11]

Although it was true that the parties took opposing sides during the great debate over the merits of the French Revolution, and thus expressed their differing hopes and fears for the future of the American Republic, the actual conduct of diplomacy by the Jeffersonians in the early 1800s differed little from that of the Federalists in the 1790s. The central theme of Henry Adams's great *History of the Administrations of Jefferson and Madison* was the inherent irony of the Republican presidents following the same foreign policies for which they had so maligned his ancestor John Adams. Jefferson's acquisition of Louisiana might well have been expected to win Alexander Hamilton's warm approval—as, indeed, it did.

This generational similarity extended to domestic affairs as well. Out of power, Jefferson spoke of freedom of the press in the elevated tones of Milton's *Areopagitica*. In power, he went after opposition newspapers and judges with a vigor comparable to that of the Federalists after the passage of the Alien and Sedition acts.

The fact is that Federalists and Jeffersonians were alike the progeny of the Revolution, not, as in nineteenth-century France, the descendants of the victors and the vanquished. Theirs was a shared commitment to the success of the Young Republic as well as a shared fear, not uncommon to revolutionaries, that opposing forces, domestic or foreign, might upset the upsetters. There is no more affecting end-of-an-era tableau than that of John Adams, on his deathbed in Braintree on July 4, 1826, declaring, "Thomas Jefferson still survives," when, just hours before, his great political opponent (and constant correspondent—can anyone imagine a rich store of Stalin-Trotsky letters?) had passed away at Monticello. With perhaps more pathos than is necessary, the scene underscores the point that there was in fact a first generation of American party politicians.

The same can be said of the Jacksonian Democrats and Whigs during the 1830s and 1840s. Historians have devoted (sacrificed would be a better word) much space and more ingenuity to the task of drawing meaningful distinctions between these two party persuasions. But the more they try, the more those distinctions become—indistinct. Of course Jacksonians and Whigs represented differing ethnic, religious, and economic groups and fought over issues as well as for place and power. But more important than these differences was their shared commitment to a democratic American nationalism, and to the distinctive political culture that resulted.[12]

Democratic and Whig politicians literally spoke the same language: the language of a popular party politics. The political vocabulary of the eighteenth century, words such as faction, junto, interest, caucus, reflected a limited, elitist political order, and not surprisingly had common currency on both sides of the Atlantic. But in the first half of the nineteenth century American political language, like the political culture that it served, took on a tone and texture all its own. It drew more and more on the activities of everyday life. Candidates were favorite sons or dark horses; appropriations bills were pork barrels; defeated officeholders were lame ducks; partisans were dyed-in-the-wool, and sometimes party wheel-horses; politicians log-rolled, stayed on the fence, built party platforms composed of planks. This was the vocabulary of a politics with deep popular roots, a politics of vitality and motion. While English candidates continued to *stand* for office, American candidates *ran*—and bolted, bluffed, backed and filled, dodged the issue, stumped for votes.

This language had no particular party, sectional, or class provenance. Nor did the parties differ in their capacity to adapt to the demands of mass politics. The Democrats pioneered in 1828 by electing Andrew Jackson, "Old Hickory," a potent amalgam of Indian fighter, substantial public figure in the Old Southwest, and national hero. The Whigs raised the techniques of electioneering to new heights in their "log cabin" campaign of 1840, electing William Henry Harrison, "Old Tippecanoe," a potent amalgam of Indian fighter, substantial public figure in the Old Northwest, and national hero. Any attempt to distinguish Jacksonian Democratic simplicity from Whig quasiaristocracy falters when one considers the humble origins and social values of Whig leaders such as Thaddeus Stevens of Pennsylvania, or New York *Tribune* editor Horace Greeley (whose family was so poor that they migrated *to* Vermont seeking opportunity), or that greatest of American democrats, Abraham Lincoln.

The generational cohesion of the Jacksonians and the Whigs is as striking as the generational cohesion of the Federalists and the Jeffersonians. A sharper distinction can be drawn between these two political generations than between their component parts. In this fashion American politics faithfully reflected underlying American realities: the rapidity of change between generations, the prevalence of shared values within each generation.

Events in the 1850s and 1860s—the rise of the slavery issue, the South's move to secession, the Civil War, and Reconstruction—created the sharpest, most explicitly ideological political divisions in American history. Yet even the Southern proslavery, secessionist challenge and the Northern antislavery, Unionist response had enough in common to illuminate in a special way the inner coherence of each American political generation.

The secessionist South and the Unionist North justified their stands by reference to the same political tradition. Southerners saw the creation of the Confederacy and the preservation of slavery as quintessentially American acts of voluntarism and local self-determination. Northerners viewed the preservation of the Union and the end, or at least the containment, of slavery as necessary to the maintenance of the same social values: freedom and individualism.

That the two sections were engaged in divergent readings of a shared political philosophy is evident in the character of the Confederate constitution. That document differed from its Federal model only in details. It forbade the African slave trade, and made no provision for the right of secession. Slavery, not government, was the distinguishing feature of the new State.[13]

Historical as distinct from biological generations move at a varied pace, determined by the course and character of events. The Civil War, like the Revolution, stepped up the rate of generational change in American politics. Between the early 1850s and 1880 the Republican party passed through three fairly distinct phases. The first was dominated by the party's founders, including Lyman Trumbull, George Julian, Charles Sumner, and Lincoln himself, who laid its organizational and ideological base. They were followed and often displaced by a postwar leadership of organization-minded inheritors such as Roscoe Conkling, John A. Logan, Zachariah Chandler, and Ulysses Grant. These were late arrivals to the party—all save Chandler had been Democrats before the war— and in consequence tended to be plus royaliste que le roi. They called themselves Stalwarts and the Old Guard, and by 1880, when Republicanism still was less than thirty years old, spoke of theirs as the Grand Old Party.

These were the classic "politicos," using the memory of the Civil War to foster strong state and national Republican organizations. Yet by the early 1880s they in turn were challenged by other, often younger, party members more attuned to the issues and conditions of postwar America, men such as James A. Garfield, John Sherman, and James G. Blaine, whom the Stalwarts contemptuously labeled Half-Breeds.

A similar process of generational change went on within the Democratic party. The Democrats of the 1860s, like the Republicans, were intensely ideological, championing the Confederacy in the South, often opposing the war in the North. But they too gave way to postwar leaders—most notably Samuel J. Tilden—who were more interested in the politics of organization than in the politics of ideas. By the 1880s "Bourbon" Democratic organizations led by close equivalents of the Republican Half-Breeds were the norm both in the North and in the South.

Just as democratic nationalism was the leitmotif of the political generation of the 1830s and 1840s, and the ideological conflict over slavery and secession dominated the politics of the 1850s and 1860s, so did organizational politics prevail in the late nineteenth century. The primacy of party-building united a generation of politicos. New York Republican leader Roscoe Conkling declared in an 1876 campaign speech: "We are told the Republican party is a machine. Yes. A Government is a machine; the common-school system of the State of New York is a machine; a political party is a machine. Every organization which binds men together for a common cause is a machine."[14]

The work of Thomas Nast, the preeminent political cartoonist of his time, vividly portrays this change in political generations. During the 1860s Nast powerfully expressed the Republican position on the great issues of the Civil War and Reconstruction. In the early 1870s he created his famous images of the rapacious Tammany tiger and the gross, porcine Boss Tweed. But as the passionate ideological politics of those years faded, so did the intensity of Nast's vision. In the mid-1870s he produced what came to be the accepted representations of the major parties: the Republican elephant and the Democratic donkey. These were undramatic, without strong symbolic meaning, perfect embodiments of a politics that relied on organization and sentiment more than on ideology and purpose.[15]

The shift in political culture can be seen, too, in that all too common event, the presidential assassination. On one level, the killing of a president is a random act, divorced from larger historical meaning. But on another level, presidential assassins in their perverse but vivid ways have reflected the changing character of American political life.

John Wilkes Booth was ardently pro-Southern. Shortly before he killed Lincoln he wrote, "I have ever held the South were right . . . This country was formed for the *white*, not for the black man." His act, part of a conspiracy to kill the other architects of Union victory, including Grant, Stanton, and Seward, was a lurid finale to a generation of ideological politics. On July 2, 1881, Charles Guiteau shot President James Garfield, declaring, "I am a Stalwart and now Arthur is President." The proximate cause of his deed was that he had failed to get an appointment in the new administration. Booth the avenger of the Lost Cause of the Confederacy, Guiteau the party factionalist and spectacularly disappointed office-seeker were benchmarks of the generational shift from a politics of ideology to a politics of organization.[16]

As before, political change proceeded in pace with the evolution of the larger society. The organizational politics of the late nineteenth century had a symbiotic relationship with American industrialization. In both realms, fierce competition conjoined with a constant quest for structural and operational efficiency.

The high levels of organization and voter turnout attained by both parties in the late nineteenth century were very costly. More than some post-Civil War moral lapse, this explains the pervasive corruption at the time. Politicos no less than industrial or financial executives expected to be well paid for their efforts. Tens of thousands of party workers had to be compensated. Expensive elections had to be paid for.

But the late nineteenth-century political system was not sustained by organization and money alone. The Republicans in the North and the Democrats in the South drew for decades on the sectional passions of the Civil War. And each party laid claim to a complex of voter affiliations based on religion, ethnicity, and ideology as well. The Democrats of the late nineteenth century were hostile to active, centralized government, to the rise of big business, to restrictions on social behavior. Their Jeffersonian, antistatist, states' rights stance appealed to urban Irish Catholics as well as to rural white Southerners. The Republicans had a no less distinctive appeal. They were both the "party of piety," favoring forms of social control such as liquor regulation, and the "party of prosperity," supporting protective tariffs and other policies designed to foster American industrialization. In this way they, too, appealed to a constituency that cut across class and occupational lines. Thus, for all their differences, the two parties offered structurally similar responses to the political needs of a people enmeshed in rapid economic and social change.

At the turn of the century the larger consequences of American industrialization fostered yet another shift in the political culture. As before, a presidential assassination cast a lurid light on the change. Leon Czolgosz, who killed William McKinley in 1901, claimed to be an anarchist, an avenger of the wrongs of industrial capitalism. His father was an itinerant immigrant laborer; he grew up in the industrial heartland cities of Pittsburgh and Cleveland; this product of an industrial-urban age used the alias of Fred Nieman—Fred Nobody.[17]

The emblematic controversy over American imperialism that went on between 1898 and 1900 also set the tone for the political generation to come. The opponents of an overseas empire were a motley group, including former president Grover Cleveland and his great intraparty opponent William Jennings Bryan; the industrialist Andrew Carnegie and the socialist Henry Demarest Lloyd; genteel reformers E. L. Godkin and Charles Eliot Norton and Republican regulars John Sherman and Thomas B. Reed. Imperialism, too, had a varied appeal, attracting conservatives such as Henry Cabot Lodge as well as the reform-minded Theodore Roosevelt, Albert Beveridge, and even (for a time) Robert LaFollette.

For all its seeming variety, each group in fact had a distinct generational (and attitudinal) character. The leading anti-imperialists were in their late sixties; the leading imperialists were in their forties. The anti-imperialists, most of whose careers had by now passed their peak, were intensely aware of the rapidly changing character of American life. Most of that change they disfavored; and they found in imperialism an attractive focal point for their discontent. As Cleveland put it, "the fatal un-American idea of imperialism and expansion" was "a new and startling phase in our national character." By the same token, to the predominantly young, ambitious, and rising imperialists, an American empire was a fit expression of the vigor and progress that they saw in their country and in themselves.[18]

This tension between an often fearful emphasis on the need to preserve the American past and a usually confident acceptance of new policies for a new America underlay the public life of the progressive period before World War I and the 1920s after. But no hard and fast political line can be drawn between these two impulses. They intertwined through the parties, the issues, the leaders of the time. It was the tension between the old and the new America itself, rather than its resolution, that characterized the political generation of the early twentieth century.

Thus the regulation of big business developed as an often confused compound of antitrust attempts to restore small-unit competition and regulatory policy designed to come to terms with rather than to dismantle big business. A similar ambiguity of purpose was evident in the conservation movement. Aesthetic conservationists sought to preserve the past through the maintenance of wilderness; scientific conservationists sought to harness nature to serve more adequately the needs of an urban-industrial society. Policies such as national prohibition and immigration restriction came to fruition at this time precisely because they served the interests both of those who sought to restore a past America and those who saw in these forms of social control means of improving the quality of the society that had come to be.[19]

The presidents of the early twentieth century, Theodore Roosevelt, William Howard Taft, Woodrow Wilson, reinforce this view of the distinctive character of the progressive political generation. For all their strong party roots and invocations of traditional American values, they differed markedly from their late-nineteenth-century predecessors. McKinley had been a Civil War officer; his successor Roosevelt as a boy of seven had watched Lincoln's 1865 funeral procession in New York. TR's executive vigor, his flamboyant efforts to turn the presidency into a "bully pulpit," his concern with issues such as labor-capital relations, the trusts, and conservation, distinguish him as well.

Taft was no less different from the organizational presidents of the late nineteenth century. A judge, solicitor general, governor general of the Philippines, and secretary of war, he never ran for a major public office before he became president. He was the first chief executive to embody the growing importance of bureaucratic expertise and the administrative state. Wilson, political scientist, university president, holder of no public office save a two-year term as governor of New Jersey before his presidency, had a not dissimilar background. For all their political and personality differences, the three presidents of the early twentieth century had more in common with each other than with any of their predecessors.

The same may be said of the major political figures of the 1920s. On the face of things, Herbert Hoover and Al Smith represented polar elements in American life: Protestant, native-born Republicanism in the one case; Catholic, immigrant-urban, Democratic America in the other. Yet beneath their cultural confrontation was a shared body of experience and attitudes. Each had made his mark as a highly competent administrator of complex governmental units, Hoover as food administrator during the First World War and as secretary of commerce during the 1920s and Smith as governor of New York, the nation's leading industrial state. Both had a strong belief in the prevailing progressive values of efficiency and expertise. And both subscribed to traditional American principles of minimal government control; by 1936 they stood together in opposition to the New Deal.

Have the traumatic events of the past half-century—the Great Depression and the New Deal, World War II, postwar suburban affluence and inner-city turmoil, the Cold War—fundamentally altered the character of American politics? Have the class conflict of the Depression, the racial tensions of recent decades, the ideological politics of the radical right and the new left broken the traditional pattern of intragenerational political coherence? Have a corporate economy, cultural homogeneity (Daniel Boorstin's "everywhere communities"), and the decline of traditional party organization and constituencies put an end to intergenerational political change?

Historians have all they can do to make sense of the past; they can hardly be expected to speak authoritatively of the present. Nevertheless, it would seem that in recent decades as much as at any time before, gulfs of experience and perception divide one American social, and hence political, generation from another. Those who experienced the Great Depression and World War II were as indelibly marked as those who experienced the Civil War. And it is more and more clear that the generation which came of age in the 1960s was not so much the first of a new breed as precisely that, a generation, shaped by the special experience of its time.

American politics since 1930 faithfully reflects this continuing generational pulse. The Depression and the New Deal of course produced major changes both in public policy and in voting patterns. One estimate is that eighty-five percent of first-time voters under the age of twenty-eight cast their ballots for FDR in 1936. It is equally clear that political identification since 1945 has been more fluid and less class-oriented than it was during the New Deal period.[20]

A shift of comparable scale has occurred in the realm of foreign policy attitudes. It is not too much to say that Vietnam was the last effort of a generation of policymakers determined not to repeat the mistake of Munich. Nor is it too much to say that for years to come, foreign policy will be shaped by a generation of policymakers determined not to repeat the mistake of Vietnam.[21]

If intergenerational differences continue, so too does intragenerational similarity. For all the divisiveness of the New Deal, FDR and Wendell Willkie in 1940 had more in common than either did with their predecessors Smith and Hoover. In retrospect, Dwight Eisenhower and Adlai Stevenson seem to have been cut from the same consensual cloth of the 1950s. And Richard Nixon and Jimmy Carter may yet be seen as exemplars of the current American political generation: men of the New West and the New South, attaining the presidency through their mastery of a politics of media imagery that has supplanted a politics of organization, interests, and issues.

Dissenters from the political mainstream of the post-1945 decades—the radical right, the new left—constitute no exception to this view. They have had a symbiotic relationship not unlike that of the secessionists and abolitionists of the 1850s. The corporate liberalism condemned by the left bears a close resemblance to the left-leaning liberalism that so frightens the right. And in structural terms the right and the left have had similar dealings with mainstream politics. The "capture" of the GOP by Goldwater in 1964, and its calamitous political consequences, had a striking reprise in the McGovern candidacy and campaign of 1972. Both events were testimony to the weakening of the traditional party system that is a distinguishing feature of the present generation of American politics.

This impressionistic review of the generational theme in American political history does not detract from the importance of other major sources of political stability and change. It seeks only to make the point that the more familiar determinants—ethnicity and religion, economic interest, sectional identification—have worked in a political culture characterized by intragenerational coherence and intergenerational distinctions. This interplay has been evident from our society's beginnings. It is one of the distinguishing marks of our political way of life, and it must be taken into account in any attempt to see that politics clearly and in the whole.

REFERENCES

[1]Mannheim, "The Problem of Generations," *Essays on the Sociology of Knowledge* (New York, 1952), pp. 276-332; Ortega y Gasset, "The Concept of a Generation," *The Modern Theme* (New York, 1961), pp. 11-18, and *Man and Crisis* (New York, 1958), pp. 50-84; Norman B. Ryder, "The Cohort as a Concept in the Study of Social Change," *American Sociological Review*, 30 (1965): 843-861, and "Cohort Analysis," in David L. Sills, ed., *International Encyclopaedia of the Social Sciences* (New York, 1968), vol. 2, pp. 546-550. See also Julián Marías, *Generations: A Historical Method* (University, Alabama, 1970).

[2]Rudolf Heberle, "The Problem of Political Generations," *Social Movements: An Introduction to Political Sociology* (New York, 1951), pp. 118-127; Marvin Rintala, "A Generation in Politics: A Definition," *Review of Politics*, 25 (1963): 509-522.

[3]Tocqueville, *Democracy in America* (New York, 1958), vol. 2, 62, 105-106.

[4]Schlesinger, "The Tides of National Politics," *Paths to the Present* (New York, 1949), pp. 77-92; Huntington, "Paradigms of American Politics: Beyond the One, the Two, and the Many," *Political Science Quarterly*, 89 (1974): 23-25.

[5]On Harvey, Thomas J. Wertenbaker, *Virginia Under the Stuarts* (Princeton, N.J., 1914), p. 79; on Bradford, "Documents," *American Historical Review*, 8 (1903): 299.

[6]Winthrop, "A Modell of Christian Charity," *Winthrop Papers* (Boston, 1931), vol. 2, p. 282; Darrett Rutman, *Winthrop's Boston* (Chapel Hill, N.C., 1965), p. 22; Penn is quoted in Gary Nash, *Quakers and Politics* (Princeton, N.J., 1968), p. 49.

[7]Pauline Maier, "Popular Uprisings and Civil Authority in Eighteenth-Century America," *William and Mary Quarterly*, 3rd series, 27 (1970): 3-35; John P. Reid, "Lawless Law and Lawful Mobs," *New York University Law Review*, 23 (1977): 32-40.

[8]Bernard Bailyn, "Politics and Social Structure in Virginia," in James M. Smith, ed., *Seventeenth-Century America* (Chapel Hill, N.C., 1959), pp. 90-115.

[9]James K. Martin, "Men of Family Wealth and Personal Merit: The Changing Social Basis of Executive Leadership Selection in the American Revolution," *Societas—A Review of Social History*, 2 (1972): 43-70; Winthrop P. Jordan, "Familial Politics: Thomas Paine and the Killing of the King, 1776," *Journal of American History*, 60 (1973): 294-308; Edwin G. Burrows and Michael Wallace, "The American Revolution: The Ideology and Psychology of National Liberation," *Perspectives in American History*, 6 (1972): 167-306, esp. "The Ideology of Parental Authority," 226 ff.

[10]Stanley Elkins and Eric McKitrick, "The Founding Fathers: Young Men of the Revolution," *Political Science Quarterly*, 76 (1961): 181-216, esp. 202-203.

[11]Schuyler is quoted in David H. Fischer, *The Revolution of American Conservatism* (New York, 1965), pp. 15-16. See also William N. Chambers, *Political Parties in a New Nation* (New York, 1963); Noble E. Cunningham, Jr., *The Jeffersonian Republicans* (Chapel Hill, N.C., 1957); and *The Jeffersonian Republicans in Power* (Chapel Hill, N.C., 1963).

[12]On Whig-Jacksonian similarities and differences, see Major L. Wilson, "The Concept of Time and the Political Dialogue in the United States, 1828-48," *American Quarterly*, 19 (1967): 619-644; Glyndon G. Van Deusen, "Some Aspects of Whig Thought and Theory in the Jackson Period," *American Historical Review*, 63 (1958): 305-322; and the seminal works of Marvin Meyers, *The Jacksonian Persuasion; Politics and Belief* (New York, 1960), and Lee Benson, *The Concept of Jacksonian Democracy: New York as a Test Case* (New York, 1961).

[13]David H. Donald, *An Excess of Democracy: The American Civil War and the Social Process* (New York, 1960); Morton Keller, *Affairs of State: Public Life in Late Nineteenth Century America* (Cambridge, Mass., 1977), Chap. 1.

[14]Keller, *Affairs of State*, p. 248.

[15]Morton Keller, *The Art and Politics of Thomas Nast* (New York, 1968).

[16]Keller, *Affairs of State*, pp. 31, 267-268.

[17]Ibid., p. 599.

[18]Ibid., pp. 593-597.

[19]Morton Keller, "Public Policy and the Large Enterprise: Comparative Historical Perspectives," *Historical Function of the Organizational Structures of Modern Business Enterprises (Zentrum für interdisziplinäre forschung*, University of Bielefeld, forthcoming); Samuel P. Hays, *Conservation and the Gospel of Efficiency* (Cambridge, Mass., 1959); James H. Timberlake, *Prohibition and the Progressive Movement 1900-1920* (Cambridge, Mass., 1963).

[20]Norman H. Nie et al., *The Changing American Voter* (Cambridge, Mass., 1976), chap. 5; but see Everett C. Ladd, Jr., and Charles D. Hadley, *Transformations of the American Party System*, 2nd ed. (New York, 1978), pp. 75-87. See also Paul R. Abramson, *Generational Change in American Politics* (Lexington, Mass., 1975).

[21]Graham T. Allison, "Cool It: The Foreign Policy of Young America," *Foreign Policy*, 1 (1970-1971): 145-160.

TAMARA K. HAREVEN

The Search for Generational Memory: Tribal Rites in Industrial Society[1]

IN 1958 CLAUDE COCKBURN RECALLED a meeting with three Ladino-speaking Jews in Sofia shortly after the Second World War. They explained that they were not Spaniards, but one of them added, "Our family used to live in Spain before they moved to Turkey. Now we are moving to Bulgaria." When Cockburn asked him how long it had been since his family lived in Spain, he responded that it had been approximately five hundred years. The man spoke of these events as though they had occurred "a couple of years ago."[2] This famous incident has been cited frequently as an example of the relativity of historical memory. It also suggests the lengthy time over which individuals associate themselves with events which occurred generations earlier.

By comparison to other cultures, for most Americans generational memory spans a relatively brief period. The term generational memory is employed here broadly to encompass the memories which individuals have of their own families' history, as well as more general collective memories about the past. Most people do not even remember, or never knew, their grandfathers' occupation or place of birth. For a small proportion of the American population memory reaches back to the American Revolution, or to pre-Mayflower England or Europe. For descendants of later immigrations, memory extends mostly to the first generation in America, or, in fewer instances, to the last generation in the "old country." A sense of history does not depend on the depth of generational memory, but identity and consciousness do, because they rest on the linkage of the individual's life history and family history with specific historical moments.

Recently, efforts in American society to stretch generational memory, namely, the search for roots, through the tracing of genealogies and through oral history, have gained considerable popularity. A touch of magic has been attached to the process since the Bicentennial, and, in the aftermath of *Roots*,[3] a number of efforts to commercialize the search have emerged as well. More traditional scholars and foundations have also begun to encourage oral history, both as a means of retrieving or salvaging vanishing historical information and as a way to spark community identity. The success of *Roots* has publically dramatized the symbolic significance of such efforts.

Genealogies originally functioned to provide pedigrees and legitimization for status, claims for property, inheritance, or access to skills or political positions. Such real and symbolic functions of genealogies have survived in Ameri-

137

can society, especially in the South, despite an increasing democratization of
society. Even the Daughters of the American Revolution, whose genealogical
efforts were initially directed towards the inclusion of common people into the
nation's ancestry (providing they were present in America in the colonial and
revolutionary period), eventually turned their pedigree into an exclusive status
grouping justified by a genealogy.

When it was founded in 1890, the DAR was reacting against the heraldic
genealogical movements of the earlier period, which tried to link Americans
with the English nobility. Applicants for membership were required to have an
ancestor who was alive during the American Revolution, regardless of rank or
status. "Lineage tracing," writes Margaret Gibbs, "was as much the rage in this
decade—and in the early 1900's as Mah-Jong and crossword puzzles in the 'roaring twenties.' "[4] Along with numerous other patriotic societies which were
founded in that period, the DAR was dedicated to the preservation and protection of patriotic ideals. Partly, the movement developed as an expression of
anxiety in face of expansive foreign immigration, a fear of "race suicide" and a
fear of loss of status for native born middle and upper classes.

On the other hand, the recent genealogical movements, especially the search
for roots and the reconstruction of family histories, involve a different constituency and fulfill an entirely different function. They encourage individuals to
locate their own life histories in the context of activities and historical settings of
family members in earlier generations. Rather than concentrating on lineages as
such, they encourage detailed knowledge of those relatives and of the historical
events and the social context surrounding their activities. In this respect, family
histories represent a recent popular version of an older generation of autobiographies or traditional biographies of great families. Whereas, in the past, formal family histories were limited primarily to the upper classes, the uniqueness
of our time lies in the democratization of the process and in the inclusion of large
segments of the population in the search. The tapestry has thus broadened from
those claiming descent from the Mayflower or from Southern aristocrats, to
include the descendants of African slaves and immigrants.

The emphasis on individual identification with genealogy has thus shifted
from the search for legitimization of exclusive status to a concern with emergent
identity. Erikson defines "identity" as the meeting between individual life history and the historical movement.[5] The process involved in the current reconstruction of individual family histories goes beyond individual identity
in Eriksonian terms. It encompasses the linkage of one's family background with
the larger historical experience, which is recognized and accepted as part of a
collective heritage. Earlier, and even today in some circles, the search for a genealogy was considered successful only if it led to high-status ancestry, but the
current populist mood encourages the search for one's origin, regardless of the
social status of one's ancestry. The discovery of ancestors who were mere com-
moners, poor immigrants, or slaves is now considered as legitimate as linkage to
nobility and great heroes. The recent acceptance of slavery as part of America's
heritage by whites as well as blacks is indicative of this change.

This is precisely why *Roots* had the impact on the American public which it
did. Its most compelling aspect was not the book's rendition of the story of

slavery in a humane and moving way, but rather, the successful trace of the
connection between a contemporary man and the origins of slavery through an
individual line of descent. In itself *Roots* offers few new insights into the history
of slavery. Its key message is the resilience and survival of African traditions,
demonstrated in the effort of Chicken George and his descendants to transmit
their family history from generation to generation. Its uniqueness lies in the
process of search and trace of the history of one family, whose odyssey fits closely
the contours of the collective experience of American slavery. Although most
reviews have praised Haley's book as a great epic of slavery, they under-
estimated the significance of the final chapter recounting Haley's journey into
the past in his effort to trace his family history back to its African origin,
prompted by several fragments of an aging grandmother's narrative.

Significant here are both the process of the historical search itself and its
successful outcome, which offered thousands of people the opportunity of a
vicarious linkage with the historical group experience. (This is one of the rare
occasions when the painstaking and tedious process of historical research has
been acclaimed in the popular culture as a heroic act.) To understand fully the
role which *Roots* has fulfilled in American culture it is important to realize that
Haley's search *had* to be successful. The process of search would not have been
recognized as important in its own right.

What if Haley had failed? Consider two hypothetical alternative outcomes.
The first alternative could have been a break in the chain of evidence. This is, in
fact, what happens to the majority of people attempting to trace their family
histories beyond two generations. Most people embarking on such efforts without Haley's ingenuity, commitment of time, networks of scholarly support, and
financial resources, could never dream to travel a similar road. Had he failed,
Haley's story of the search itself, without the final linkage to Africa, would not
have electrified the public. Alternatively, suppose Haley had been successful in
tracing his ancestry, but the tracks did not lead back to the kind of ancestor he
found. Suppose the story diverged, and Haley discovered an ancestor, who,
rather than being an innocent victim captured and sold as a slave, had himself
been a collaborator in the buying and selling of slaves. The search itself would
still have been historically meaningful and personally satisfying, but it would
not have had the same impact on the American public, because it would have
lacked the direct link with collective experience of slavery. In short, the significance of Haley's book for American culture of the seventies lies not merely in
the successful tracing of a line of ancestry back to Africa, but rather in the fact
that this ancestor's history was characteristic of the mainstream of the slave
route to North America and of the slave experience.

It is no coincidence that Haley is also the author of the *Autobiography of
Malcolm X*.[6] Both the *Autobiography* and *Roots* are American success stories. In
both, the hero follows a progression which he views as destined to culminate in
the ultimate triumph. Earlier life events lead in an almost linear sequence to the
moment of triumph and redemption. In Malcolm X's biography, as in the *Confessions of St. Augustine*, the entire life sequence leading to the moment of conversion is viewed as providential. Even Malcolm's devastating life experiences,
his "sins" and suffering, were justified as steps toward the final redemption.

Similarly, in Haley's story, the memory of the suffering of Kinte and that of his descendants in slavery were redeemed in the historical moment of rediscovery and linkage between past and present.

Both individual stories fulfilled significant public functions: at the height of the Black Power movement, Malcolm X's story and conversion performed a symbolic function, purging Black Americans from repressed anger reaching back into several generations. Haley's story provided a symbolic route for rediscovery of a past and, with it, a historic identity for Black Americans. The two had to occur in this sequence. First, the anger had to be purged in order to reverse a negative into a positive identity. Then came the search for roots, the discovery of a past, and the acceptance of this past as a significant part of America's heritage. Appropriately, the subtitle of Haley's book is *The Saga of an American Family*.

Roots also represents another important historical linkage, namely, that of the informal family narrative transmitted from generation to generation, which is not intended as a formal source of history, with the formal oral tradition of Gambian society—the official chronicle recited by the Griot. In Africa and in other nonliterate societies both types of oral traditions coexist, each performing a different function. The oral history genre which has survived in the United States, especially in black culture, is personal and informal. One of the most remarkable of Haley's discoveries was the survival of fragments of an oral tradition in his grandmother's memory in 1950s America. By that time, these fragments had lost their specific significance, but they were still being transmitted with a purpose; so that one's children and children's children would remember.

In modern American society, archives and formal histories have long replaced oral chronicles as official history. As the rich collection of folklore in Appalachia, or the very moving account of *All God's Dangers* suggests, generational memory and real traditions have persisted as historical sources in islands of local folk culture throughout the United States, though most prominently in black culture.[7] There is, however, a significant difference between the informal oral tradition which has survived in the United States and the official oral tradition in nonliterate societies. In such societies, the oral tradition has an institutionally recognized place and purpose in the culture, and whether it constitutes an official chronicle, a family narrative, a fable, or other types of memories, it is structured and presented in specific formulae. The function of oral testimony may range from myths aimed at providing an explanation of the creation of the world and of society as it exists, to those providing a pedigree for tribal rulers or to a justification of the political structure. The oral testimony can be legalistic, didactic, or explanatory, and its structure and mode of presentation may vary accordingly. Whatever its function, its social purpose is officially valued in these cultures.

In modern American society, although, in the absence of such a well-defined tradition as in nonliterate societies, it is difficult to find a formal place for oral history, informal oral history as a historical source is not a new phenomenon. It has been utilized systematically as an archival and research tool especially to record the memories of public figures who have been active in political and social life, as evidenced in projects of Columbia University and the Kennedy Library. Such projects have been carried out with historical scrupulousness, where the process of interviewing itself was preceded by research in written documents. Informal oral history has been employed effectively also in more modest historical projects, where the oral evidence was linked with written records and interpreted in conjunction with them.

Oral history also has an important social science heritage, which has developed since the 1930s, namely, the use of the individual life history for the "study of lives," which Dollard and subsequently Allport and White had developed as a major research method in psychology.[8] More recently, Oscar Lewis and Robert Coles have demonstrated the power of this method when applied to the urban poor, to Puerto Ricans and Mexicans, and the children of migrant workers and sharecroppers.[9] Inspired by this approach, radical historians have utilized oral history as a means to record the experiences of workers, activists, and participants in social protest movements, not only to retrieve and record information, but also as a way to form group consciousness through the process of interviewing itself.

More recently, oral history has been used on the community level for a similar purpose, namely, that of firing collective historical consciousness through the discovery of a common past. Some oral history efforts which emerged in recent years are filiopietistic and attach a mystique to the process because of the encounter with the living past which it represents. The Bicentennial, in particular, gave an impetus to oral history projects which are intended to stimulate "community awareness" and "identity." Such undefined slogans, which have been used rather indiscriminately, do not explain how community consciousness would be raised through such projects and *whose* history is actually being recovered. The widespread use of the cassette tape recording machine over the past decade has contributed considerably to the popularization of oral history interviewing. Like the computer, the recorder has not only facilitated the gathering and preservation of data; it has also generated a mystique of authenticity which is conveyed through the magic of technology. Oscar Lewis somewhat glorified its role: "The tape recorder used in taking down the life stories in this book has made possible the beginning of a new kind of literature of social realism. With the aid of the tape recorder, unskilled, uneducated and even illiterate persons can talk about themselves and relate their observations and experiences in an uninhibited, spontaneous and natural manner."[10] People using the tape recorder, like those using the computer, discover quickly, however, that it does not have intrinsic magic. Without the historical and sociological imagination shaping the interview, one can end up recording miles of meaningless information.

Little attention has been paid to two aspects of oral history which are central to its role, namely, the nature of the interview process itself and the function of oral traditions in a modern, literate society.

First, the interview process. During an extensive oral history project in a large New England industrial community,[11] we became acutely aware of the fact that oral history is not strictly a means of retrieval of information, but rather one involving the *generation* of knowledge. Essentially, an oral history narrative is the product of an interaction between interviewer and interviewee. By its very nature such a process determines what is going to be recalled and how it will be recalled. The interviewer is like a medium, whose own presence, interests, and questions conjure corresponding memories. Even if the interviewer tries to remain inconspicuous, the very process is intrusive.

Oral history is therefore a subjective process. It provides insight into how people think about certain events and what they perceive their own role to have been in the historical process. "A testimony is no more than a mirage of the reality it describes," writes Jan Vansina, the leading scholar of oral tradition in Africa. "The initial informant in an oral tradition gives either consciously or unconsciously a distorted account of what has really happened, because he sees only what he has seen."[12]

Oral history is an expression of the personality of the interviewees, of their cultural values, and of the particular historical circumstances which shaped their point of view. This is precisely its great value, rather than its limitation. Similar arguments could be made about written documents; diaries and personal letters are also highly subjective, though their subjectivity is of a different origin. A diary reflects a person's individual experiences or observations, whereas an oral history is the individual's experience as evoked by an interviewer who has an intentional or unintentional influence on what is remembered and the way in which it is remembered. Oral histories are also distinguished from diaries or letters in their retrospective construction of reality. Like autobiographies, oral histories are past experiences presented from the perspective of the present.

The dynamic interplay between past and present in an individual's reminiscences can take different forms. At times, interviewees temporarily immerse themselves into a past episode as they recount it. This is especially true for childhood memories. On such occasions, the individual reminiscing slips back into the past, and recounts vibrant memories without any consciousness of the present. The interviewee becomes like an actor fully playing the role in his or her own past. On most occasions, the person remembering maintains a conscious separation between the account of the past and the present, though hindsight provides a contemporary perspective on past experience.

On many other occasions, interviewees find it difficult to distinguish past from present, or earlier from subsequent events. Interviewees also misrepresent or reinterpret actual events or situations through faulty memory or repression of difficult experiences. Traumatic experiences also lead to the reinterpretation of events. For example, when we interviewed former workers of the Amoskeag Mills, some of them said they had finished working in the Amoskeag in 1922. When we pointed out to them that their work records in the corporation files indicated they had worked until 1930 or later, the typical reply was "Oh yes, but that was after the strike. Things were not the same anymore." The strike of 1922 represented to the majority of people who worked there at the time the destruction of the world to which they had become accustomed. Even though they returned to work after the strike, they associated the strike with the end of their career.

Sometimes people just forget experiences; other times they *care* to forget, or, if they remember them, they do not want to talk about them. As Gunhild Hagestadt points out, in many families there are prohibited zones, which most family members choose not to tread in, as if by unspoken agreement. An interviewer can sense the invisible electrified fences when approaching such areas, but can do very little about them.

Oral history is a record of perceptions, rather than a re-creation of historical events. It can be employed as a factual source only if corroborated. The difficulty of cross-checking information does not detract, however, from its value for understanding perceptions and recovering levels of experiences which are not normally available to historians. It offers almost the only feasible route for the retrieval of perceptions and experiences of whole groups who did not normally leave a written record. The major contribution of *Akenfield* and of *Hard Times* is not in their historical accuracy, but rather in their contribution to an understanding of human experiences and social conditions.[13] As long as one understands this, rather than assumes, as some do, that oral history is the closest to "unadulterated human memory" we can approach, it can be valued for what it is and utilized creatively.[14]

The second major feature of oral history involves its very significance in modern industrial society. In the absence of an established oral history tradition in American society, it is difficult to define its place and to justify its meaning to individual interviewees. It is almost impossible to stimulate *spontaneous reminiscing* as many community identity projects suggest one should. To make oral history meaningful, one has to find a link between an individual life and a broader historical context. Such links are exceedingly difficult to identify unless the individuals participated in a common distinct cultural activity, organization, or group with a shared interest or if their lives were affected directly by a common dramatic event.

Even in the black community, where the oral tradition is alive, particularly in the South, it is often difficult to link informal experiences and memories to a larger picture, unless the interviewees themselves are aware of a common focus.

Without such linkages, in most instances in the United States, oral history interviewing remains a private exercise. In Africa, by contrast, Vansina points out, "Every testimony and every tradition has a purpose and fulfills a function. It is because of this function that they exist at all."[15] In nonliterate societies the functions of an oral tradition are socially defined and are recognized by all members. In modern America there is no such established tradition, except in regional oral traditions which survive in isolated localities. Within the larger community, the public role and social significance of oral history are not automatically understood.

People who have not been "famous" or who have not participated jointly in a specific movement, such as a labor movement, or a strike, or in an organized political or social activity, would find it difficult to achieve such an identification. Such people experience great difficulty in making the connection between their own lives and the historial process. Community organizers who expect the emergence of "instant identity" through the interview process face an instant disappointment.

In societies where the oral narrative is part of the formal culture, no explanation is needed as to why a certain story is significant. The very time-honored practice and the setting within which the oral tradition takes place lend it strength and meaning. In modern America, except for historically conscious individuals or groups and unusually articulate and interested individuals, most people do not see an immediate significance in being interviewed. Although they might be inclined to reminiscence privately, telling stories to their own grandchildren or sharing memories of past experiences, most people are rather bewildered when requested to tell their life histories to strangers.

When approaching the former workers of the Amoskeag Mills in Manchester, New Hampshire, for interviews, we frequently encountered the questions: "Why ask me? My story is not special," or "What is so important about my life?" Except for a few people, those who consented to be interviewed did so, not because of their understanding of the importance of this process, but because, prompted by their own work ethic, they wanted to help us do "our job."

Attitudes changed drastically after the exhibit "Amoskeag: A Sense of Place, A Way Of Life" opened in Manchester.[16] Although this exhibit was primarily architectural and was aimed at professionals and preservationists rather than at the larger public, it evoked an unexpected response from former and current textile workers in the community. It provided the setting for the former workers' public and collective identification with their old work place and it symbolized the historical significance of their work lives. Thousands of people, mostly former mill workers and their families, came to see the exhibit. Most striking were recurring scenes where old former workers searched for their relatives in huge historic group portraits of the workers, and where grandparents led their grandchildren through the exhibit, often describing their work process of thirty to forty years earlier. Even though they had privately cherished many memories associated with their work experience, they felt that industrial work, especially textile work, was generally looked down upon. The sudden opportunity to view their own lives as part of a significant historical experience provided a setting for collective identification. Under these circumstances, interviewing ceased to be an isolated individual experience. It turned, instead, into a common community event. Former mill workers recognized each other at the exhibit, some not having seen each other for thirty years. Although the exhibit was not designed to serve this purpose, it turned into a catalyst.

The oral histories which followed were of an entirely different character from the earlier ones: people we approached were willing to be interviewed. They related their work and life histories with a sense of pride. Many individuals who had heard about the project volunteered to be interviewed. Identification with the work place and with the buildings thus provided a more direct and immediate stimulation of memory and interest in the process than isolated interviewing. The exhibit established our credibility as interviewers and laid the foundation for a continuing series of interviews with the same individuals. This is not to suggest that every successful oral history requires an exhibit or some other external device to engender identification. It suggests, however, how tenuous oral history is among those elements of the population who do not have an oral tradition. It is also becoming clear that, except for the search for roots through the reconstruction of one's own family history, the quest for oral history is more common among the educated, the professional, and the semi-professional, especially among second- or third-generation ethnics, than as a "folk movement."

Why this exercise of "tribal rites" in an advanced technological society? Today, when the printing and circulation of information have reached an all-time peak, and when computers generate and objectify knowledge, scholars, foundations and cultural organizations, and the general public are reviving genealogy and the oral tradition—the tools of transmission of collective memory in nontechnological societies. Among scholars, this revival represents a revolt against "objective" social science and a shift from an emphasis on strictly formal knowledge to existential process. Oral history and the search for roots also fit into the effort of recent scholarship to integrate the experience of large segments of the population into the historical and sociological record. On a more popular level, the oral history revival is connected with an effort to authenticate the experiences of different ethnic groups in American culture. It thus represents a commitment to pluralism and expresses the reemergence of ethnicity and its acceptance as a vital aspect of American culture.

The current search is also prompted by a realization that the traditions which one is trying to record are about to become extinct. *The World of Our Fathers, The Godfather*, and many other ethnic monuments were generated at the moment when the last living links with the world are about to disappear.[17] Most of these efforts to capture ethnic traditions do not bring back the heritage from the old country, but rather the experience of the first generation of immigrants in America.

The search for roots in our time is not entirely new. An earlier centralized effort of this sort took place in the 1930s in the midst of the Great Depression. Current popular oral history projects are miniscule by comparison to the undertakings of the Works Progress Administration's Federal Writer's Project in most American communities. Some of its achievements include the American Guide Project, which generated a massive collection of local guides, the recording of over two thousand narratives of former slaves, the compilation of numerous volumes of local oral histories, and the assembling of a number of major collections of folklore. The national folklore project under the direction of John Lomax was intended to capture the surviving oral traditions and folkways. It produced a national volume entitled *American Folk Stuff*, designed as a collection of readable tales. "All stories must be narrated as told by an informant or as they might be told orally with all the flavor of talk and all the native art of casual narrative belonging to the natural story-teller," read the instructions of the national program director to all state directors.[18]

The folklore project stressed the collection of materials from *oral* sources with reference to the life of the community and the background of the informant. It captured urban and ethnic folklore as well as rural. "All types of forms of folk and story-telling and all minority groups—ethnic, regional and occupational are to be represented for two reasons: first to give a comprehensive picture of the composite America—how it lives and works and plays as seen through its folk storytellers; second, by the richness of material and the variety of forms to prove that the art of story-telling is still alive and that story-telling is an art."[19] Under the auspices of the Farm Security Administration, some of that generation's master photographers, such as Dorothea Lange, James Agee, and Walker Evans, recorded the words and faces of sharecroppers, "Okies," migrants, and

Appalachians, bringing the faces of rural America into the center of the nation's consciousness. Thus, through a concerted government effort, rural roots were exposed and recorded for posterity.

Much of the social documentation of rural life resulted from the recognition that that world was fast disappearing, and from the fear that some of its wholesome values would be swept out by a new industrialism. To a large extent, this passion to document rural life was stimulated by the discovery of chronic poverty and deprivation in the rural South and Midwest, which had been ignored while the "pathology" of cities had occupied the limelight during the first three decades of the twentieth century. While they conveyed the suffering and deprivation of their subjects, the photographs and narratives in *Let Us Now Praise Famous Men* and in other kindred documentaries also conveyed the resilience and wholesomeness of this group.[20] The faces of the "Sharecropper Madonna" and of the Okies also had a sobering effect on those who idealized the myth of self-reliance and frontier life. In addition to the strong humanistic empathy for the subjects and their ways of life, these projects also expressed the period's longing for a lost mythical past of innocence and wholesomeness. The very launching of these projects in the midst of a catastrophic depression resulting from the "industrial plant being overbuilt" was a reaction against "progress" and with it, the destructive pace of modern, industrial life.

The 1930s was the era of the discovery of rural native American and black roots. The day of the immigrant was still to come. The WPA writers' project also attempted to record urban folklore. The New York City folklore project, for example, was intended to reveal "the epic of construction, excavation and wrecking, transportation . . . and the symphony of New York night life . . ." Similarly, the social ethnic project which the WPA launched was intended to shift the emphasis from "the contribution of ethnic groups to American culture" to their participation in various aspects of community life. However, the definition of ethnicity which the WPA introduced was one very different from the ethnic revival today: "Immigrants and the children of immigrants are American people. Their culture is American culture."[21] Generally, the images and experiences which captured the imagination of the thirties were the documentaries of rural life. The earlier documentation of life and poverty in immigrant slums in New York, Chicago, and Baltimore, which was carried out in the late nineteenth and early twentieth centuries by Jacob Riis, the Russell Sage Foundation and the *Survey*,[22] and Lewis Hine's prolific photographic record of child labor, was documenting the plight of urban immigrants and the deterioration of social and economic life as part of a social protest movement, not in order to capture ethnic "roots." Immigrants who had flooded American cities between the 1880s and World War I were still too recent and still represented undigested alien masses.

The current quest for roots holds in common with that of the 1930s a genuine concern for recovering the historical experience as it was viewed and perceived by participants. As in the thirties, the search emerged from a crisis in values, and from a questioning of the very foundations of American society. Both in the 1930s and in the 1960s, the search for roots came in response to a disillusionment with technology, industrialism, and materialism. In the thirties the effort led to a reaffirmation of the qualities and strengths of American folk culture. Alfred Kazin, one of the unemployed writers in the WPA project, described the interview experience as "A significant experience in national self-discovery—a living record of contemporary American experience."[23] The current search is aimed more specifically at the recovery of ethnic group identities. In the 1960s and 1970s the search for roots has been individual as well as group oriented. Unlike the 1930s, when the effort was organized and supported by the government, in the current decade it represents a more spontaneous movement. Its very emergence is part of an aftermath of the Civil Rights and Black Power movements and is part of the recent acceptance of ethnicity as part of American culture.

Ironically, we are now engaged in recovering generational memory, after much of it had been wiped out in a century-long effort to assimilate immigrants. As Lloyd Warner pointed out, the symbols which dominated the historical rituals and pageants of Yankee City's Tricentenary were those of the colonial period and the era of the American Revolution.[24] An entire century of Yankee City's history had been almost completely ignored. Despite the fact that they already comprised a significant element of the city's population, the ethnic groups were expected to choose themes from the colonial and revolutionary era for the floats which they sponsored in the historical pageant (the Jews choosing an episode in the life of Benedict Arnold). Even in 1976, during the Bicentennial celebration in one of the historic mill buildings in Lowell, Massachusetts, the majority of the participants from the community (who were of different ethnic origins) were wearing revolutionary era costume, though Lowell was founded in 1820 and symbolized the beginning of the new industrial order. Similarly, a recent follow-up study on Yankee City in the 1970s finds that the new owners of the Federalist houses in Newburyport are reconstructing the genealogies of these houses, rather than their own family histories.[25]

The current return to ethnicity in American culture is possible precisely because so much has been forgotten already and because of the distance in time between the current generation and the two generations of immigrants who came to the United States between 1880 and 1920. Before ethnicity could be recognized as a permanent feature in American culture, the different ethnic subcultures had to go the full cycle of assimilation and come close to extinction.

In some ways we are now witnessing the final consequences of the closing of the gates in the 1920s. The end of immigration at that point facilitated the absorption of immigrants who had arrived earlier into the United States. Had there been a continuous influx of new immigrants, it is doubtful whether ethnic diversity would have been accepted today as a genuine part of American culture. The current search for ethnic roots is in itself a rebellion against the concept of the melting pot; it is an effort to salvage what has survived homogenization. In the process, it is also likely to create new identities, new heritages, and new myths. Part of this process represents an effort to counteract alienation and to seek comfort and reassurance in memories of close family ties and community solidarity which are generally attributed to the lost ethnic past. For most ethnic groups this past represents the world of the first generation of immigrants in the United States, rather than the old country. The search for an ethnic past becomes especially significant for our times because of the generational watershed which we are currently experiencing: the two generations of

European immigrants which had come here from the old country in the late nineteenth and early twentieth centuries are now dying out, while the generation which is now reaching the prime of its adulthood has no personal memory of World War II. What this would mean for the generational memory of the children of this age group is an interesting question in itself.

In assessing the significance of the current search for roots from a historical point of view, we must ask where this all leads. In 1911, confronting the DAR, Jane Addams warned them: "We know full well that the patriotism of common descent is the mere patriotism of the clan—the early patriotism of the tribe—and that, while the possession of like territory is an advance upon that first conception, both of them are unworthy to be the patriotism of a great cosmopolitan nation . . . To seek our patriotism in some age rather than our own is to accept a code that is totally inadequate to help us through the problems which current life develops."[26]

It would be a historical irony, of course, if the groups which had been excluded for so long from the official cultural record, would fall into a similar trap of exclusiveness and separatism when recreating their own history. Some of that danger would be present if the reclamation is particularistic and parochial. Is the current individualism and ethnocentrism going to result in a retreat and withdrawal from a common culture and common social goals? Will it eventually lead to fragmentation rather than a balanced pluralism? Whatever the outcome might be, the current search inevitably has to take place first within the subcultural compartments, since until very recently, the larger society has tried to mold the identity of different ethnic groups in its own image.

REFERENCES

¹In the process of writing this essay, I have benefited from a number of enlightened conversations and from the insights of the following people: Randolph Langenbach, Richard Brown, Ronald Grele, Nancy Chudacoff, John Modell, Frank Fustenberg, and Carol Stack and Robert LeVine. I am indebted to Stephen Graubard for valuable comments, to Howard Litwak for editorial assistance, and to Bernice Neugarten and Gunhild Hagestadt for their insights.

²Quoted in M. I. Finley, "Myth, Memory and History," in *History and Theory* (1965), pp. 281-302.

³Alex Haley, *Roots* (Garden City, N.Y.: Doubleday, 1976).

⁴Margaret Gibbs, *The DAR* (New York: Holt Rinehart and Winston, 1969), p. 21.

⁵Erik Erikson, *Identity: Youth and Crisis* (New York: Norton, 1968); *Life History and the Historical Moment* (New York: Norton, 1975).

⁶Alex Haley, *Autobiography of Malcolm X* (New York: Grove Press, 1965).

⁷Theodore Rosengarden, *All God's Dangers: The Life of Nate Shaw* (New York: Knopf, 1974).

⁸John Dollard, *Criteria for the Life History* (New Haven: Yale University Press, 1935); Gordon Allport, *The Use of Personal Documents in Psychological Science* (New York: Social Science Research Council, 1942); Robert White, *Lives in Progress* (New York: Dryden Press, 1952).

⁹See Robert Coles, Children of Crisis series, particularly *Migrants, Sharecroppers, Mountaineers* (Boston: Little, Brown 1967); Oscar Lewis, *Five Families: Mexican Case Studies in the Culture of Poverty* (New York: Basic Books, 1959); *La Vida: A Puerto Rican Family in the Culture of Poverty—San Juan and New York* (New York: Random House, 1966).

¹⁰Lewis, *La Vida*, p. 2.

¹¹This project involved extensive and repeated interviews of approximately three hundred former workers in the Amoskeag Mills in Manchester, N.H. (once the world's largest textile company). The people we interviewed represented all levels of skills and came from different ethnic groups. In addition to the workers, we also interviewed people from management, as well as people from different programs, including the clergy, and in the community. This oral history project grew out of extensive research in historical records. The reconstruction of most of each interviewee's work history and family history preceded the interview itself. Edited selections from this project

were published in Tamara K. Hareven and Randolph Langenbach, *Amoskeag: Life and Work in an American Factory City* (New York: Pantheon Books, 1978).

[12]Jan Vansina, *The Oral Tradition; A Study in Historical Methodology* (Chicago: Aldine, 1965).

[13]Ronald Blythe, *Akenfield* (London: Allan Lane, 1969); Studs Terkel, *Hard Times: An Oral History of the Great Depression* (New York: Pantheon, 1970).

[14]Cullon Davis et al., *Oral History From Tape to Type* (Chicago: American Library Association, 1977).

[15]Vansina, *Oral Tradition*, p. 77.

[16]The exhibit, funded by the National Endowment for the Arts and by local foundations, was created and produced by Randolph Langenbach at the Currier Gallery of Art in Manchester, N.H. It documented the development of the architectural design and the urban plan of Manchester, N.H., by the corporation which founded the city and continued to control it until the corporation's shutdown in 1936. Through eighty mural-size photographic panels by Langenbach, as well as historic photographs, the exhibit documented the connection between the architectural environment, corporate paternalism, and the experience of work. Unexpectedly, 12,000 people came to see the exhibit during its five weeks. Most of them were former mill workers.

[17]Irving Howe, *The World of Our Fathers* (New York: Harcourt Brace Jovanovich, 1976).

[18]Instructions from Henry Alsberg, director of the writer's project to all state directors, quoted in William F. McDonald, *Federal Relief Administration and the Arts* (Columbus, Ohio: Ohio State University Press, 1969). p. 7.

[19]Ibid., p. 11.

[20]James Agee and Walker Evans, *Let Us Now Praise Famous Men* (Boston: Houghton Mifflin, 1941). For slave narratives see George P. Rawick, ed., *The American Slave: A Composite Autobiography*, 19 vol. (Westport, Conn., 1972). On local oral history projects, see for example: *These Are Our Lives: As Told by the People and Written by Members of the Federal Writers' Project of the Works Progress Administration in North Carolina, Tennessee, and Georgia* (Chapel Hill, N.C., 1939).

[21]On the ethnic program see McDonald, *Federal Relief Administration and the Arts*, p. 725.

[22]Jacob Riis, *How the Other Half Lives* (New York: Scribner's, 1890); *The Children of the Poor* (New York: Scribner's, 1892). The Russell Sage Foundation sponsored and published studies of poor and working people; its most notable publication was Paul Kellogg, ed., *The Pittsburgh Survey*, 6 vols. (New York: Charities Publication Committee, 1909-14). *The Survey* was the best of a number of social reform journals.

[23]Alfred Kazin, *On Native Grounds: An Interpretation of Modern Literature* (New York: Reynal and Hitchcock, 1942), p. 378.

[24]Lloyd Warner, *The Living and the Dead* (New Haven: Yale Univ. Press, 1959).

[25]Communication to author from Professor Milton Singer, Department of Anthropology, University of Chicago.

[26]Jane Addams, quoted in Gibbs, *The DAR*, p. 2.

MARY DOUGLAS

Judgments on James Frazer

"TIMES HAVE CHANGED AND SO HAVE OUR EARS." This line from Tacitus is the first reference in Roman antiquity that E. H. Gombrich finds to the psychology of perception and its relation to styles. His extraordinarily rich discussion of this whole subject, *Art and Illusion*, treats the history of art as a continuing tension between the stability of a style and the struggle against it, the struggle of an artist "to win freshness of vision."[1] He gives many examples of the artist's ambivalence towards tradition,[2] cites the many exercises in copying the masters, and the common fear of becoming a slave to tradition.[3] Like other great art historians his powers are taxed to account for innovation, but this is not the principal task of his book. Rather the other way, he deploys the psychology of perception to explain why innovation is so difficult. A current style imposes a closure on the possibilities of perception. A style is a contemporary organization of experience: "A style, like a culture or climate of opinion, sets up a horizon of expectation, a mental set which registers deviations and modifications with exaggerated sensitivity."[4] Constable succeeded in establishing a new way of transposing our awareness of brightness into painting, but beside Corot's work the brightness of Constable's painting is eclipsed: "It recedes behind the ridge which separates, for us, the contemporary vision from that of the past."[5]

This essay explicitly seeks to use Gombrich's ideas about style as a framework within which to discuss the changes in the reputation of James Frazer as one generation has succeeded another. One hundred years ago Frazer took finals in classics and then prepared to compete for the fellowship in Trinity College, Cambridge. He won it, aged twenty-four, with a dissertation entitled "The Growth of Plato's Ideal Theory."[6] In that hundred years his reputation grew so that he completely dominated a large area of European thought. He dominated classics—no small feat—and he dominated archeology. Above all, he dominated the whole horizon of thoughts about man and his nature, his origins, his capabilities and destiny, within which the widest literary efforts were engaged. No one reputation in the subject rivals his until we reach Lévi-Strauss. In his inaugural lecture to the Collège de France, Lévi-Strauss remarks that fifty years had elapsed between the founding of his Chair of Social Anthropology in 1958 and Frazer's inaugural lecture[7] in Liverpool on taking the first university post in the world ever to be thus entitled. Fifty years earlier still, Lévi-Strauss also remarked, were born Franz Boas and Emile Durkheim, the founders of modern anthropology, the one American, the other French. This pretty trilogy of dates is enclosed in a century, and frames a Franco-Anglo-Saxon dialogue on Frazer's chosen subject. But note that the contemporary vision held within this horizon does not count Frazer as a founder. It would be difficult for Lévi-Strauss to salute him as such. Nothing matches the greatness of Frazer's fame so well as the completeness of its eclipse among anthropologists today. Malinowski recognized him as a powerful influence in his own work. But there will be few now to say that standing on the shoulders of this particular giant they were able to get a longer view.

Frazer is now attacked as a theorist. He is attacked as a serious thinker. He is even attacked as a stylist, the one reproach that would really have surprised him and hurt his feelings. On the first count we shall see that the theoretical field he was confronting was a very different one from that in which we work now. On the score of the profundity and scope of his thought, his ghost might expostulate that he is taken out of context and sadly misunderstood. For settling the question of style there is the lack of any general theory of style. Without understanding the problems of style that Gombrich has discussed, it is difficult even to judge the seriousness of a thinker. All in all, it is obviously difficult to set a writer in the perspective which he perceived himself to be in. When we follow Gombrich's discussion of how the prevailing culture or style closes the possibilities of perception, we can be sure that the painters who carefully copied admired past masters were not fully understanding or faithfully copying what they saw. "All thinking is sorting, classifying. All perceiving relates to expectations and therefore to comparisons . . . We have to speak of expectations, guesses, hypotheses, which can become so strong that our experience runs ahead of the stimulus situation."[8] This being so, the following account given by Gombrich of the transmission between generations has something missing: "If Constable saw the English landscape in terms of Gainsborough's paintings, what about Gainsborough himself? We can answer this. Gainsborough saw the lowland scenery of East Anglia in terms of Dutch paintings which he studied and copied . . . and where did the Dutch get their vocabulary? . . ."[9] What is left out is the whole history of art and the series of misunderstandings each generation takes for its starting place. According to Gombrich, it is only the vocabulary and probably only a part of it that stays, while at each historical stage there cannot be a real seeing in terms of another viewpoint. Lawrence Gowing has called attention to the creative aspect of that misunderstanding:

> One might write the history of that order of originality which this century identifies as the essence of art—and eventually it must be written—as a history of inveterate misunderstanding. We cannot claim that the view of Delacroix that inspired Cézanne represented a true evaluation of him. The guiding star that Cézanne followed shone far more steadily than the flawed jewel of Romanticism ever did. And Delacroix himself, how shallow his interpretation of Rubens! Then Rubens—was not his merely sensuous appreciation of physical rhythms as the basis of style a gross misconstruction of the philosophical meaning that the human body held for Michelangelo? And so on . . . Yet this succession of creative misunderstandings was nothing by comparison with the way that the 20th century used Cézanne.[10]

Within each new dimension of understanding the project of passing judgment on another generation's work seems necessary. The judgments partake initially in what Lawrence Gowing calls the "apparent arbitrariness of a continued and unending process of redefinition, on the basis of a past which is itself in a perpetual state of rediscovery and revaluation."[11] But if later judgments upon one-time achievement are not themselves to be devalued and arbitrarily dismissed, we should seek laboriously means for reconstructing the old dimension of understanding.

In 1910, when Frazer remarked, "My sun is westering,"[12] he was more likely referring to his expected life-span (he was then fifty-four years old) than to his reputation, which was nowhere near its zenith. He did not listen to his critics. If he had wished to answer them, he might have said: First, mythology is my subject matter, I have rescued it from the toils of philologists; second, my insight has opened a unitary vision of human history, and supported a noble view of human progress. Above all else, I am writing literature, my work is largely an imaginative effort, my greatest achievement is in the development of a style in which to present my insight. The things he took seriously were literature and human destiny, the one in the service of appreciating the other.

I shall try to establish these three points, starting with his subject matter, the strange state of mythology as he found it. In 1878, the Ninth Edition of the Encyclopaedia Britannica was launched. Its editorial announced a new policy of expansion for "the modern sciences of anthropology and sociology." It guaranteed that henceforth "Mental Philosophy and the important topics concerned with Biblical Criticism, Theology and the Science of Religion" would be treated "from the critical and historical rather than the dogmatic point of view.[13] Indeed, when the volume for S was reached in 1886, there was Robertson Smith's famous article on sacrifice, which subverted many pious presumptions. In due course Frazer himself wrote the article on taboo in 1888. This was his first major step towards transforming the study of mythology, and closely modeled on Robertson Smith's ideas.

We can hardly imagine now the high excitement that focused on the origins and fate of human culture. A modern audience misses the emotional violence of Ibsen's play when Hedda Gabler stuffs into the stove her lover's manuscript on the future of civilization. In 1890 the horror of the deed was that she had deprived humanity of profound insights into its very self. Not a mere petty act of caprice or jealousy, it must have ranked as an irreparable crime, a public tragedy for all posterity.

To recapture that mood of intense interest we should realize what a great race was on. In France, Germany, America, and in England the researchers were competing on work deemed of the utmost importance. In the apparent nonsense of beliefs in ghosts, female deities, instant transformations and transportations, there had to be some systematic sense that would show us how we humans here and now are constituted. Whoever solved the riddle would be sure of fame. So completely had the literary public taken the project to heart that writers could use it to enhance their dramatic moments. How else could George Eliot have convinced anyone in 1872 that the ardent clever heroine of Middlemarch should have ever consented to marry the dreary Mr. Causabon? Only by showing the girl dazzled by his noble enterprise: "with something of the archangelic manner he told her how he had undertaken to show that all the mythical systems or erratic mythical fragments in the world were corruptions of a tradition originally revealed. Having once mastered the true position and taken a firm footing there, the vast field of mythical constructions became intelligible, made luminous with the reflected light of correspondences . . ." Later, when the plot has to discover Mr. Causabon's egotism and plain unworthiness, the trick is done by showing that he is not seriously working on the Key to All Mythologies, distracted from his high mission by envy of other scholars. But long before that denouement, the worst blow had fallen: Mr. Causabon did not even read German. "The Germans have taken the lead in historical enquiries, and they laugh at results which are got by groping about the woods with a pocket compass when they have made good roads . . . the subject Mr. Causabon has chosen is as changing as chemistry: new discoveries are constantly making new points of view. Who wants a system based on the four elements, or a book to refute Paracelsis? Do you not see that it is no use now to be crawling a little way after men of the last century . . . and correcting their mistakes?—living in a lumber room and furnishing up broken-legged theories about Chus and Misraim?"[14] So the man is first built up as a hero and then demolished as a fraud—all on the strength of his dealings with mythology.

In the history of ideas, before some major figure has arrived on the scene, the old perspectives often seem littered with a crazy jumble of broken bits and loose ends. Just such a state is summed up in a critical article on mythology by Andrew Lang in the same edition of the Encyclopaedia Britannica. He singled out the central puzzle of mythology as follows. The myths of civilized peoples, for example those of the Greeks and Aryans, contain two elements, rational and irrational. The first are completely intelligible, but the second constitute the puzzles: "The rational myths are those that represent the gods as beautiful and wise beings . . . there is nothing not explicable and natural in the conception of the Olympian Zeus . . . or in the Homeric conception of Zeus as a god who 'turns everywhere his shining eyes' and beholds all things. But Zeus . . . who played Demeter an obscene trick, by the aid of a ram, or the Zeus who, in the shape of a swan, became the father of Castor and Pollux, or the Zeus who deceived Hera by means of feigned marriage with an inanimate object . . . is a being whose myth is felt to be unnatural and in great need of explanation." Max Muller called this irrational, unnatural element "the silly, senseless and savage element in mythology."

That great philologist proposed to solve the puzzle by tracking the names of deities back to the original meanings of words common to all the Indo-European languages. Traced to its Sanskritic form, Athene is revealed as the word for dawn and Zeus as the word for sky. Now, according to Muller, at the beginning of human life and language, in a premythopoeic period, those words could have been chosen to mean powerful spiritual beings. But it is in the nature of abstract ideas that they are difficult to hold on to, and it seemed likely that the religious meaning would have been lost in the course of time and only the particular material reference of words be left. So the word Zeus from a sky god with male gender would have degenerated in the mythopoeic period to something like the shining ones (male) and the word for Athene to something like the burning one (female). Muller thought that the rough-hewn language of our forebears would only be able to say "the sun follows the dawn" in a way that might also be interpreted as "the brightly shining man pursues the ardent woman." And so to explain the odd result, the myth of the sun god pursuing a female would be invented. The argument almost anticipates jokes about translation machines that turn "the spirit is willing but the flesh is weak" into "the wine is good but the meat is bad." But quite certainly Andrew Lang was being very unfair on Max Muller. His general idea that false theories circulate as a result of a concretization of abstract ideas has many resonances today. But his actual theory had technical difficulties.

Lang, in his article, went on to compare Muller's theories with those of Spencer, who had a similar speculation about the inadequacies of first human speech. As Lang said of them both: "The chief objection to these processes is that they require as a necessary condition a singular amount of memory on the one hand, and of forgetfulness on the other." But he was in real sympathy with the questions expressed by Muller: "was there a period of temporary madness which the human mind had to pass and was it a madness identically the same in the south of India and north of Ireland?" Lang answered affirmatively to both.

Against these protagonists with their convoluted schemes, bristling with technical difficulties, Frazer entered one simple theory adapted from Robertson Smith. Partly because he far surpassed his colleagues with sheer narrative skill, he succeeded in absolving mankind from the charge of an ancient temporary madness. The savages were philosophers, poets, not simpletons. Incidentally, he also absolved his contemporaries from any dilemma posed by their attitude to dogmatic religion. Frazer's theory was that all religions tend to deify kings and to make their gods die as sacrificial victims; all teach that by the ritual act of king-killing the world will be renewed. The central doctrine of Christianity was that god incarnate was put to death under the label of king; the same god is treated doctrinally as sacrificial victim: the rite of the sacrifice is credited with powers of renewal. The analogy with Christianity is there, very complete and compelling. But Frazer had too much respect for the poetic aspect of religion to press it home offensively. He never explicitly made the parallel between Christianity and the ancient beliefs he reclassified.

If anyone now seeks to convict Frazer's enterprise of superficiality, surely anyone in his time would have been astonished. What else could be more profound? It would surely always be thought serious to explore this unitary experience of the human race and to find all humanity, even in its dimmest, remotest past, meditating upon the relation of man and nature and developing an understanding of that relation which culminates in emotional power and beauty in the great religions. Anatole France declared: "Il nous fait entrer dans la pensée des barbares d'aujourd'hui et des temps lointains; il a éclairé d'une lumière nouvelle cette antiquité grecque et latine que nous pensions connaitre; il a substitué aux fables que l'homme imagine pour expliquer sa propre origine, les premières données d'une science rigoureuse qui n'existait pas avant lui."[15] Called upon to address the Société Ernest Renan in 1920, Frazer declared his loyalty to the same project at which Renan had labored: a rediscovery of true religion, divested of archaic trappings.[16] The contrast he drew between Renan and Voltaire is revealing of his own methodological preferences: Voltaire was more prosaic, more analytic; Renan, the Breton, more poetic. He insisted that Renan was deeply religious, destroying images which he loved, to put better ones forward. He took to heart Renan's judgment that the Christian historic effort represents "half the poetry of mankind." There is no question that he was dealing with matters judged profound by his contemporaries, whether they disagreed with his conclusions or not. There is a question whether he would have liked Anatole France's description of his contribution to a rigorous science—for he frankly preferred the path of poetry.

It was from Renan, he said, that he got the idea of ending the *Golden Bough* with the tolling of bells from Rome.

In the 1890 edition he describes his journey at an end; he climbs the Appian Way to the Alban hills and sees the sunset behind St. Peter's; then he pursues his way, darkling, along the mountain side to Nemi, to look once more at the lake of Nemi. Finally, "There comes to us, borne on the swell of the wind, the sound of the church bells of Rome, ringing the Angelus. Ave Maria! Sweet and solemn they chime out from the distant city and die lingeringly away across the wide Campagnan marshes. *Le roi est mort, vive le roi! Ave Maria!*" But in the foreword to the 1900 edition he notes:

> To a passage in my book, it has been objected by a distinguished scholar that the church bells in Rome cannot be heard, even in the stillest weather, on the shores of the lake of Nemi. In acknowledging my blunder and leaving it uncorrected, may I plead in extenuation of my obduracy the example of an illustrious writer? In *Old Mortality* we read how a hunted Covenanter, fleeing before Claverhouse's dragoons, hears the sullen boom of the kettledrums of the pursuing cavalry borne to him on the night wind. When Scott was taken to task for this description, because the drums are not beaten at night, he replied in effect that he liked to hear the drums sounding there, and that he would let them sound on as long as his book might last. In the same spirit I make bold to say that by the lake of Nemi I love to hear, even if it be only in imagination, the distant chiming bells of Rome . . .

However, in the last edition, strict geographical scholarship prevailed over imagination. He confided to the Société Ernest Renan that a friend made him change the bells to the church of Aricia from which they could really be heard at the lake.[17]

Having dealt with the theory of mythology as Frazer found it and touched upon the greater philosophic seriousness of his view compared with the other mythologists, I will return to the question of seriousness when I have said something more about his interest in the literary imagination, on which the tribute to Renan gives a hint.

Frazer's early essay "The Growth of Plato's Ideal Theory" used stylistic criticism for attributing chronology to the different parts of the corpus. From this beginning his later prejudices on style are already clearly formulated: "in the later Dialogues . . . The vivacious manner of a great dramatist, enthralling his hearers by the alternate play of high tragedy and light comedy, is exchanged for the dry as dust manner of a professor lecturing to his pupils . . . it is a transformation like that of a Shakespeare into a Kant . . ." Later in the essay, he suggests that Plato lost by being "guided by the pale cold light of Reason, instead of by the purple glow of the Imagination." In the many volumes of the *Golden Bough*, meticulously footnoted on obscure places and peoples, he never gave up his own light touch and dramatic contrasts. He also managed to write on purely literary themes: an essay entitled "London Life in the Time of Addison, 1672 to 1719," a "Biographical Sketch of William Cowper," a series of imaginative reconstructions on Sir Roger de Coverly give some idea of his stylistic preferences.[18] In the same volume an essay on Condorcet is a good example of his mixing tragedy with farce. He greatly admired the philosopher, and saluted his calm survey of human progress and his firm trust in the essential goodness of mankind and the glorious future awaiting it. Revolutionary Paris was at the height of the terror then. Frazer describes the paradox of the philosopher politician who had actually prepared a new constitution in the legislative assembly, but was now condemned to death himself because he had criticized Robespierre. He describes his hiding for several days: "On the third day, driven by the pangs of hunger he entered a humble tavern and called for an omelet. They asked him how many eggs he would have in it. As a philosopher and secretary for many years for the Academy of Science, Condorcet knew much but unluckily he did not know how many eggs go into the making of an omelet. He answered at random, 12. The reply excited surprise and suspicion. He was asked for his papers, but he had none, nothing but a copy of the Epistles of Horace." And so Condorcet was hustled off. However much he admired his hero and felt the heroism and tragedy of his life, he could not resist recounting the famous, farcical ending. With Addison and Steele for his models, why should he?

Now we can begin a more serious consideration of the style and of the seriousness of the writer. The passage cited from Lawrence Gowing describes a happily creative misunderstanding between generations. But the theory of Gombrich implies that there must at the same time be unhappily destructive misunderstandings. Could it be pleaded for Frazer that he exposed himself to this misunderstanding when he chose his version of the light amusing style of eighteenth-century essayists for a life-work which required no less than twelve ponderous volumes? Or in the period from the 1880s to 1910, when he was most creative, was that read by his contemporaries as exactly the appropriate style for his great themes?

Gombrich says of painting that it is never a copy, always a transposition of nature. The success of the transposition depends on the artist's and the viewers' learning a notation. Our response is not to color as such, but to relationships, to gradients in light intervals. The proper business of mind is "assessing gradients and relationships."[19] He uses the metaphor of being attuned. Our expectations of style are as receivers already attuned: "When we step in front of a bust we understand what we are expected to look for. We do not, as a rule, take it to be a representation of a cut-off head . . ."[20] This becomes a problem in the case of copying, because a change in scale changes all the relationships. "We can speak of a real facsimile only when the copy is of the same size as the original. For size affects tone . . . since the same color will look different when the size of the area changes, a facsimile reduced in scale will look false when all colors are identical with the original."[21]

To illustrate the difficulty our generation has in assessing Frazer's work, we can use the adverse judgment of a philosopher who always wrote in a highly condensed, elliptical style and can ask whether his complaints against Frazer arise out of the constraints of a different cultural horizon. Wittgenstein exclaimed: "What narrowness of spiritual life we find in Frazer. And as a result:

how impossible for him to understand a different way of life from the English one of his time." And then, pettishly, he adds, "Frazer cannot imagine a priest who is not basically an English parson of our times with all his stupidity and feebleness."[22] He was pondering on the *Golden Bough* and using it as an illustration of the difference between explanation and a way of life.

Every explanation is an hypothesis.
But for someone broken up by love an explanatory hypothesis won't help much. It will not bring peace.
Frazer's account of the magical and religious notions of men is unsatisfactory: it makes these notions appear as *mistakes*.
Was Augustine mistaken, then, when he called on God on every page of the *Confessions*?
Well—one might say—if he was not mistaken, then the Buddhist holy-man, or some other, whose religion expresses quite different notions, surely was. But *none* of them was making a mistake except where he was putting forward a theory.
Even the idea of trying to explain the practice—say the killing of the priest-king—seems to me wrong-headed. All that Frazer does is to make this practice plausible to people who think as he does. It is very queer that all these practices are finally presented, so to speak, as stupid actions.
But it never does become plausible that people do all this out of sheer stupidity.
When he explains to us, for example, that the king must be killed in his prime because, according to the notions of the savages, his soul would not be kept fresh otherwise, we can only say: where that practice and these views go together, the practice does not spring from the view, but both of them are there.

Frazer says it is very difficult to discover the error in magic and this is why it persists for so long—because, for example, a ceremony which is supposed to bring rain is sure to appear effective sooner or later. But then it is queer that people do not notice sooner that it does rain sooner or later anyway.
I think one reason why the attempt to find an explanation is wrong is that we have only to put together in the right way what we *know* without adding anything, and the satisfaction we are trying to get from the explanation comes of itself.
And here the explanation is not what satisfies us anyway. When Frazer begins by telling the story of the King of the Wood at Nemi, he does this in a tone which shows that something strange and terrible is happening here. And that is the answer to the question "why is this happening?": Because it is terrible. In other words, what strikes us in this course of events as terrible, impressive, horrible, tragic, etc., anything but trivial and insignificant, *that* is what gave birth to them.
We can only *describe* and say, human life is like that.

Frazer is much more savage than most of his savages, for these savages will not be so far from any understanding of spiritual matters as an Englishman of the twentieth century. His explanations of the primitive observances are much cruder than the sense of the observances themselves.

These comments on Frazer amount to a grave charge of superficiality, of failure to match interpretative powers to the depth and height of human experience to be interpreted. Wittgenstein strives to seize the true nature of the human predicament: "the crush of thoughts that do not get out because they all try to push forward and are wedged in the door."[23] His criticism of Frazer parallels the oft-told story of John Constable's argument with Sir George Beaumont. The older man is saying that the greenness of grass has to be shown within the mellow tonalities of the whole picture; Constable is saying that nature is not like that, but is much lusher, much greener, more alive. He seizes an old violin whose soft hues are like those used then to transpose natural greenery to the picture's painted range. Laying it on the lawn he triumphantly demonstrates that the green in nature is nothing like the brown violin. No doubt about it; but Gombrich points out that Beaumont never said it was. The problem of transposition between the natural and the painted set of gradients still remained. What Constable had to do was to work out "how to reconcile what we call 'local colors' with the range of tonal gradations which the landscape painter needs to suggest depth."[24] This he succeeded in doing.

The very success which Frazer enjoyed argues that he was working in a well-understood style and that his transposition from life to book form, with its self-imposed constraints, successfully picked up the great themes and related them to lesser ones, so that he seemed to his generation to be talking very seriously about religion and half the poetry of the world. Wittgenstein's complaints are background to his own attempt to break through the prison of style, and to come to a fuller awareness of nature. Wittgenstein was one in a movement of many thinkers who won and to whose eyes Frazer has a fusty, narrow view.

To stop here would be to espouse the negative relativity which some of Wittgenstein's followers adopt. We can go a little further by exploring the nature of the change in perspective. Wittgenstein himself used his reflections on the *Golden Bough* to illustrate his idea about a special kind of explanation, the concept of perspicuous presentation: "a way of setting out the whole field together by making easy the passage from one part of it to another . . . the way in which we see things. . . . This perspicuous presentation makes possible that understanding which consists in just the fact that we 'see the connexions'."[25] The translator notes that Wittgenstein constantly used "*übersichtlich*" in writing of logical notation and mathematical proof: "It is clear what he means. So we ought to have an English word. We have put 'perspicuous' here, but no one uses this in English either." Others have used "transparent proof." But in the context of the remarks on anthropology it seems to a modern ear that Wittgenstein was thinking of a form of presenting a proof by showing the fit between all the steps. He was groping for structural analysis before it had become available in anthropology. His words recall Bartlett's remark: "Perhaps the mathematician or thinker in any form of closed system, who quickly stops doing something that he has begun in error, has something of a pre-perception of the 'fitness' of the structure he is building to that of the complete structure within which he is working. Exactly how or through what mechanism such pre-perception can be achieved is still exceedingly hard to understand; but the process is, in function, precisely that of 'matching' . . ."[26] A philosopher has recently placed Wittgenstein's thought on Frazer in the larger context of his philosophy and shown the direct influence of the latter on Clifford Geertz.[27] The process of matching and searching for intermediate links is the process of finding metaphorical structures. Wittgenstein would obviously have encouraged structural anthropologists to seek the cultural pattern of metaphors with the deepest, widest scope for human meaning. This need to enlarge the canvas presents, no doubt, the problems of facsimile we have noted already. Clifford Geertz responds wholeheartedly by deepening his tonal range, enriching his hues and by using a very powerful literary style. His discussion of the moral imagination uses the case of Balinese practice of burning the widows of a great man.[28] The whole colorful, emotive style escapes the reproach which Wittgenstein leveled against Frazer's account of the burning of a man in Fire Festivals. It is not frivolous; it is not superficial; it does try to grasp the intervening links which make sense of the events for the people who organize them. By comparison Frazer's style alone makes him seem to be trivializing. This has nothing to do with his attempt at explanation. He could always find a minor superstition among frolicking harvesters or New Year celebrants to match any more grandiose theme. The switches of scale give us a sense of flippancy.

If we ask why this scale-switching was acceptable to his contemporaries, we recall that at that time his readers had as much ambivalence as he did about the value of religion. Frazer firmly believed that the *Golden Bough* recorded a long history of human folly—the trail of religious institutions and wars prosecuted and crimes committed in their name. To treat these horrors delicately and to show their universal origin in man's prehistory was the stylistic challenge which he met by switching from lofty to the humble scale, from tragedy to humor.

I would conclude this question by suggesting that the glass he held to nature was the glass in which his contemporaries were prepared to see, that he was not more superficial in moral imagination than they, and not mistaken as to the style in which to present his version.

Though our present generation reacts against that perspective, there is a part of Frazer's work which they accept quite happily. I can explain the paradoxical influence of Frazer's distinction between two kinds of magic on present-day thought by comparing Frazer with Lévi-Strauss. The two scholars, their theme, their method, and their achievement are interesting to compare. "The deeper philosophy of the relation of the life of man to the life of nature" was Frazer's main concern. Lévi-Strauss seeks to reveal the functioning of the human mind, especially its age-long meditation on the difference between nature and culture.

The pair run in double harness on other points as well. Each generated in his turn an industry of imitators who collected materials according to the master's scheme and who found it made sense that way. Both are rebuked for taking their material out of context and for imposing the pattern of their own thought upon it. Each is accused of lacking sociological insight and political sensitivity. Both are especially liable to be misunderstood unless they are recognized to be speculating on the origins of thought.

When it comes to comparing their methods, the modern tool kit does not seem all that superior to Frazer's method of analyzing magical thinking. Leach has remarked that Lévi-Strauss uses much the same analytical methods as Frazer, emphasizing resemblance and contiguity, though he calls them metaphor and metonym, while Frazer calls them similarity and contagion.[29] Of course there are important differences. Frazer focused on resemblance. He thought that the likeness between two stories jumped to the eye of the reader, just as readily as likeness between two colors or two parts of the body struck the mind of the primitive. He did not think that resemblance needed analysis, and there he was naive. The method of modern structuralism focuses on difference, particularly upon close contrasts, for example between relatively up or down, hot or cold, wet or dry, dark or light. Tracing the pattern of such binary distinctions, the method traces how a whole system of symbols is constructed of similarities and juxtapositions. It is extraordinary to see Frazer's two favorite tools sharpened up and put to new use by his severest critics. But the modern mythologists did not get their idea of the structure of a symbolic system from Frazer, nor is it a coincidence that they should rely so heavily on similarity and contiguity for their work. With the aid of linguists,[30] they have raided the same old attic storeroom of ideas, the long traditions of European philosophy, but without really knowing where the furniture came from.

When Frazer taught that there are two ways of looking at the world, one modern, scientific, and the other primitive, and that the latter divides again into two, religious and magical, and that magical principles are also just two, similarity and contagion, he was making a series of binary distinctions. Binary distinctions are an analytic procedure, but their usefulness does not guarantee that existence divides like that. We should look with suspicion on anyone who declared that there are two kinds of people, or two kinds of reality or process. The self-same European tradition which we all draw upon makes an old favorite division of mental faculties, one slow, logical step-by-step reasoning, the other quick, pattern-perceiving, intuitive. Often the second is called feminine and the first masculine. Pattern-perception is contrasted with linear reasoning. Two kinds of computer thinking are often compared, analog with digital. Among the structural analysts you will find echoes of this in their use of the two axes of analysis, whose names are switched over and over again. For Frazer's principle of similarity you will read metaphor, paradigm, resemblance, substitutability, equivalence, classes, system, and for his principle of contiguity you will find continuity, juxtaposition, syntagm, syntax, structural proximity, sequencing rules, metonymy. Just like Frazer, the practitioners admit it is often difficult to tell which one applies, and then some of them sink into a morass of metonymic metaphors contrasted with metaphoric metonyms, paradigmatic syntagms, and syntagmatic paradigms. Never mind; when it comes to practicing the analysis (instead of saying how it is done), they forget the clumsy apparatus and invent delicate ways of tracing cross-references back and forth and nesting layers of meaning, from smallest to greatest. This bears out the justness of William James's view that there is no elementary principle of mental association other than contiguity.[31] How can you tell whether two patterns are similar except by tracing the internal positioning of parts? How can you compare except by prior sorting of like properties? According to James there is only one elementary principle of association, and to follow it means tracing and numbering all the connections that can be identified:

> The manner in which trains of imagery and consideration follow each other through our thinking, the restless flight of one idea before the next, the transitions our minds make between things wide as the poles asunder, transitions which at first sight startle us by their abruptness, but which, when scrutinized closely, often reveal intermediating links of perfect naturalness and propriety—all this magical, imponderable dreaming has from time immemorial excited the admiration of all whose attention happened to be caught by its omnipresent mystery. And it has furthermore challenged the race of philosophers to banish something of the mystery by formulating the process in simpler terms. The problem which the philosophers have set themselves is that of ascertaining *principles of connection* between the thoughts which thus appear to sprout one out of the other, whereby their peculiar succession or coexistence may be explained.[32]

For James the important explanatory principle about how ideas sprout up or saunter carelessly into our minds is habit, association by being frequently connected in our experience:

> Seen things and heard things cohere with each other, and with odors and tastes, in representations, in the same order in which they cohered as impressions of the outer world. Feelings of contact reproduce similarly the sights, sounds, and tastes with which experience has associated them. In fact, the "objects" of our perception, as trees, men, houses, microscopes, of which the real world seems composed, are nothing but clusters of qualities which simultaneous stimulations have so coalesced that the moment one is excited actually it serves as a sign or cue for the idea of the others to arise. Let a person enter his room in the dark and grope among the objects there. The touch of the matches will instantaneously recall their appearance . . . the feeling of the garments or draperies which may hang about the room is not *understood* till the look correlative to the feeling has in each case been resuscitated . . .[33]

William James sums up the law of mental association by contiguity by saying that "objects once experienced together tend to become associated in the imagination, so that when any one of them is thought of, the others are likely to be thought of also, in the same order of sequence or coexistence as before."[34] He sticks to the traditional word "contiguity," though recognizing that perhaps "association by continuity" or "external association" might be better. James places everything in this process upon habit, and this he traces to laws of habit in the nervous system. He refers to able writers on the subject who rely on two principles of association, one contiguity, the other similarity, but he dismisses the claims for similarity to be treated as an elementary law[35] for interesting reasons which I shall need to refer to again. So there it is, a long European and American tradition of analyzing the association of ideas, and of classing them by laws of contiguity and similarity. According to James, Frazer was wrong in distinguishing similarity from contagion as principles of thought. But if so, he erred in good and modern company.

Frazer and Lévi-Strauss, both using a tone of voice that suggests the awe and splendor of their subject, diminish the meaning it holds. Frazer belittles the faculties of the primitive mind. Lévi-Strauss uses heavy equipment for dredging up nearly vacuous thoughts. He claims to reveal how the human mind has been reflecting on the differences between nature and culture. Ask bluntly, well, what *does* it say about the difference? Usually all that structural analysis reveals is that the myths are saying over and over again that there is a difference. All we have is the possibility of a structure on which possible meanings could be hung. However much Frazer is castigated by a succeeding generation of anthropologists, they do not see that where they uncritically use his ideas they get their most disappointing result. Gombrich enables us to locate a blind spot.

Among all the other bric-a-brac we were lumbered long ago with a division between the passive and the active faculties of the mind. The first, the association of ideas, merely fed into the mental machinery the stuff for logic to work upon. It was hardly Frazer's fault that he took up this theory, for it was widely accepted in his formative period. So it is understandable that he should use the accepted division between two mental processes, and credit the active one with the achievement of gradually overcoming the delusions which the association of ideas is likely to introduce when left uncontrolled. But more recent writers have a better chance. The separation of passive and active faculties is now realized to be a much more dubious line to draw. The whole process of recognizing, comparing, classing, and performing other logical operations is seen much more as a unitary process, an active organizing effort by the perceiving subject, a pressure towards transparency and match. Any myth analyst who just sets up the framework of contrasts and similarities and stops there, claiming to have discovered something that is happening in the mind without the knower being actively involved, is espousing a passive theory. He is applying his craftsmanship to an old store of broken-legged materials, rather passive himself in his attitude to what means are available. Meanwhile the lumber room is being cleared and sorted and daylight shows up the dust. Gombrich shows that there cannot be making without matching, innovation without copying. First there has to be a model, then the critical dissatisfaction and the struggle to improve upon it. He also shows that there is no way of making all experience available at once. Any awareness depends on areas of invisibility and insensitivity. Blind spots there must be. If they surface on the periphery of vision, it can only be because some new synthesis is ready.

To return to the matter of judgment between generations: I clearly have profited greatly from Gombrich's applying the theory of perception to style in painting. But I have only found a few not especially illuminating things to say about the misunderstanding of Frazer by his successors. It might not have been necessary to refer to Gombrich in order to say that the theoretical field had changed, that Frazer thought of himself as a stylist and literary scholar, and that his style is a clue to his mood and thought. The importance of Gombrich's contribution is more precisely his demonstration of how the theory of perception, established in its main outlines at the beginning of this century, itself has led to a new horizon of expectations.

In writing so lucidly about the constancies between gradients and relationships, and about judgment and perception as the attuning of the mind to a particular key, Gombrich reintroduces a theory of rationality to a twentieth century that has always had access to it, but still has not been able to adjust to its depths. Reintroducing is the word. Admittedly it was only anticipated by Newman's account of the illative sense. But it has been here, as Gombrich shows, for a long time. Perspicuous presentation or transparent proof in Wittgenstein, preperceptual matching in Bartlett, structuralism in Jakobson and Lévi-Strauss—there is a convergence of meanings in our generation which is gradually setting up a cultural ridge, as it were, which will separate the contemporary vision from that of the past.

This should enable us to take the next step. So far we are limited to a very general statement about swings of the pendulum, creative and uncreative misunderstandings, stabilizing and constraining pressures, and the individual thrust towards innovation. At this stage we seem to be limited to agnosticism. No judgment can be passed, either on the past generation, or on the rejecting or admiring judgments of the present. But if this approach to style and culture is hanging over us as the new style, with all its closures and constraints, but fully available, a priority immediately appears among projects for this generation. Nothing else will prosper more than an examination of our own style, pushing its possibilities of comparison to their limits. When such a project is developed, it may be possible to say convincingly that Frazer was a flawed jewel of neo-classicism, or a perfect gem for all time, or a stumbling block.

REFERENCES

[1]E. H. Gombrich, *Art and Illusion: A Study in the Psychology of Pictorial Representation*, the A. W. Mellon Lectures in the Fine Arts, 1956, Bollingen Series/Princeton (Princeton, N.J.: Princeton University Press, 1960), p. 33.

[2]Ibid., p. 174.

[3]Ibid., p. 175.

[4]Ibid., p. 60.

[5]Ibid., p. 58.

[6]J. G. Frazer, "The Growth of Plato's Ideal Theory," an essay, New York, 1930.

[7]Claude Lévi-Strauss, *Anthropologie Structurale Deux* (Paris: Plon, 1973), p. 12.

[8]Gombrich, *Art and Illusion*, pp. 301, 303.

[9]Ibid., p. 316.

[10]Lawrence Gowing, "The Logic of Organized Sensations," chapter in *Cézanne, The Late Work*, ed. William Rubin (New York: Museum of Modern Art, 1977), p. 66.

[11]Ibid., p. 70.

[12]James G. Frazer, *Totemism and Exogamy, a Treatise on Certain Early Forms of Superstition and Society*, 4 vol (London, 1910), p. ix.

[13]Thomas Baynes, Editorial for *Ninth Edition of Encyclopaedia Britannica* (Scotland, 1878).

[14]George Eliot, *Middlemarch* (London, 1872).

[15]Anatole France, Preface to J. G. Frazer's *The Gorgon's Head and Other Literary Pieces* (London, 1927).

[16]James G. Frazer, "Sur Ernest Renan" (Paris, 1923).

[17]Ibid., p. 66.

[18]James G. Frazer, *The Gorgon's Head and Other Literary Pieces* (London, 1927).

[19]Gombrich, *Art and Illusion*, p. 57.

[20]Ibid., p. 50.

[21]Ibid., p. 326.

[22]Ludwig Wittgenstein, "Remarks on Frazer's *Golden Bough*," trans. A. C. Miles and Rush Rhees. Originally published in *Synthese*, 17, 1967, quoted from *The Human World*, No. 3, (May 1971): 28-41.

[23]Ibid., p. 30.

[24]Gombrich, *Art and Illusion*, p. 44.

[25]Wittgenstein, "Frazer's *Golden Bough*," p. 35, note.

[26]Frederick C. Bartlett, *Thinking: An Experimental and Social Study*, (New York: Allen and Unwin, 1958), p. 151.

[27]Richard H. Bell, "Understanding the Fire-Festivals: Wittgenstein and Theories in Religion," *Religious Studies*, 14, (1978): 113-124.

[28]Clifford Geertz, "Found in Translation: On the Social History of the Moral Imagination," *Georgia Review*, 13 (1977): 787-810.

[29]Edmund Leach, *Lévi-Strauss* (London: Fontana Modern Masters, 1970), p. 49.

[30]Roman Jakobson and Morris Halle, *Fundamentals of Language*. (The Hague: Mouton, 1956).

[31]William James, "Principles of Psychology," chapter on *Association of Ideas*, first published 1880.

[32]Ibid., pp. 551-552.

[33]Ibid, pp. 555-556.

[34]Ibid., p. 561.

[35]Ibid., pp. 581-582.

DOUGLAS BUSH

Literature, the Academy, and the Public

THERE IS, IT MAY BE SURMISED, a common if vague assumption that, whereas scientists have no obligatory concern with the past and are wholly committed to the discovery of new knowledge, the study of literature follows a static, fore-ordained pattern in which the great writers of all ages remain fixed stars, as in old metaphysical astronomy, above the sublunary world of unceasing change. If that supposition is quite mistaken, it will nonetheless be a reminder of the vital commonplace that great literature, the most generally accessible and potent of the humanities, is ageless and can never go out of date. But the aim of this article is to show, in a very summary sketch, that the approach to literature, especially in our century, has been subject to many changes of purpose and focus—to such a degree, in fact, that a superannuated veteran, while recognizing a large and many-sided enlightenment, may regret the apparent loss or obscuration of the traditional, simple-minded, humanistic conception of literature. I may add that I shall be concerned mainly with the American scene but shall often be glancing elsewhere, especially at England.

In speaking of the academic study of English literature—a relatively modern phenomenon, we may remember—and the course of scholarship and criticism, I claim no authority beyond the very limited fact that I have lived through all the changes in theory and practice of the last eighty years. Such a retrospective survey will doubtless be seen to place me somewhere between Nestor and Lewis Carroll's Father William; I may as well admit now what will become evident later, that I have returned in age to the wide-eyed innocence of childhood. At any rate, one who feels something of a stranger in the present world may be allowed to indulge in enough autobiography to recall academic experience of a time to which most memories do not reach back. In a village high school in Ontario in the early 1900s I had five and six years respectively of Greek and Latin, along with French, German, and the usual other subjects. To add a statistic about special requirements, in the scholarship examinations for admission to the University of Toronto I had twenty-one papers of three hours each; that exacting system (which left a scar in my memory) has, I believe, long ceased to operate.

At the university nine-tenths of my undergraduate work was in Greek and Roman literature, philosophy, and history, plus weekly translation into both languages. Despite that most rewarding experience (which, apart from the last item, I have tried to carry on ever since), I decided that, for teaching, English would be more enjoyable, and, by way of transition, I took a postgraduate year in Old and Middle English. My two years at Harvard, 1921-23, came during what was, there and elsewhere, the first phase of modern literary scholarship. Since a number of American pioneers before and after 1900 pursued advanced work in Germany, that long first phase was naturally a German importation; it owed much to nineteenth-century science and had an overwhelming philological and medieval emphasis. In my two years I had to get in the full complement of eight courses, write a thesis, and prepare for the oral. The required philological courses consumed so much time and labor that not much literature could be squeezed in. My thesis, like many theses of the period, was devoted to source-hunting, but I can say that, except for the pressure of time, it was rather exhilarating, at least to write. The oral examination began with some forty minutes on Indo-European philology, which normally turned our nervousness into paralysis. Professor von Jagemann (whose face was seamed with what were said to be duelling scars) had provided his classes with mimeographed sheets listing the various forms of roots from Sanskrit through the Western languages, and I, who had no philological aptitude whatever, memorized the whole by brute force; unfortunately, if asked a question that touched on something on page 15, I had to start mentally on page 1—which, in an oral, was difficult. After that opening ordeal, transfixed with more arrows than St. Sebastian, we took a wholly factual journey through English literary history, in the last twenty minutes skittering over the modern centuries.

Some of our professors—notably my illustrious mentor, John Livingston Lowes, author of the most distinguished of source studies—could be highly stimulating and warmly encouraging, but the department as a whole seemed unaware that most of us, both as persons and as prospective teachers, wanted and needed a different diet. For instance, they themselves had had more or less classical training, but the program laid out for us made no provision for such study: our appointed road to the promised land led through the wilderness of Gothic and the like. We found occasional relief in mutinous talk about the doctoral regimen, and some of my best friends were ardent disciples of Irving Babbitt, a vehement crusader against "the system"; but I was then an unregenerate Romantic (strange as that later appeared) and could not share their allegiance. In the half-century or more since I was a student, graduate work at Harvard and elsewhere and the general level of teaching have changed greatly for the better. Yet there were and are some things to be said for the old ways. They made solid, accurate knowledge a prime requisite and laid firm foundations for literary study and indeed for criticism; and critical dissertations were sometimes permitted. We may respect such limited virtues when we think of the amount of loose, strained, and faddish interpretation and speculation and murky writing that have attended the later age of enlightenment.

Irving Babbitt, the philosopher Arthur Lovejoy, and others did much to replace the primacy of philology and an external conception of literary history with the history of ideas and to inspire a host of young scholars dissatisfied with dusty answers. Although Babbitt had more ethical earnestness than literary sensibility (hence the rise and fall of the "New Humanism"), his unceasing concern with moral ideas won respect even from students who reacted against his dogmatic opinions. Philosophical, religious, political, social, economic, and scientific ideas had inevitably affected writers and their readers in some way or degree, and the re-creation of old—or surviving—ideologies did, and continues to do, a great deal to fertilize our understanding of individual writers and of the whole past and the present. Dozens of large labels, such as Calvinism, Puritanism, Anglicanism, Arminianism, have been closely reexamined and have yielded precise discriminations of significant diversities within supposedly monolithic sects and parties. So too with other areas and movements: the impact on thought and literature of various sciences, astronomy, geology, and biology, has been studied in dozens of books and hundreds of articles—most of them, it may be noted, written by literary scholars. The study of ideas, at its best, has come much closer than external literary history to the central and enduring interests of man as man, has quickened understanding of religious, political, social, and ethical creeds and dreams for which through the centuries people lived and fought and died. (Much valuable work of this kind, to be sure, had been done in the nineteenth century; for later students of English, however, that activity had been checked by what I called the first phase of scholarship.) The revived history of ideas, with all its fructifying power, could at times suffer from a quantitative approach, since small writers might be more serviceable witnesses than great ones; the scale of intellectual and artistic values could be neglected. We may see an unfortunate reversal of the historical study of ideas in occasional efforts to modernize an author, Milton for instance, by reinterpreting his religious beliefs out of all likeness to his auctorial and actual self.

The arrival of a polar opposite, aesthetic and technical criticism, requires a preliminary glance backward. With Romantic liberation from Neoclassical "rules," criticism from the late eighteenth to the early twentieth century was mainly impressionistic and appreciative; these terms are descriptive, not disparaging. This body of criticism, from Coleridge to Pater and Wilde, could include perceptive evaluation, though it commonly stopped short of close analysis. And it could express an emotional involvement which our rigorous modernism seems to consider beneath its scientific dignity. Before and after 1900, it may be added, there was also a swarm of casual and chatty "bookmen" who, though not real critics, had a gift for luring young or general readers into enjoyment of good literature. But the time was ripe for amateurs, small or great, to give place to a new tribe of professionals.

The so-called "New Criticism" had begun before the history of ideas was well launched. It was engendered in the 1920s and 1930s by the principles and practice of two powerful innovators, T. S. Eliot, in his double role as poet and critic, and I. A. Richards, a student of psychology, language, and poetry who was deeply concerned with sharpening and refining mental and communicative processes (and who was in his later years to become a poet himself). The New Criticism was actively developed—and christened—by their American followers, who, though not a unified school, were united in their insistence on close reading of literature, especially poetry, with precise analysis of the effects achieved and of the means employed. This kind of intensive study proved a very salutary aesthetic discipline. But, for some influential exponents, such refinement of perception entailed unwarranted limitations: the assumption that poetry was not poetry unless it was composed of imagery, ambiguity, paradox, and irony, and the conception of a poem as an autonomous object, more or less independent of history and the author's life and background. Thus the New Criticism could focus its concentrated light too narrowly and sometimes warp interpretation.

During the 1940s a very different, "Neo-Aristotelian" school developed at the University of Chicago under the leadership of Ronald S. Crane, a conventional historical scholar who had experienced conversion. Whereas the New Critic would, with microscopic eye, scan the texture and imagery of *Macbeth*, Crane, viewing the play in its wholeness, would as an Aristotle of modern sophistication study in depth the function of the "plot," a procedure which could correct centrifugal aberrations but could also be rather cumbrous. Crane was, however, an avowed pluralist who did not prescribe any one road to salvation.

The scholarly and critical phases so far noticed might seem enough to have filled a couple of generations, and, while they began roughly in succession, the various aims and methods have been carried on side by side. Even source-hunting became respectable when the mines to be quarried were the works of Eliot and Joyce. But there remain other distinct and, to my increasingly blurred vision, less distinct phases. One has gone under the name of "archetypal" or "myth-and-symbol" criticism. There is no space, even if I were qualified, to outline the growth and ramifications of this complex movement, but one must salute the chief contemporary theorist, Northrop Frye. In his two *Summas*, *Anatomy of Criticism* (1957) and *The Secular Scripture: A Study of the Structure of Romance* (1976), Professor Frye mapped out the panorama of modes, symbols, myths, genres, and romance, in fact all literature, in a network of related patterns. For him, in the words of W. K. Wimsatt, "There is one basic and inclusive myth, which takes the shape of a divine quest, death, and rebirth, following the cycle of the four seasons." We are dazzled by Frye's range of active knowledge, inexhaustible fertility in ideas, and taxonomic genius, although we may feel undernourished in his objective, schematic, and purely verbal or literary universe which seems to have no clear ethical or aesthetic base and only a tenuous connection with life—a universe of the mythic imagination from which, however, its creator can at times look down into a more human one.

"Myth" is used nowadays in the broad psychological-anthropological sense of a story which embodies primary, universal actions, situations, emotions, wishful dreams, and can therefore be endlessly re-created. Of course Greek myths made popular by Homer were elaborated and reinterpreted by the Greek dramatists and have been ever since by innumerable poets of all the literary nations. Many of these, treated as Greek myths, retained their original story and characters, with or without interpretative overtones. Others, especially in modern times, have been transposed into modern terms and settings, as in Joyce's *Ulysses* Irish people in Dublin have unheroic or antiheroic experiences and feelings in parallel contrast with those of Homer's characters. T. S. Eliot spoke in his dual role when he hailed *Ulysses* as giving imaginative writers, who face the infinite complexities of the modern outer and inner worlds, a model of the "mythic" presentation of life, an escape from the traditional narrative pattern and texture of composition, now felt as cramping, blunt, and inadequate. (To venture a marginal remark on Molly Bloom, the archetypal Earth Mother, Chaucer in a fraction of the space achieved a far more vital and moving creation in the Wife of Bath.)

Eliot himself, in *The Waste Land* of the same year, 1922, created a "mythic" mosaic out of ancient and modern allusions and vignettes, with no perceptible "story line" except as these fragments are unified in the brooding consciousness of the seer Tiresias. The unconscious or conscious use of myth and symbol is at least as old as the Bible and Homer, and criticism has enriched appreciation in discerning and defining this poetic and parabolic or semiallegorical element in literary art, in Shakespeare, Milton, the later works of Dickens, and many others. But the single-minded quest can mislead as well as illuminate, can indulge in triumphant discovery of the obvious or the fallacious, and can find especially Freudian symbols in anything and everything. Some critics carry the game to such fantastic extravagance that, to borrow a happy coinage from Edward Le Comte, their interpretations are mainly or wholly "phallacious." On the higher levels of psychoanalysis, in my limited experience, Freudian critics commonly follow a method both fanciful and Procrustean, forcing a formulaic and reductive pattern upon an author or a work. In general, one may think, or an old codger may think, that assimilation of Freud (or bits of him) has done much more harm than good in criticism. A splendid exception is W. J. Bate's *Samuel Johnson*, in which independent knowledge and insight guarantee judicious use of Freud.

To turn for a moment to another line of criticism, it has been noted that Karl Marx, even in a book enforcing his rigorous socioeconomic creed, could make such a concession as this: "It is well known that certain periods of highest development of art stand in no direct connection with the general development of society, nor with the material basis and the skeleton structure of its organization."[1] But modern Marxist criticism, despite such a philosophical luminary as Georg Lukács, seems normally to be content with more or less blunt applications of the party line. It—like much Freudianism—recalls Bacon's Idols of the Theater.

A third Idol of the Theater, in my opinion, is what goes under the name of numerology; a more inviting label would be Sir Thomas Browne's phrase, "the mysticall Mathematicks of the City of Heaven." The long tradition and its literary and other developments are so very complex that it is hard to be at once brief and intelligible. The Western tradition began with Pythagoras, whose "music of the spheres" reminds us that he conceived of the universe as a mathematical structure. The Christian Kepler, the first great lawgiver of modern astronomy, brought scientific knowledge to his similar conception of the universe as a divine and mathematical harmony. Biblical exegesis had for centuries enlarged the scope of mystical numbers by finding in them allegorical meanings. The venerable tradition became, modern expositors feel assured, part of the Renaissance man's mental furniture. But that, even if true, is, one may think, a very different thing from what these scholars have made of it. They have carried this mode of interpretation into many poems of the sixteenth and seventeenth centuries, from Spenser's *Epithalamion* and other short poems and *The Faerie Queene* to Milton's *On the Morning of Christ's Nativity, Comus, Lycidas*, and *Paradise Lost* and even his long treatise on Christian doctrine. We are asked to recognize hidden significances in numbers of cantos (or books), stanzas, and lines and in the placing of allusions. I, a heretic whose skepticism has attracted brickbats from sundry dedicated experts, cannot believe that early readers counted lines, even up to thousands, compiled all sorts of data, and, with a handbook beside them, brooded on their possible meanings—which had the advantage or disadvantage of being decidedly variable. I cannot believe, either, that great poets in deeply serious or religious poems would have played numerological games purely for their private gratification. Nor, if they did base not only minutiae but their whole conceptual structures on numerology, do I understand why they did not provide some clue to their purposes but left it to modern scholars, with nothing but internal "evidence," to impose such arcane and complex schemes upon the works. Finally, even those who can suspend disbelief and accept the experts' findings must grant that they have set up around the poems a barricade which the mass of otherwise qualified—and humane—readers cannot scale.

I am not disposed, for a reason to be explained in a moment, to linger with what are nowadays the most formidably fashionable schools and subschools of criticism. Even the many related or overlapping labels may baffle the ordinary student of literature: structuralism (an umbrella name for operations in various fields), formalism, genre-criticism, comparatism, linguistics, stylistics, semiotics, and other "isms" and "icses," of European and especially French origin. These modes of theorizing, for which literature supplies occasional laboratory specimens, have obviously far outdistanced our earliest phase of literary study in their ultrascientific aims and methods and their highly technical vocabulary. I have tried to read in this mass of writing, some of it by first-class minds, but with small success. In short, I am a benighted laggard who has fallen far behind the growing army of illuminati. However, my embarrassing predicament may underline the conclusion toward which this discourse has been slowly moving, namely, that a glance over the modern evolution of scholarly literary criticism makes clear its increasing, self-created isolation from the general reading public. Moreover, in some quarters it seems to have assumed independent status as a literary genre above the plane of imaginative creation—out-Patering Pater, we might say.

The modern critical scene, apart from much journalism, is very different from that of the great amateurs of the past; the last notable American amateur was Edmund Wilson, who belonged to no school but followed his own interests wherever they led him. We took brief account of the newer, abstruse phases of critical theory and may look at the more traditional activities of the great majority of scholars and scholarly critics. During the last two generations serious criticism has increasingly become the preserve of academic, professional students of literature, specialists in this or that period or area or individual author. This extreme specialization, one must say at once, has made possible an unprecedented illumination of the whole body of literature, both in philosophical depth and in fullness and precision of aesthetic and technical analysis. That is an incontrovertible fact which is proof against literary journalists' sneers at "the professors," "the drones of Oxbridge and the M.L.A." But my present concern is with the liabilities entailed by that truly great achievement. One is the obvious fact that among the multitude of workers a good many, inspired mainly by professional ambition and pressure, turn out so many articles and books that are, to put it mildly, unnecessary. Such wastage, to be sure, attends all kinds of learned inquiry, even in the sciences. The vigilant Senator Proxmire has included among his "Golden Fleece" awards such peculiar grants as $84,000 from the National Science Foundation for a study of why people fall in love, $46,000 from the Agriculture Department for a study of the length of time needed to cook breakfast, and $27,000 from the Law Enforcement Assistance Administration for an explanation of prison inmates' desire to escape.

What matters most is that scholarly specialists write almost wholly for fellow specialists. Like the critical theorists we noticed, and increasingly under their influence, they remain aloof from the interests and grasp of common readers. Many of the sheep may not be very hungry, but many presumably are, and they are not much fed; it is surely part of a scholar's duty, in writing as in the classroom, both to arouse and to satisfy hunger. Or are some modern classroom operations related to the declining appeal of the humanities? I have no notion. Whatever the actual state of affairs, it seems an indisputable proposition that, if highly specialized literary work dominates the academic scene and loses touch with the fundamental questions and values of literature, the health, even the survival, of the humanistic tradition is seriously threatened. We might think of the late Lionel Trilling, a lineal heir of Matthew Arnold, who was deeply concerned with literature, education, and culture and society at large, and who addressed the general public as well as the literary in language unspoiled by jargon. I refrain from naming other authentic literary humanists among the living.

The withdrawal of intellectuals to a plane on which they could think their thoughts without the handicap of making them intelligible and attractive to inferior minds has been a general movement not confined to the literary. Philosophers, Josiah Royce wryly remarked in a far-off time, were expected to spiritualize the community; but they (that is, professors of philosophy) long ago abandoned the quest of the good life for what particles of unquestionable truth could be found in semantics and mathematical and symbolic logic. The spiritual and ethical vacuum that movement left seems to have been filled by apostles of Dionysus. The new race of historians, scorning the narrative and literary virtues of writers from Herodotus to Samuel Morison, have likewise gone in for quantitative and statistical analysis of the past, a method which doubtless can correct some erroneous views but doubtless also ensures a considerable loss of readers. In a larger context, we might recall the campus explosions of a decade ago, set off by righteous anger against the Vietnam war and other discontents, which somehow included a violent rejection of all concern with the past and a demand for a spurious kind of "relevance." Of late years revolt against the establishment has apparently given way to eager striving for a secure place within it.

To return to literature, we have nowadays, in this country alone, scores of more or less gifted poets, of whom a few have won a sort of popularity as public performers, but in general their themes and techniques have been too subtle and sophisticated to attract more than fellow poets and devotees happily attuned to the right wavelength. And a good many critics seem less concerned with what they say than with how they say it; the first question may be harder to answer. Modern poets, like all others, must, as Keats said, work out their own salvation, a process especially difficult in the present world, and no outsider could presume to suggest what they should be and do. We may, though, observe some external facts or apparent facts. Whatever the abundance of contemporary talent, and whatever deposits of older poetry may linger in some minds from college courses, it seems safe to infer that for most of the educated public poetry simply doesn't matter. A century ago, we may think, it did matter, to a much larger proportion of the public. The poet A. H. Clough spoke otherwise, in a review in 1853 of his friend Arnold and Alexander Smith. People, he said, much prefer *Vanity Fair* and *Bleak House* to highly literary and academic poetry (which was hardly fair to Arnold). Is it, Clough asked, "that to be widely popular, to gain the ear of multitudes, to shake the hearts of men, poetry should deal, more than at present it usually does, with general wants, ordinary feelings, the obvious rather than the rare facts of human nature?"—a question he expanded at some length. But, though some mediocre poets, English and American, were popular, the really great Tennyson was immensely popular too, and not always for wrong reasons. Wallace Stevens, who in sophisticated opinion appears to stand at the head of modern American poets, has not had, and never could have, a position even remotely comparable to Tennyson's. Robert Frost, of course, was very popular, but largely because his outward simplicity masked his real complexity and his disturbing message; he was stereotyped as the homely New England sage. A number of contemporary poets might possibly be willing to enjoy popularity on the same terms, but, to put it crudely, they have priced themselves out of the market—a most regrettable situation for which the public must bear part of the responsibility, though perhaps not the larger part.

Current fiction is so preoccupied with sex that it is assured of a loyal following. Half a century ago, if my memory does not exaggerate, there was in liberal journals something like a flood of individual and group discussions on the theme: "Can the artist live in America?" The consensus, as I recall, was that the only hope for honest fiction depended on the abolition of censorship. The zealous activities of Anthony Comstock and others were stupid and often ridiculous, though the advertisement "Banned in Boston" brought its financial rewards (a general principle recognized by the old vagabond in *Huckleberry Finn*). Censorship did expire, but no tidal wave of great novels followed. The enormous popularity of Dickens was due in part to his early faults but mainly, as always, to his unique creative and comic genius and, for some readers, to his profound concern about the evils in English society (recent generations have been taught to appreciate the superb artistry he attained). Our chief—and subcritical—best-sellers seem to owe their status to their ample provision of erotic titillation; indeed that has become an indispensable ingredient of fiction on all levels. Last spring, by the way, it was reported that the commercial networks, whose barometric vision is fixed on ratings and profits, had decided to turn from violence to sex.

Two years ago the serious and philosophical Saul Bellow, in accepting the Nobel prize, looked squarely at our world of outer and inner crises and disorder and rejected intellectuals' doctrine of the extinction of the individual person and, with that, the death of the novel of characters. The modern novelist must take a more penetrating and responsible view of his art, must try to fulfill mankind's need "for a broader, more flexible, fuller, more coherent, more comprehensive account of what we human beings are, who we are, and what this life is for." Mr. Bellow cited Dostoevsky and Tolstoy, Conrad (a lifelong favorite of his) and Proust, "who would not give up the connection of literature with the main human enterprise." "A novel," he affirmed, "is balanced between a few true impressions and the multitude of false ones that make up most of what we call life . . . What Conrad said was true, art attempts to find in the universe, in matter as well as in the facts of life, what is fundamental, enduring, essential."[2] Such art, such an assertion of good against evil, is not an illusion, in spite of intellectuals' negativism.

With Mr. Bellow may be linked another witness, the novelist-scholar John Gardner, whose *On Moral Fiction*[3] appeared just after I finished this article. Mr. Gardner also upholds a lost orthodoxy, in no tame or moralistic way, and maintains the "eternal verities" against the reign of flux (what Aristophanes called the god Whirl):

> My basic message throughout this book is as old as the hills, drawn from Homer, Plato, Aristotle, Dante, and the rest, and standard in Western civilization down through the eighteenth century . . .
> The traditional view is that true art is moral: it seeks to improve life, not debase it. It seeks to hold off, at least for a while, the twilight of the gods and us.[4]
> Real art creates myths a society can live instead of die by, and clearly our society is in need of such myths. What I claim is that such myths are not mere hopeful fairy tales but the products of careful and disciplined thought; that a properly built myth is worthy of belief, at least tentatively; that working at art is a moral act; that a work of art is a moral example; and that false art can be known for what it is if one remembers the rules. The blank abyss stirs a certain fascination, admittedly, or we would not pay so many artists so much money to keep staring at it. But the black abyss is merely life as it is or as it soon may become, and staring at it does nothing, merely confirms that it is there. It seems to me time that artists start taking that fact as pretty thoroughly established.[5]

As for criticism, Mr. Gardner, listing some of the schools we have noticed, sees them as in the main not meeting our needs, "first, because they're all too neat, too theoretical, too 'scientific' to deal with so lively and unpredictable a creature as art, and second, because they ignore the very essence of art, which is emotional affirmation."[6]

In this connection I cannot omit the name of the late F. R. Leavis, who, with all his quirks and quiddities, earnestly maintained the fundamental primacy of literature as a moral force.

We have observed some varieties of modern professional intellectualism in the humanities, chiefly in literary criticism, and their increasing aloofness from traditional aims and from the reading public. Of course orthodox specialists and adventurous explorers are necessary in all branches of learning, but one may think that, at least in the literary domain, they should not be overwhelmingly predominant. To recall earlier ages, from Sir Philip Sidney through Dryden, Johnson, Coleridge, Arnold, and others, is to remember that they all, even Coleridge, addressed the whole body of educated readers, the public to which they themselves belonged. As men of letters—and poets as well—these and other critics, endowed with superior knowledge, insight, and powers of utterance, shared their experience and ideas with the public, thereby raising the general level of understanding and taste and enlarging the community of humane readers. However much they differed from one another, they all, openly or tacitly, upheld the ancient axiom that it is the function of literature to teach and delight (not, of course, didactically).

In all ages, and especially in the last two hundred years, many serious writers have been moved by the urge to self-expression or to art for art's sake,

but the greatest, from Homer down into our own century, have exemplified the
traditional ideal or principle. To some people that ideal seems the only solid
ground on which responsible writers can stand. There are contemporary critics
who dismiss the idea of the moral and spiritual power of literature as an obsolete
superstition, a Victorian soothing-syrup concocted by Arnold. In this century,
it is said, explosions of new knowledge, along with two world wars, mass murder, and the threat of total destruction, have annihilated our classical-Judeo-
Christian heritage, fragmented the modern mind, and left a civilization animated chiefly by greed and fear. Such clichés of despair are not altogether new,
even in their presumed finality, but mankind has hung on, if only by the skin of
its teeth. But there are people, whether relatively few or many, who cannot
acquiesce in our supposedly bankrupt moral vision and who believe that it is or
should be a prime obligation of imaginative and critical writers to keep before us
the unique and essential function that so much great literature has long fulfilled
and can again fulfill.

REFERENCES
   [1]*A Contribution to the Critique of Political Economy* (New York, 1904), p. 309.
   [2]I quote from the text, copyright© The Nobel Foundation (Stockholm, 1977), kindly furnished
by Mr. Bellow's office at the University of Chicago.
   [3]John Gardner, *On Moral Fiction* (New York: Basic Books, 1978).
   [4]Ibid., p. 5.
   [5]Ibid., p. 126.
   [6]Ibid., p. 129.

JONATHAN LEAR

Going Native

POSITIVISM CASTS A LONG SHADOW. The attempt to escape from its penumbra has been an arduous task.

In the early 1930s two young philosophers, A. J. Ayer from Oxford and W. V. Quine from Harvard, traveled to Austria to attend meetings of the Vienna Circle. Ayer is now retiring as Wykeham Professor of Logic at Oxford. His *Language, Truth and Logic*, first published in 1936 when Ayer was only twenty-five, is the classic English statement of positivist dogma. It faithfully reflects both the positivists' faith in the methods of the natural sciences and their naive notion of what those methods were.

Since the beginning of the century, metaphysics had been linked with meaning: both Frege and the young Wittgenstein understood that one's view of the world, of what there is, will be determined by one's theory of language. Ayer turned this insight into a serious weapon. The meaning of a sentence was supposed to be given by its method of verification—and verification was taken to consist solely in possible sensory experience. This method admitted as meaningful those sentences which could be used to make assertions about the empirical world, the so-called synthetic sentences. The only other sentences rescued from the netherworld of senselessness were those of logic and arithmetic. Though they could not be confirmed by any sensory experience, they were taken to be analytic: true in virtue of their meaning, embodying rules of language which "simply record our determination to use symbols in a certain fashion."[1]

Positivist metaphysics is dramatically odd. Discourse fundamental to human experience—about how one should act toward others, about how one should live a life, about what is beautiful, about religion—was banished as meaningless. Further, Ayer rejected the common conception that our immediate experience is of a world of physical objects and simply insisted that our experience was of "sense-contents" and that physical objects must be definable in terms of them.[2] Why did Ayer get away with such a bizarre metaphysical position? It was partly because he disguised the fact that he *had* a metaphysical position by using "metaphysics" as a pejorative term, partly because he claimed to be on the side of natural science. Positivists allied themselves with the forces of light and objectivity against those of mysticism and darkness. A champion of scientific method need not sully his mind with metaphysics. In the development

175

of philosophy in this century, the big battalions are on the side not of God, but of Science.

It fell to Quine, the other young man who made the pilgrimage to Vienna, to write the classic refutation of Ayer's positivism. Quine has just retired as Edgar Pierce Professor of Philosophy at Harvard. Though he was in Vienna in the early 1930s, he did not publish his famous critique, "Two Dogmas of Empiricism," until 1951. In this essay Quine reveals himself as a man under the sway of positivist doctrine who has over time gained perspective. That the man who offered the classic critique of logical positivism was himself deeply influenced by it has, I think, hampered the efforts of a generation to abandon positivist metaphysics.

For Quine, the fundamental flaw of positivism was its misconception of what a verification theory of meaning should be. In Quine's now famous metaphor, our total theory of the world is like a field of force on which experience impinges only at the periphery.[3] In the interior lie theoretical beliefs; toward the periphery lie beliefs about immediate experience. Our beliefs are linked by inferential connections, both deductive and inductive, but our whole theory is so underdetermined by experience that no recalcitrant experience will dictate exactly what revisions must be made. The positivists were wrong to think that an *individual statement* could be subjected to empirical confirmation or refutation. 'Water boils at 212° F' for example, cannot be confirmed by a unique sensory experience: if anything should go wrong we might decide that the thermometer was inaccurate, or that the 'water' had impurities, or that the water *was* boiling although it was not bubbling, or that at certain air pressures water does not boil at 212° F, and so on.

Quine responded to positivism not by discarding a verification theory of meaning, but by offering a more sophisticated model. What had to go was not empiricism (whatever that is) but its two dogmas. First, one had to give up the analytic/synthetic distinction because there were no sentences that could be considered "truths of meaning" immune from revision in the light of experience. Nor were there sentences whose meaning could be given individually by specifying a unique range of confirming sensory experience. So, secondly, one had to forego the reductionist belief that a meaningful sentence about the empirical world must be a construct out of a unique chunk of immediate "sense data." Experience still plays a crucial role in the determination of meaning, but, for Quine, the unit of confirmation is our entire theory. The meaning of an individual sentence is dependent on its position in the total network, its inferential connections with other sentences, as well as on experience.

Quine's positivist heritage emerges in his belief that the underdetermination of theory by experience implies what he calls "the indeterminacy of translation." According to Quine, two translation manuals could be set up between English and some radically alien language such that each manual would accommodate all the natives' dispositions to speech behavior and yet the manuals themselves would be incompatible.[4] There would simply be no answer to the question of which manual provided the correct translation. Quine has never been enthusiastic about offering examples. His standard case is of the jungle linguist hearing a native say 'Gavagai' in the presence of a rabbit. Our initial guess that 'gavagai' means rabbit assumes that the natives, like us, are interested in medium-sized enduring physical objects, rather than in space-time rabbit-processes or undetached collections of rabbit-parts. The attempt to ask the native whether he meant rabbit would already require setting up a scheme of translation, using a set of "analytical hypotheses" about their grammar, which would in effect impose a "frame of reference" on the natives' speech behavior.[5] In order for us to question the natives in their own language, one manual might have us saying, 'Is this the same gavagai as that?' while the other interprets us as saying, 'Does this gavagai belong to that?'[6]

Indeterminacy is supposed to be a consequence of Quine's verificationist model of language.

> When . . . we take a verification theory of meaning seriously, the indeterminacy would appear inescapable. The Vienna Circle espoused a verification theory of meaning but did not take it seriously enough. If we recognize with Pierce that the meaning of a sentence turns purely on what would count as evidence for its truth, and if we recognize with Duhem that theoretical sentences have their evidence not as single sentences but only as larger blocks of theory, then the indeterminacy of translation of theoretical sentences is the natural conclusion. And most sentences, apart from observation sentences are theoretical . . . Should the unwelcomeness of the conclusion persuade us to abandon the verification theory of meaning? Certainly not. The sort of meaning that is basic to translation, and to the learning of one's own language, is necessarily empirical meaning and nothing more.[7]

> The crucial consideration behind my argument for the indeterminacy of translation was that a statement about the world does not always or usually have a separable fund of empirical consequences it can call its own.[8]

It is important to realize that the indeterminacy thesis does not need to be posed in terms of a translation between English and an alien language. It can be stated as a thesis about the speakers of a single language. Quine claims that English sentences could be translated directly into *nonequivalent* English sentences, yet the translation as a whole would preserve a speaker's dispositions to verbal behavior.[9] We seem to be faced with the possibility that as we speak our mother tongue, there is no fact of the matter as to what we mean by our utterances.

One has only to state the indeterminacy thesis in this way to begin to become suspicious. Why should Quine have presented it as a problem of radical translation of an alien language? My own view is that Quine wished to provide an empiricist theory of meaning but, because of his positivist background, had a narrow vision of what it would be to do this. Only with the metaphor of radical translation could Quine impose such rigid constraints on what was to count as "empirical evidence." And only with such an unduly limited conception of what constituted the empirical evidence for a translation would the indeterminacy thesis begin to look plausible.

Quine's theory of meaning contains a core insight which is both valuable and true. Language is essentially a social tool, used primarily for communication. Language is learned by public promptings and encouragements to respond to publicly observable circumstances. Quine, like Wittgenstein, categorically rejects the notion that meaning can essentially involve anything private to an individual, such as a hidden mental image. This is the myth of the museum—that words name specimen mental objects—which Quine rightly urges us to reject. If we are to explain language-mastery, and thus the meaning our words and sentences have, we must do it on the basis of our experience: the sensory evidence of all types to which we have over time been exposed and our sensitivity to it. Positing interior mental objects that are named by words only gets in the way of an explanation, for it merely papers over the gaps in our understanding of how language-mastery is acquired.

Where Quine errs is in his belief that in avoiding the pernicious myth of the museum we are led inescapably to the indeterminacy of translation. The cost of a nonmystifying empirical theory of meaning is, Quine thinks, indeterminacy. His argument is unconvincing. The jungle linguist is supposed to have available all the empirical evidence which prompts the natives' assent and dissent to native sentences. Quine identifies the visual stimulation that prompts native assent to 'Gavagai' with the pattern of chromatic radiation of the eye.[10] This has the aura of scientific precision, dear to Quine's heart, but it takes us further away from rather than closer to an empiricist theory of meaning. If language is learned by public promptings in publicly observable circumstances, why interpret visual stimulation in terms of something as hidden as ocular irradiation? Why not simply say that the native assents to 'Gavagai' in the presence of a rabbit or other circumstances which would reasonably lead him to believe a rabbit was present?

Precisely because ocular irradiation of the retina is such a scientifically ideal notion, our access to it is limited. A light meter may be able to give exact readings of light refracted off an opaque screen. But humans are not screens and do not have light meters attached to their retinas. What the linguist does know is what is publicly observable; for example, that a rabbit has just crossed his and his native friend's visual field. He does not know whether he and the native are experiencing similar chromatic irradiations—perhaps the native has learned to dilate or contract his pupils in certain hunting situations—or whether the irradiation is similar, on the microscopic level, to previous irradiations caused by rabbits. That is at best plausible conjecture. To assume that there must be a constancy and coherence at the microlevel of ocular irradiation which can be used to give an analysis of our sensory experience is to flirt with a reductionism which one might have expected the author of "Two Dogmas" to find objectionable.

Further, as Crispin Wright pointed out, there is the problem that the predicates we apply in observational circumstances tend to be irremediably vague.[11] The relation 'x is perceptually indistinguishable from y' is nontransitive: x may look just like y and y may look just like z while x and z do not look exactly alike. But we learn to apply observational predicates on the basis of the way things look to us, so the extensions of many observational predicates will not be determinate. This, of course, is no evidence for indeterminacy of translation. One should just try to translate a vague predicate into a predicate which exactly preserves the vagueness. It does, however, give cause for doubt as to whether visual stimulation should be conceived in terms of ocular irradiation. For example, the native might be willing to assent to a sentence as he is gradually, imperceptibly, drawn across an entire spectrum of ocular irradiation, which he would never be willing to do if he simply leapt from one end of the spectrum to the other.[12]

Quine is not unaware of such problems:

> In taking the visual stimulations as irradiation patterns we invest them with a fineness of detail beyond anything that our linguist can be called upon to check for. But this is all right. He can reasonably conjecture that the native would be prompted to assent to 'Gavagai' by the microscopically same irradiations that would prompt him, the linguist, to assent to 'Rabbit', even though this conjecture rests wholly on samples where the irradiations concerned can at best be hazarded merely to be pretty much alike.[13]

It is *not* all right. Given that we learned our language without such attention to detail, that the native learned his language without such attention to detail, is not the attention to "detail" misguided? We wish to explain how language-acquisition is possible on the basis of experience. To this end, it is not advantageous to construe sensory experience in such a way that it cannot be checked by the field linguist or, for that matter, the language-learning infant.

The fascination with "scientific method" may thus be obstructing the development of an empiricist theory of meaning. The jungle linguist is supposed to be noting native assent and dissent under varying patterns of ocular irradiation. But why settle for native assent and dissent as the sum total of permitted cooperation with the native? It is as though the natives are pygmies who have been stuffed into oversized Skinner boxes and allowed to push one of two buttons in response to sensory stimulation. Why not talk to them?

Quine's response is that by the time we are able to talk to them we have already begged the question in favor of one of the translation manuals. We have imposed a set of analytical hypotheses on native linguistic behavior which will translate them as saying that they mean what we think they mean. The response is inadequate. For we are not forced to interpret the native via a translation manual: we always have the option of going native. Human languages are learned, and they seem to be learned on democratic principles. Any baby who has the capacity to learn the language of the community of which he is a member is thought to have the capacity to learn the language of any (human) community whatsoever. On the old-dogs/new-tricks principle, it may be a bit more difficult for the adult linguist to go native than for the baby, but the difficulty is not overwhelming. However, Quine thinks the bilingual is not essentially better off, for he too is using analytical hypotheses albeit unconsciously.[14] In trying to go native he has in effect set up a translation manual between his original language and the native language. In fact, Quine thinks the bilingual may be somewhat worse off, since he has, figuratively, ingested the native and thus hidden him from public view.[15]

This is untrue to the phenomenology of the acquisition of a second language (whether acquired in radical or nonradical circumstances). Though we may begin with a few rough and ready translations, remarkably quickly we simply speak and think in our newly acquired tongue. We do not owe undying conceptual allegiance to our first language; we are not forced to treat the mastery of another language as an implicit translation into our original language. In fact, it is not incoherent to imagine someone who could speak two languages fluently yet feel uneasy about translating between them. Quine has often pictured our conceptual scheme as a ship at sea: we may replace planks but we must stay afloat while doing so. An apter metaphor for the multilingual may be a flotilla.

He has various ships at sea, and the crews of each may or may not have thrown lines over to the others.

Whether or not a bilingual is able to translate between the two languages over which he has mastery is irrelevant to the indeterminacy thesis. For, as we have seen, the translation between alien languages is not essential to the indeterminacy thesis. Our concern is not with translation per se. We are native speakers among native speakers: our task is not to translate other speakers, merely to understand them.[16] The difference is important. For Quine, even when we are among native English speakers we are still essentially engaged in a process of translation. This is to misconceive the situation. Language is essentially shared, social and public. We do not normally translate a native English-speaker into our own (private) language: we talk to him in our common tongue.

But what about the possibility of some ingenious permutation of the entire language? If we wished to find out whether by 'rabbit' some fellow English-speaker meant rabbit and not undetached collection of rabbit-parts, our natural inclination is simply to talk to him about it. Suppose he responds, "By 'rabbit' I mean rabbit and not undetached collection of rabbit-parts." Might it not *still* be the case that he is unwittingly under the influence of a weird and cunning permutation of the language such that by 'rabbit' he means undetached collection of rabbit-parts and by 'undetached collection of rabbit-parts' he means rabbit? This is Quine's *malin génie:*

> It is meaningless to ask whether, in general, our terms 'rabbit,' 'rabbit part,' 'number,' etc., really refer respectively to rabbits, rabbit parts, numbers, etc., rather than to some ingeniously permuted denotations. It is meaningless to ask this absolutely; we can meaningfully ask it only relative to some background language. When we ask, "Does 'rabbit' really refer to rabbits?" someone can counter with the question: "Refer to rabbits in what sense of 'rabbits' "? thus launching a regress; and we need the background language to regress into. The background language gives the query sense, if only relative sense; sense relative in turn to it, this background language. Querying reference in any more absolute way would be like asking absolute position or absolute velocity, rather than position or velocity relative to a given frame of reference.[17]

The translation metaphor has here come to tyrannize Quine's thinking. We do not need a background language to regress into; the questions can be asked and answered in English. Quine has, I suspect, misconstrued the significance for natural language of a certain result in mathematical logic. Tarski proved that in order to provide the semantics for a *formalized* language L_0, of a certain character and expressive power, one must use a metalanguage L_1 that is essentially richer in expressive power than the original language.[18] To provide the semantics for L_1, we must, in turn, retreat to a language L_2 which is essentially richer than L_1, and so on. To try to provide the semantics of L_0 within L_0 leads to paradox. Thus to interpret the sentences of one language, there must always be a background language to regress into. However, it is doubtful whether Tarski's formal languages provide an accurate model for natural language. For instance, every sentence of L_0 is assumed to be either true or false, and it is questionable whether every English sentence enjoys that status. If we are willing to admit that some of our declarative constructions—for example, 'I am now lying'—may not be either true or false, then there is no objection in principle to providing the semantics of a language within a language.[19] For anyone impressed by the methods and results of natural science it would, of course, be attractive to do for linguistic space what Einstein did for physical space—to become the Heisenberg of discourse. But one risks becoming hostage to a metaphor.

Quine's problem, stripped of translational imagery, is that we seem to get more out of experience than is given to us. That is, Quine's problem—give or take a concern with language rather than the mind—is Hume's problem:

> [The] human subject is accorded a certain experimentally controlled input—certain patterns of irradiation in assorted frequencies, for instance—and in the fullness of time the subject delivers as output a description of the three dimensional world and its history. The relation between the meager input and the torrential output is a relation that we are prompted to study for somewhat the same reasons that always prompted epistemology; namely, in order to see how evidence relates to theory, and in what ways one's theory of nature transcends any available evidence.[20]

Is the relation really that of *meager* input to *torrential* output? Suppose, for a moment, that we think of the output in the same physicalistic terms in which Quine wishes us to conceive the input. That is, instead of input of irradiation by photons, and so on, and output of people speaking a language, we conceived of the whole process as merely a field of atoms interacting. For Quine there would, presumably, be no paradox on this homogeneous microlevel. Atoms would be interacting as atoms are wont to interact. Only when we flip between micro- and macrolevels does there appear to be a slack between output and input. But this does not necessarily mean that we have gotten more out of experience than has been given to us, it may only mean that our conception of what is given to us in experience needs revising (and fleshing out). Our "torrential output" may be evidence that what is meager is not our input, but Quine's idea of sensory experience. The current generation needs philosophers who are willing to play Kant to Quine's Hume.

What is sensory evidence? Quine says that is all we have to go on in constructing our picture of the world. But Quine already has a picture of the world which dictates his view of how we construct pictures of the world. His view of how we construct a picture of the world is not constrained by the sensory evidence, whatever that is, but by his theory of what sensory evidence is. Quine is an ardent physicalist, so he tries to explain our construction of a theory of the world in those terms. His inability to do so is taken to be *our* failure: meaning is said to transcend experience. Here Quine's position is in deepest tension with his own favorite metaphor of the ship at sea. There is no pure, theory-independent notion of what is "out there" stimulating us.[21] In our comprehensive theory of the world one of the things we must explain is how we learn the language we do. If physics makes language-acquisition appear a mystery, then so much the worse for a purely physicalistic conception of sensory evidence.[22]

Quine makes it look as if to deny indeterminacy is to turn one's back on an empiricist theory of meaning. He says that although a verification theory of meaning leads inescapably to indeterminacy, we should not abandon verificationism, because in learning a language all we have to go on is empirical evidence.[23] But what constitutes "empirical evidence"—the evidence on the basis of which we construct our theories—is itself a theory-laden question. Yes, we want to remain empiricists because we do not want language-mastery to be an ineffable mystery. However, we should not, for that reason, make language-mastery *another* type of mystery, by construing "empirical evidence" so narrowly that we are landed with indeterminacy.

But even if we are generous in our construal of empirical evidence, might we not *still* be faced with indeterminacy? I do not think we can answer that question before we have been presented with a compelling argument for indeterminacy; and Quine has not provided one.

One of the most eloquent critics of Quine's "translational" approach to the theory of meaning is Michael Dummett, who has recently been named to succeed Ayer as the Wykeham Professor of Logic at Oxford. For Dummett, the consequences of a theory of translation for the theory of meaning are obscure. Precisely because a translational theory makes no explicit mention of meaning, it is unclear what lessons should be learned from it.[24] Quine focused on the relation of translation between sentences rather than on their meaning in order to avoid appeal to such shadowy entities as meanings.[25] Yet one ought to be able to avoid the myth of the museum and nevertheless embrace a less impoverished conception of meaning than Quine's.

Dummett's suggestion is that a theory of meaning ought to be a theory of understanding.[26] That is, a theory of meaning for a language should tell us what a speaker knows when he understands the language. It would be hard to overestimate the helpfulness of this suggestion, for it enables us to address ourselves directly to the question of meaning and to see this as a question about the abilities of those who use the language.

However, to explain what it is to understand a language is, for Dummett, a highly problematic task. This is revealed most clearly in his critique of the relation between truth and understanding. Since Frege, it has been thought natural to suppose that one understands a sentence when one knows what it would be for the sentence to be true. As plausible as this idea may seem, Dummett finds great difficulty in accepting it. For example, consider the sentence α: 'There is no number n, greater than 2, such that $x^n + y^n = z^n$ (for any integers x, y, z).' The mathematician Pierre Fermat (1601-1665) wrote in the margin of his own copy of Bachet's *Diophantus* that he had discovered a proof of α. Unfortunately, there was not enough room in the margin to write out the proof. This may, for all we know, be one of the greatest practical jokes in the history of human thought. Since Fermat's time, mathematicians have tried without success either to prove or to disprove Fermat's "last theorem." If Fermat's last theorem is true, the only way we could come to know it is by some form of proof. Since there are infinitely many numbers it is impossible to check every one to ensure that α is true. No computer has yet found a set of numbers which shows that α is false; that is, some $n > 2$ such that $x^n + y^n = z^n$. But we do not yet know whether this is because there are no such numbers or because the computer has simply not gone far enough. Until someone comes up with a proof or disproof we have no way of knowing whether we shall ever learn whether Fermat's last theorem is true.

Such a sentence Dummett calls *undecidable*. What is meant by this is *not* that the truth of the sentence could never be determined. For all we know, a mathematician will come up with a proof of Fermat's last theorem tomorrow or a computer will crank out a set of numbers which shows it to be false. A sentence is undecidable if: 1) we do not now know whether it is true; and 2) the meaning of the sentence does not give us a recipe for determining whether it is true or false. When we understand the sentence α, the only suggestion we are offered for determining its truth is to check all numbers to make sure there are none such that $x^n + y^n = z^n$; but since there are infinitely many numbers this is not a task which we could, even in principle, perform.

Fermat's last theorem is undecidable because there are infinitely many numbers to be checked, but it is easy to form other types of undecidable sentences. For example, consider β: 'Fermat really did prove his last theorem.' How could we ever come to know whether the sentence is true or false? Well, if we found among Fermat's papers a proof of his last theorem, that would show that β was true; or if we found in his diary a confession that his marginalia were a bit of mischief, we would know that β is false. But there is no guarantee that if we continue to search his papers we will uncover any such treasure. Here the undecidability of β is due to the past's limited accessibility to us.

Someone understands a sentence when he knows what it would be for it to be true: it is this claim which Dummett finds incoherent in the case of an undecidable sentence. If to understand a sentence one must know what it is for it to be true, on what basis can we ascribe such knowledge to a person? Two beliefs are crucial to Dummett's own position. First, a person must be able to manifest his knowledge by some observable behavior. Knowledge of a language is practical knowledge; the ability to speak a language is a practical ability. A theory of meaning, Dummett thinks, should provide a theoretical representation of this practical ability.[27] Of course a native speaker need not explicitly know the theory, but Dummett thinks we can interpret his language-mastery as manifesting *implicit* knowledge of the theory. So if we are to describe linguistic ability in terms of the (implicit) knowledge a speaker has, there must be some exercise of this ability which is seen as a manifestation of the knowledge.

Second, someone cannot always manifest what he understands by a sentence by *stating* what it is for the sentence to be true. For Dummett, one cannot simply repeat the sentence, for the whole question is what one understands by it. A reformulation of the sentence in other words must sometimes be inadequate. For the question arises how to manifest one's knowledge of the verbal reformulation. One will be led either into an infinite regress or, if one is ultimately led back to the original sentence, a vicious circularity. So the knowledge someone has when he understands a sentence cannot, in general, be merely verbal.

How then can one manifest one's knowledge of what it is for a sentence to be true? For decidable sentences the answer is easy enough. If a decidable sentence is true one can *recognize* it to be true. So a person can show that he knows what it is for a decidable sentence to be true by assenting to it whenever he recognizes it to be true.

There is no comparable activity which could demonstrate knowledge of what it is for an undecidable sentence to be true. We cannot check every number to see if Fermat's theorem is true, so, it seems, we cannot always recognize an undecidable sentence to be true when it is true. Dummett thinks there is nothing we can do to manifest a knowledge of what it is for an undecidable sentence to be true. If we had such knowledge, however, we should be able to manifest it. Therefore we are unjustified in claiming knowledge. The understanding of an undecidable sentence can never consist in a knowledge of what it is for it to be true.

What then *do* we know when we understand a sentence? To answer this question Dummett follows Wittgenstein and focuses on what we learn when we learn a language. We do not emerge from the womb speaking a language. (We cannot say, "Thank goodness, people to talk to at last.") Rather, the ability to speak a language is an acquired skill. In learning to use a language we learn on which occasions we are entitled to assert the sentence, or accept it as true. We understand a sentence, Dummett thinks, if we know when it would be permissible to assert it. And we learn that it is permissible to assert a sentence when we can recognize it to be true.

For a simple decidable sentence, we can recognize it to be true whenever it is true. Truth and the grounds for asserting a sentence coincide. But for an undecidable sentence, like Fermat's last theorem, we can assert it only if we can prove it and we may never be clever enough to think up a proof. The claim that the sentence is definitely true or false independently of whether we know it, goes beyond anything we may justifiably be said to know.

Dummett's great contribution to the philosophical community is to make us aware to what extent our metaphysical picture of the world will depend on our theory of meaning. *Realism* is the belief that the indicative sentences of our language are true or false, independently of our knowledge of them. For Dummett, it is *because* we assume arithmetical sentences to be true or false that we find it natural to adopt a picture of the numbers standing in a row which stretches out to infinity. One then imagines that either there are numbers in the row which falsify Fermat's theorem or there are not. Similarly, it is *because* we assume that past tense sentences are true or false, independently of our knowledge, that we tend to picture the past as stretching out behind us. We are convinced that either Fermat did prove his theorem or that he did not, even if we do not know which. However, if we abandon the realist beliefs that every arithmetical or past tense sentence is true or false, then these metaphysical pictures should cease to exercise such a hold on our imaginations. And Dummett has urged us to find these realist beliefs problematic. In a language that contains undecidable sentences, we simply do not know whether every sentence is true or false. We *think* we know what it would be for an undecidable sentence to be true: and we think we know it must be true or false, even if we do not know which. This, Dummett argues, is because we imagine a superhuman being with observational powers which transcend our own.[28] This being is able, even if we are not, to check an infinity of numbers or to see into the past and determine whether these sentences are true or false. It is our conception of what this being would have to do that is supposed to embody our understanding of what it is for such sentences to be true. Such a defense Dummett correctly sees as inadequate. The language we are trying to describe is spoken by humans, not superhumans, and as such must be related to human abilities. Dummett has thrown down the gauntlet to the current generation of young philosophers. His antirealism challenges us to justify our commonsense beliefs that the world exists independently of our knowledge of it, that the past is determinate even if we do not know exactly what happened, and that basic arithmetical sentences are definitely true or false even if we do not know how to prove or disprove them.

It is fitting that Dummett has been named to succeed Ayer. For the core of Dummett's critique is that verification rather than truth must be the central concept of a theory of meaning. Of course, Dummett's verificationist theory of meaning is far more sophisticated than Ayer's. The question which remains, however, is whether Dummett has succeeded in extracting what is valuable in the positivist tradition or whether his own theory is encumbered by unjustifiable positivist assumptions.

Dummett's positivism emerges in his demand that a theory of meaning be deeply explanatory:

> If a theory of meaning gives an account of the working of the language to which it relates, then, it seems, it must embody an explanation of all the concepts expressible in that language. . . Hence, if a theory of meaning is a theory of understanding, as I have claimed, it would appear to follow that such a theory of meaning must, in *explaining what one must know* in order to know the meaning of each expression in the language, simultaneously *explain* what it is to have the concepts expressible by means of that language [my emphasis].[29]

Why should we accept this? According to John McDowell, a Fellow of University College, Oxford, Dummett demands too much of a theory of meaning. Dummett conceives of speakers of a language as manifesting *implicit* knowledge of the theory. The ability to speak a language is a practical ability: it is a knowledge *how* to do something. The point of a theory of meaning, for Dummett, is to provide a theoretical representation of this practical ability. Of course the speaker need not explicitly know the theory in order to be able to speak, but we can view his ability to speak as a manifestation of an implicit knowledge of the theory. That is why the theory must be so explanatory: it must tell us what a native speaker must know in order to understand an expression.

The idea that a theory of meaning should be seen as an explicit statement of what every native speaker implicitly knows is one McDowell urges us to reject.[30] For one is easily misled into viewing native speakers as proceeding according to the rules of the theory which they have somehow internalized. If we picture the theory as internalized, as providing us with the rules we follow when we ordinarily speak, then of course the rules could not be given to us linguistically. For it would only be by having already internalized them that we could understand them.

However, a theory of meaning should have little to do with what is going on "inside" a speaker. A theory of meaning for a language ought to enable someone who explicitly knew the theory to understand speakers of the language. Someone who explicitly knew the theory could, by manipulation of the theory, come to understand what native speakers were saying. This is not the way native speakers come to understand each other: they unreflectively comprehend what their fellow native speakers are saying. The theory should provide *a* way of coming to understand speakers, not *the* way speakers use in ordinary discourse.

How speakers come to exercise linguistic competence is an interesting psychological question; and it is for psychologists to answer it. The point of a theory of meaning, for McDowell, is to describe linguistic competence, not to explain how it is exercised. If a computer with a very different internal makeup from our own were able to speak English, the theory of meaning should be able to interpret its utterances as it does those of any other English-speaker. The question of how the computer came to have the ability or how it manages to exercise it, while of deep psychological interest, would be irrelevant to a theory of meaning. Dummett often insists on this himself,[31] but McDowell contends that the desire to view a theory as implicit knowledge leads Dummett into a contradictory position. If we think of the theory of meaning as something native speakers implicitly know, it becomes tempting to see native speakers as guided by the theory. But this is to fall victim to the very psychologism Dummett condemns: it is, in effect, to postulate an internal mechanism for which we have no empirical evidence.

Dummett demands that a theory be able to explain, for each sentence, what it is to know the meaning of that sentence. This demand for an explanation is essentially a demand for a reduction. Dummett condemns as unexplanatory the attempt to use the language to describe what someone understands by a sentence. The theory must give us some behavioral manifestation of what it is to know the sentence. The theory must provide some sort of *reduction* of language to nonlinguistic behavior. One's understanding of a sentence is manifested in the activity of verifying it. Reductionism, in one guise or another, has been fashionable since the heady days of Vienna. It is Dummett's own brand of reductionism that McDowell finds objectionable, and it stems directly from Dummett's demand that a theory of meaning ought to state the implicit knowledge of a native speaker.

Language is a public tool for communication and so, for a given sentence, one ought to be able to manifest what one understands by it. However, what counts as a manifestation is not settled in advance of a theory of meaning. There is scope for construing manifestation broadly or narrowly. Dummett wants to construe manifestation narrowly, but it is worth noting just how slippery is the slope on which he wishes to take his stand. According to Dummett, one is supposed to manifest one's understanding of a sentence by verifying it. But in fact we go through life without verifying most of the sentences we uncontentiously take to be true or false. For example, consider the sentence, 'The Mona Lisa is hanging in the Louvre.' This seems to be a paradigm decidable sentence. Even if I do not know whether it is true, I do know what I would have to do to find out—and this is a task I could *in principle* carry out: I could go to the Louvre and look. So I do know the sentence is true or false, even if I do not know which. Or do I? Suppose I cannot afford the trip to France, or that I have a dreadful fear of traveling. What does it mean to say that it is a task I could in principle perform? Well, one might say, other people could in principle go to the Louvre and look. But why should my linguistic abilities have anything to do with the tasks other people can perform? According to Dummett, I am not allowed to call on God's ability to see into the past to justify my knowledge that the past is determinate, that sentences about it are true or false. Why should I be able to call on the ability of other people to see into the Louvre to justify my knowledge that a sentence about the Mona Lisa is true or false, even if I do not know which? It is no good answering that God's abilities, in contrast to the abilities of other people, are very unlike my own. If other people can travel to the Louvre, while I cannot, then their abilities may appear to me to be radically different than mine. In short, there is no fixed answer to what we could in principle verify. If we wish to take a verificationist argument to its radical extreme, it begins to look as though the only sentences which are in principle decidable are those sentences which have been or will be decided by me.[32] If pushed, Dummett's verificationism seems to collapse into a radical solipsism.

If we decline the reductionist gambit, then Dummett's argument loses much of its force. We are freed from the obligation to provide for each sentence taken individually a purely behavioral manifestation of what it is to understand it. That we do not know how to verify a particular undecidable sentence does not necessarily imply that we do not know what it is for it to be true. For example, we can take an understanding of a particular past tense sentence to be manifested in a competence with the past tense as a whole.[33] Even if we do not know whether *that* sentence is true or false, our experience of the past and overall reaction to it—linguistic and nonlinguistic—counts as a manifestation of our knowledge that the past is determinate: it manifests our knowledge that the past tense sentence is true or false, even if we do not know which.

I can both imagine and sympathize with Dummett's frustration with this response. If we assume we understand the language, how is a *critical* theory of meaning possible? How could we ever come to criticize our own usage? How could we ever discover that we do not have a clear idea of what we mean by a sentence? Dummett stands in a great philosophical tradition which tries to offer a critique of thought; his own critique is filtered through a concern for language. A verification theory of meaning is vital to Dummett's program, for it enables him to criticize language and thought. The inability to verify an undecidable sentence is supposed to reveal that we cannot mean by it what we, perhaps naively, think we mean. Dummett thinks that unless we go along with his reductionism a critical theory of meaning is impossible: we simply have to say that in order to understand the language one must already understand the language. This, in Dummett's view, is to admit defeat in the philosophy of language. Since we are still in the early days of theorizing about meaning, Dummett thinks defeatism premature.[34]

Defeatism *is* premature, but even more premature is Dummett's conviction that in abandoning reductionism we are abandoning critical philosophy. From the assumption that we must understand the language about which we are theorizing, it does not follow that we must accept the language uncritically as spoken. Nor does it follow that we must abandon any systematic inquiry into what we understand when we understand a language.[35] To show exactly how one can criticize language while using it would be to show how a nonpositivist theory of meaning is possible. And that, I think, would be a valuable contribution from the current generation of young philosophers.[36]

REFERENCES
   [1] A. J. Ayer, *Language, Truth and Logic* (Harmondsworth, England: Penguin Books, 1971), p. 41.
   [2] Ibid., p. 71.
   [3] W. V. O. Quine, "Two Dogmas of Empiricism," in *From a Logical Point of View* (New York: Harper and Row, 1963), pp. 42-43.
   [4] W. V. O. Quine, *Word and Object* (Cambridge, Mass.: MIT Press, 1970), pp. 26-27.

[5]W. V. O. Quine, "Ontological Relativity," in *Ontological Relativity and Other Essays* (New York: Columbia University Press, 1969), p. 48.

[6]Ibid., pp. 33-34.

[7]W. V. O. Quine, "Epistemology Naturalized," in *Ontological Relativity*, pp. 80-81.

[8]Quine, "Epistemology Naturalized," p. 82.

[9]Quine, *Word and Object*, p. 27.

[10]Ibid., section 8.

[11]See Crispin Wright, "Language-Mastery and the Sorites Paradox," in G. Evans and J. McDowell, eds. *Truth and Meaning: Essays in Semantics* (Oxford: Clarendon Press, 1976).

[12]Cf. *Word and Object*, pp. 125-128.

[13]Ibid., p. 31.

[14]Ibid., section 15.

[15]Ibid.

[16]See G. Evans and J. McDowell, "Introduction," *Truth and Meaning;* D. Davidson, "Radical Interpretation," *Dialectica* (1973). Compare, e.g., *Word and Object*, pp. 59, 78.

[17]Quine, "Ontological Relativity", pp. 48-49.

[18]A. Tarski, "The Concept of Truth in Formalized Languages," *Logic, Semantics and Metamathematics*, (Oxford: Clarendon Press, 1956).

[19]See Saul A. Kripke, "Outline of a Theory of Truth," *The Journal of Philosophy* (1975).

[20]Quine, "Epistemology Naturalized," pp. 82-83.

[21]See Richard Rorty, "A World Well Lost," *The Journal of Philosophy* (1972). For an application of this insight to moral philosophy, see John McDowell, "Are Moral Requirements Hypothetical Imperatives?" *Proceeding of the Aristotelian Society, Supplementary Volume* (1978).

[22]Or we could *stretch* our conception of the physical, which after all is not a hard and fast notion, to encompass the evidence needed to explain language-mastery.

[23]Quine, "Epistemology Naturalized," pp. 80-81.

[24]Michael Dummett, "What Is a Theory of Meaning?" in Samuel Guttenplan, ed., *Mind and Language* (Oxford: Clarendon Press, 1977), pp. 98-99; "The Significance of Quine's Indeterminacy Thesis," *Truth and Other Enigmas* (London: Duckworth, 1978).

[25]Cf., e.g., W. V. O. Quine, "The Problem of Meaning in Linguistics," in *From a Logical Point of View*, pp. 47-64.

[26]Michael Dummett, *Frege: Philosophy of Language* (London: Duckworth, 1973), pp. 92-95; "What Is a Theory of Meaning?" pp. 99-101; "What Is a Theory of Meaning? (II)" in *Truth and Meaning*, pp. 69-71.

[27]Dummett, "What Is a Theory of Meaning? (II)" pp. 69-71.

[28]Cf. e.g. Michael Dummett, *Elements of Intuitionism* (Oxford: Clarendon Press, 1977), pp. 375-380; "What Is a Theory of Meaning? (II)" pp. 98-101.

[29]Dummett, "What Is a Theory of Meaning?", p. 101.

[30]See John McDowell, "On the Sense and Reference of a Proper Name," *Mind* (1977), and "On 'The Reality of the Past,' " in P. Pettit and C. Hookway, (eds.), *Action and Interpretation* (Cambridge: Cambridge University Press, 1978).

[31]Cf. e.g. Dummett, *Frege: Philosophy of Language*, p. 681, and "What Is a Theory of Meaning? (II)," pp. 70-71.

[32]A similar point is made by Colin McGinn in "Truth and Use," forthcoming in M. Platts, ed., *Essays in Philosophy of Language* (London: Routledge and Kegan Paul, 1979). In the philosophy of mathematics this position is advocated by strict finitists. See A. S. Yesenin-Volpin, "The Ultraintuitionistic Criticism and the Antitraditional Program for the Foundations of Mathematics," in A. Kino, J. Myhill, and R. Vesley, eds. *Intuitionism and Proof Theory* (Amsterdam: North Holland, 1970).

[33]John McDowell, "On 'The Reality of the Past.' "

[34]Cf. e.g. Michael Dummett, "The Justification of Deduction," in *Truth and Other Enigmas*, p. 309.

[35]Dummett conflates these beliefs in his discussions of holism in the philosophy of language. Cf. e.g. "The Justification of Deduction," pp. 302-305, 309, "What Is a Theory of Meaning?" p. 115; "What Is a Theory of Meaning? (II)" pp. 79ff; *Frege: Philosophy of Language*, pp. 593ff; *Elements of Intuitionism*, pp. 3, 365-367. Dummett's remarks on holism are extremely confusing and deserve detailed criticism. I believe that Dummett offers valuable criticisms of certain theses advanced by Quine and Davidson, but that he unfairly assumes that these criticisms will apply to any theory of meaning which does not take verification as its central concept.

[36]I would like to thank Cynthia Farrar and Jennifer Hornsby for offering extensive comments on the initial draft, and John Dunn, Quentin Skinner, Timothy Smiley, and Bernard Williams for taking the time to read and discuss a later version.

HAROLD R. ISAACS

Bringing up the Father Question

THERE CAME A TIME in my middle forties when I first began to notice that almost all writing about fathers and sons was done by sons. Our shelves are filled with what I came to call son novels in which writers across the generations have tried to deal with the experience of wrenching free from their fathers or have written sad or tender memoirs about what their fathers were like as they finally came to remember them. Samuel Butler's *The Way of All Flesh* can stand as a more or less classic model of the first, and the one that comes to mind as an example of the latter is James T. Farrell's *Father and Son*. Where, I began to wonder, were all the father novels, the father plays, the father poems, in which fathers speak for themselves? Had I in my earlier years, not being tuned to the necessary wavelength, simply missed all there was about fathers going through the other side of this experience of conflict, rejection, changing relationship? What had happened to all these son-writers when they had become fathers themselves and had run the course of the experience through to the time when *their* sons had become adults? Where was this experience recreated as seen through fathers' eyes, felt at fathers' nerve ends, carried on through to fathers' outcomes?

Surely, I thought, it had to be there, ready to be discovered when one was finally ready to discover it. I began to look, but only through the corner of my eye turned once in a while from other working/writing concerns. I began to ask, but only now and then through the years, when at odd times I would put my question to better-learned, better-read friends. I came to expect the first rush of a ready answer and then the nonplussedness as the thrust of the question came more slowly home: where was the writing about the father-son theme as it unfolds between fathers and growing and grown sons written *from the fathers' point of view*? Then would come a slower, more puzzled reaching into the stacks of memory and the most common first mentions: the Old Testament, that great father book, the Greeks and their gory generational myths, Turgenev's *Fathers and Sons* (which is essentially a son book that is kinder to fathers than it is to sons), Lear. After that would come a few snatches here and there, references that would go in scribbled notes into folders I kept to pursue when, if ever, I would take the time.

Speaking of Lear, I of course do not ignore how heavily daughters also figure in this matter, or mothers. There is a good deal of daughter writing about fathers and mothers; how much mother writing there is, with writers conveying mothers' sensations and perceptions, is another question. However, I have found that writing *about* mothers, especially in the scholarly and professional disciplines where these matters have been studied, far outruns what there is about fathers. I even have some computer-supplied numbers to illustrate this unsurprising fact. No, only at obvious perils of several kinds could one ignore mothers and daughters in dealing with our generational complexities. I have had the considerable influence of a mother of my own, a daughter, and most of all, my son's and my daughter's mother in shaping my own changing awarenesses of this subject. But the question I am raising just now has to do with fathers, with the remarkable rarity of the father's point of view in so much that has been written, whether as art or as "science," about the generational experience. I focus my question even more narrowly, moving it beyond the relations between fathers and small children—a subject on which there has been a newly swelling literature in recent years—to the father as he moves into his own ripening years and his children into their own mature adulthood.

I raise the question because having been a son and become a grandfather and having a sense of some tolerable grasp on both those roles, I still am pressed by questions about what it is to be a father. I found that none of the reading I had done or the conditioning I received in the several traditions of which I am heir had provided me with adequately usable or satisfying answers with which to inform my own experience. It may very well be in myself and not in the stars of my culture or its literature that I still have to seek such answers. But still I raise my question—and all I shall do here is raise it—in the spirit of setting out to discover what the mix might be. I do so also, obviously, because I think it has some general interest and application, particularly in the context of the present *Daedalus* volume. It used to bother some of my colleagues whenever I remarked that all inquiry is autobiographical, even, perhaps especially, in academic life, and maybe most of all in the so-called social sciences. Yet there could be no denying that all inquiry is subject to the nature of the inquirer. The distance between the questions he asks and the facts of his own life is a matter of individual particulars, even style. I hasten to add that I have no intention of inflicting any more explicit autobiography on these pages, but am simply noting that in my own case in this essay, that distance now becomes considerably narrower than it was during all the question-asking years I spent with all those other working/writing concerns.

The generational experience, to be sure, suffused those other concerns, which had mainly to do with the wars, revolutions, and nationalist movements of our time. I well remember being disconcerted one day nearly forty years ago by the bald view—in a little book by Arthur Koestler called *Arrivals and Departures*—that all revolution comes down in the end, the individual particular end, to an acting out of the revolt of sons against fathers. I thought that the politics that interested me came to more than that. But Koestler had also caught the full taste of the bitter ashes of this generational sequence in its Russian outcome where, in *Darkness at Noon*—as it was played on the stage—Rubashev, the Old Bolshevik, summoned for the last time from his Lubianka cell, pauses to look at the executioner-guard who has come for him. "My son," he greets him, and goes on out to be shot in the head, like so many other fathers of the revolution, devoured by their young.

In China, revolution began most literally and directly as rebellion against the authority of fathers encrusted in Confucian tradition and practice. Wrenching China around from its traditional past toward a modernizing future, a process underway for more than a century now, has been to a unique degree a matter of generational confrontation. In the lives of those who have figured in this history, ten hundred times ten thousand individual dramas have been played out on the larger stage of great events. Among these many actors, the name of Mao Tse-tung came eventually to lead all the rest. Of Mao as son we know little enough; of Mao as father, scarcely anything has ever been written. His children do not figure in the iconographic treatment of the hero by his army of reverent biographers. Only in Lucian Pye's psychobiographic study[1] have I seen brought together the remarkably scattered fragments about Mao's abandoning and ignoring of his children—no one is even sure how many there are— suggesting a Mao who never wanted to be a father to his sons and daughters, deserting and expending them one after another as he went his way toward becoming the Heaven-Mandated Father of his People instead.

Before Mao, there was Chiang Kai-shek, who seized and held that mandate himself for awhile, and whose son, Chiang Ching-kuo, now holds a minitoken of it, successor to his father as ruler of a phantom Chinese Republic on the island of Taiwan. Of what lay between this father and this son across these years a strong tale waits to be fashioned, a peculiarly dramatic example of the point and counterpoint of personal and political generational change and conflict in the Chinese experience of this century. In 1927 from Moscow, where Chiang Kai-shek had sent him to study the new revolutionary ways, son Ching-kuo bitterly denounced his father for the betrayal and mass slaughter through which he became ruler of the land. At that moment of his victory, like many another Chinese rebel before him, Chiang Kai-shek put aside his first, traditional wife, mother of Ching-kuo, and married the modern and well-connected Mei-ling Soong instead. After some years, came reconciliation between father and son, Ching-kuo returning to become a member of his father's staff, then war, victory over Japan swiftly turned into defeat at the hands of the Communists, flight to Taiwan. There followed years of living together in their palace-in-exile in Taiwan, the family group made up of Chiang Kai-shek and the wife who had displaced Ching-kuo's mother, Ching-kuo and the Russian wife who had come back with him from Moscow, a setting and a cast in which art could scarcely be expected ever to outdo nature, the story ending with Ching-kuo's coming into the shrunken legacy of the power he had once so despised his father for winning. Across the strait in China itself, meanwhile, the Chinese Communist "sons" of their Russian Communist "fathers" had gone through a generational severance of their own and were proceeding to make China over, as far as they could, in their own shifting image.

A comparably dramatic generational treatment of the Indian political experience of this century also waits to be done in a study of the Nehrus, Motilal the patriarch, Jawaharlal the son, Jawaharlal's daughter Indira, and Indira's son Sanjay. The father-son-daughter-son dynamics of this family story are intimately woven into the main design of this history, nationalism born, burgeoning, rampant, triumphant, decaying—from ripening to rotting in four generations. Even more striking, possibly, are the dynamics of the Gandhi story, the story of Gandhi the saint and political leader and the story of Gandhi the son, husband, and—most fleetingly touched in the great mass of mostly reverent literature about him—Gandhi the father. Gandhi wrote more about himself as son than most of his admiring biographers have wanted to know. Very few of them have been able to show much of this Gandhian-style candor in dealing with Gandhi as father of his sons. The difficulty admirers have had in dealing with this theme is notably illustrated by the quality of stifled anguish in the treatment given to it by Erik Erikson in *Gandhi's Truth*, a matter worth pursuing in more space than we have for it here, especially since we must shortly come to Erikson again on the same subject in another context.

But whether in China or India or across all of Asia and Africa, the generational theme remains a master key to much recent history. With it one passes from the prenationalist fathers who submitted to foreign dominance to the nationalist sons who defied their fathers to challenge it and who now have been largely displaced by *their* postnationalist sons and daughters.[2] No one can count the numbers of fathers slain in near or distant defiles across these many passages or the crimes subsequently committed, knowingly or unknowingly, by their young slayers. Nor is there any oracle to say what has been gain or loss, who has been victor or who victim. In this history too, as in so much else, the question is how much of it we may yet hear from surviving fathers themselves, or will they too, as fathers seem to do, leave the writing of it to their sons?

The question here has to do with the rarity of literature about the fathers' experience as seen from the father's point of view. Pursuit of this question also turns up a not uncommon pattern of slighting, scanting, or ignoring the subject altogether, even in work where one might expect it to have an important place. Consider, appropriately enough, the example of two recent issues of *Daedalus*, "The Family" (Spring 1977) and "Adulthood" (Spring 1976).

(Apropos of *Daedalus* in this connection, it is impossible not to cite here the myth as set down by Robert Graves wherein Daedalus, escaping the wrath of Minos, fashioned those waxed wings for himself and his son Icarus and warned the boy not to fly too high or too low. As they flew off, Daedalus cried out to his son: "Follow me closely, do not set your own course!"[3] There is plainly nothing new under the sun that melts the wax on the wings of disobedient or heedless sons. The lesson has to be that *Daedalus* has even less call than most to be scanting or avoiding the subject of fatherhood.)

Of the twelve articles in the issue on "The Family," only one deals with "parenting" as such, though in a specifically limited way. The author was trying to remind feminist ultras of some physiological facts of life that put certain current life-style fads and notions "at odds with the biology of our species." That biology imposes its own greater demand on motherhood than on fatherhood, she points out, and anybody who wants to change things had better adjust his or her clocks to evolutionary time. An article entitled "The Child in the Family" is written explicitly "from the child's perspective"; the word "father" appears in it twice, both times in the same sentence in a quite inconsequential reference. In "Family Time and Historical Time," the author notes that in real time "a son becomes a father." This mention of a fact of family life is modest enough, but it has to serve as the only such through the next one hundred twenty pages (on family economic problems, the child-care debate, income support policies, housing, etc.) until we come to Hiroshi Wagatsuma's report on the current shift from "Confucian" to "fatherless" family styles in Japan. This finally does introduce the subject, after its fashion, though here too its many references come overwhelmingly, with only one or two exceptions, from material written by sons and daughters.

In the issue on "Adulthood," the object was to try to elevate the subject to the level of childhood and adolescence as a distinct subject worth separate scholarly attention. Its seven articles look at the matter from medical, philosophic, religious, and cultural points of view, locating it in a variety of settings, Christian, Islamic, Confucian, Japanese, Indian, Russian. The "medical" or biological treatment duly notes development of reproductive capacity as a feature of the passage to adulthood and refers briefly to Erikson's "generativity vs. stagnation" stage where the purpose is to create a next generation "by way of generativity and genes." But "the same purpose," the author hastens to add, "may also be achieved by some who forego parenthood and express their generativity through other altruistic and creative acts."

In somewhat the same spirit, most of the articles that follow deal mainly with standards of "maturity" as the prime feature of adulthood, taking us far aloft from the earthy business of becoming and being a parent. This is true even of the treatments of the "Confucian" and "Japanese" traditions. Both ascend to more general or abstract philosophic and cultural considerations, barely managing to mention the heavy concern in these cultures with actual fathers in actual families. The "Christian" and "Islamic" discussions are dominated by the religiously metaphoric use of the "father-child" relationship, the "father" God or his surrogate priest, and the "child" the obedient, faithful, submissive believer of whatever age. Not metaphorically but in a kind of evolutionary sequence, this too forms part of the stuff of Jung's father-archetype, which is associated with strength, power, and authority, as the mother is with all that is protecting, warming, nourishing. "As the growing consciousness becomes more capable of understanding . . . in the place of the father comes the society of men, and in the place of the mother, family and clan. Finally, instead of the father, the image of God appears . . ."[4] Christ, of course, was and is, before everything, a *Son* and the New Testament is the son book of all son books in our culture with incalculable effects on its concepts of fatherhood. The central character in the Islamic story is of an earthier sort, to be sure, but in neither of these particular studies is any attempt made to deal with the actualities of parenthood on earth except to suggest that it is subordinate to the Parenthood in heaven.

Similar elements appear in an article on Tolstoy and his Russia where the great masses of Russians were cast as children to all their assorted "little fathers"—their noble masters, the priests, and beyond them to the big Father himself in heaven. Tolstoy, a young man with "bull-like" sexual appetites, married and sired a manor full of children, went on to write of human growth and decay, finally concluded that human love led only to a dead end, that resurrection of the spirit lay in the embrace of a moral absolute. The author says that up to this point Tolstoy was "successful" as father as in everything else, but gives us no picture of this "success" at any stage. When he abandoned all, Tolstoy abandoned his children too, all except daughter Sasha, and took himself off into his sky-blue yonder.

The only authors in the collection who actually deal with adulthood in terms of family and the generational experience are Lloyd and Suzanne Rudolph, who report a diarist's description of life in a noble Rajput family of the turn of the century, and his passage, as he became an adult, through its various stages and levels. Here too, however, the stress is on his experience as a son, adjusting to the several varieties of parental or surrogate-paternal authority in the extended family system and the complexities of a mother-son relation that took precedence over that of husband-wife. Of Rajput Singh as father himself, we learn practically nothing.

The major contribution is by Erikson, whose vehicle for treatment of the theme of adulthood is Ingmar Bergman's film *Wild Strawberries*, an account of an old Swedish doctor's journey to receive honors crowning his lifetime of work. In a series of encounters and fantasies, the journey becomes one back into his childhood and through the stages of his life, in which Erikson finds a vivid illustration of his own view of the life cycle, its crises, its outcomes. "It demonstrates," he says, "how a significant moment in old age reaches back through a man's unresolved adulthood to the dim beginnings of his awareness as a child."

As so often in Erikson, there are glinting marvels of insight in his tracing of his own themes through the experience of old Dr. Borg as shown by Bergman. But what is remarkable is what he passes by as he goes. Bergman gives Dr. Borg's experience as a father only the most fleeting sidelong glance, and even then not in the old man's own fantasies or memories on this journey through his life, but only in a glimpse or two through the eyes of the young, his daughter-in-law, who thinks he's an ogre, and some youthful hitchhikers, who think he's beautiful.

To trace this single strand, let me, for economy's sake, focus on the single most relevant exchange. Borg is driving with his son Ewald's estranged wife Marianne. They are estranged because she is pregnant and Ewald does not want to have a child because his own childhood and the marriage of his parents were so wretched. Marianne has vainly tried to get Dr. Borg to help her. She keeps prodding the old man, making Erikson think "of Cordelia, driving Lear's despair to the surface." Erikson's account of what follows:

> It all begins . . . with small even petty items which yet betray basic attitudes. She, nervous, wants to smoke, he stops her, nastily . . . Suddenly she asks him his "real" age—for no "real" reason. But under the impact of his dream, he knows that she, too, wonders when he will die. Pettily, he still thinks of the money her husband owes him, pleads principle: "a bargain is a bargain." Ewald, he is sure, understands this for they are "alike," as she, indeed, admits they are. Then the bombshell: "But he also hates you." An indescribable horror appears on his face, but he keeps calm. Asked why she doesn't like him she (says) . . . she has now stayed with him a month with the "idiotic idea" that he might help Ewald and her, but that he had refused adamantly to hear about their marital trouble.[5]

In the published version of the screenplay there are some variations to be noted. In the exchange about smoking, in a line that Erikson passes over, Dr. Borg says smoking is a "manly vice" not for a woman. Marianne asks, "And what vices may a woman have?" Borg replies: "Crying, bearing children, and gossiping about neighbors." So much for children in the "unresolved" outlook of Dr. Borg. In the lines about the loan, Borg says, "I know that Ewald understands and respects me." She replies, "That may be true, but he also hates you." The Bergman text, written as first person narration by Borg, then goes on: "Her calm, almost matter-of-fact tone startled me. I tried to look into her eyes but she stared straight ahead." Borg says, "Ewald and I never coddled each other," and then, as his very next line, asks Marianne, "Tell me, what do you really have against me?"[6]

I do not know whether Erikson was writing from this or some other text of the screenplay, or whether that "horrified" look—merely "startled" in the text—was what he saw on the screen rather than in the text. In any case, we have here a rather remarkable sequence. Daughter-in-law tells old man his son hates him. At this "bombshell" either "indescribable horror" or a "startled" look comes on the old man's face. Although he is on this journey through his life, Borg does not ask why his son hates him, he makes no comment on it, does not move into any dream or fantasy that deals with it as he deals here with so much else in his life. No, he goes past it, or at least Bergman takes him past it, and Erikson, without remark, goes past Bergman going past it. And the old man turns to Marianne and asks why *she* doesn't like him. Next subject, next take. In the reliving of Borg's life, we never do see him as father, never do hear anything more about his son hating him or how he felt about it, only old Borg in his dream finally "finding" his own father and mother again, and "in a truly primal scene," winning a silent smile and wave from them before he enters upon his own problematic second childhood.

Presumably this tells us something about both Bergman and Erikson. Bergman clearly has his own "unresolved" problems about parenthood and love. In a film interview shown along with a recent TV replay of his *Scenes from a Marriage*, Bergman talked of his adolescence, how hatred had grown between him and his father, ending in a violent quarrel in which he knocked his father down and also hit his mother, leaving home that night not to see or speak to them again for four years. In a much milder passage, in his introduction to *Four Screenplays*, Bergman thanks his parents for creating "a world for me to revolt against." In his family "there was an atmosphere of hearty wholesomeness which I, a sensitive young plant, scorned and rebelled against." What he did get from his family, he goes on, were the values of "efficiency, punctuality, a sense of financial responsibility—which may be bourgeois but are nevertheless important to the artist."[7] The sensitive young plant apparently did not absorb any of that "hearty wholesomeness," it would appear, going on to make films which, if *Scenes from a Marriage* is a fair sample, are nonhearty to a degree. Indeed, the husband in *Scenes* is so childishly "unresolved" that he cannot even find a love to keep in a marriage with Liv Ullman, and neither he nor Liv appear capable of even playing the role of parents. Bergman "deals" with the existence of their children by keeping them out of sight. Bergman's own "unresolved" problems appear, it seems, no matter what the age or stage of his chosen characters.

Erikson, for his part, has always recognized that as inquirer he is undetachable from his inquiry, indeed he is almost always close to the center of it. His personal experience, his preoccupations, his identifications fill many of his pages as he has tried, more than most, to be as forthcoming as he could with his reader on this score while unfolding and refining his concept of the life cycle. Thus again, in his article on *Wild Strawberries*, he notes and lightly turns aside the "friendly suspicions" of some of his Harvard students that he was in some fashion identifying himself with Dr. Borg. "I can only register such suspicion," he writes, "as an essential aspect of any conception of the whole of life; for can our concepts and can our terms ever transcend the observations and values that are part of our limited existence—and of the illustrations that we chose?"[8] At the same time, Erikson has elsewhere disarmingly acknowledged the limits of candor. "Nobody likes to be found out," he wrote in a 1970 essay, "not even one who has made ruthless confession a part of his profession. Any autobiographer, therefore, at least between the lines, spars with his reader and potential judge."[9]

There is no intent here to spar with Erikson as "reader" much less as "potential judge"; he needs no one, surely not this question-asker, to drive any of *his* despairs to any surface. Yet it is precisely because Erikson has supplied so much insight into so much that he opens himself more than most to questions on the issues of fatherhood raised here. From his own occasional autobiographic references, it is plain that Erikson has constructions of his own to deal with when it comes both to sonhood and fatherhood. There is his "stepson identity."[10] There are his identifications with Freud and Gandhi, both occurring at certain distances, giving to both, he suggests, the "mythical" quality he assigns to his own unknown natural father.[11] In Gandhi, he tells us, he sought a "spiritual fatherhood" and as *Gandhi's Truth* indicates on so many of its pages, this became a most intense identification indeed, all the more remarkable in view of the clashing sets of values in this encounter. Erikson as aspiring prophet himself could identify with Gandhi the saint. But as everything we know about Gandhi as husband and father suggests, and as Erikson himself clearly shows in his "Dear Mahatmaji" letter in *Gandhi's Truth*, this "spiritual" identification had to be able to transcend almost every other value we must assume Erikson to hold, as an analyst, and as man, husband, and father himself. Perhaps some closer reader of Erikson's work and all his self-scrutiny, perhaps Erikson himself in adding to it, will provide a clearer picture than we now seem to have of how Erikson does perceive the father theme, the father experience.

Of course there has been a great deal written *about* fathers, not as much by far as about mothers, but still quite a bit. My own first reconnaissances made years ago across the cluttered study-strewn fields of psychology and sociology turned up many pages of titles which appear at least to have touched on the father subject from almost every conceivable angle, and some inconceivable, and from almost every point of view except the particular one that interests me. I am bound to say that the quantities of wrecked, useless, obsolete, and just plain forgotten material on these scarred landscapes is staggering. Broken slabs of impenetrable prose and shattered tables of loose statistics lie about everywhere and severed coefficients hang rotting forlornly from every scraggly bush.

In literature about child-rearing, notes an unusual father-focused review written in 1965, "attention given to fathers is scant indeed." In much of it, the word "father" never appeared at all, and "only distantly and indistinctly" when it did, even then hardly ever being assigned any "essential or crucial importance." "Fathers, it would seem," this author concluded, "are generally undervalued, at least by psychologists, in our culture. The strong interest in mothers to the neglect of fathers seems to have a long history in technical writings."[12]

Actually, a whole new body of writing about fathers was beginning to appear having to do, symbolically enough, with fathers who were not there. The separations of World War II had produced an interest in the effect of the *absent* father in young families. This interest has continued, fed by the steeply rising numbers of fatherless families at the lower ends of the socioeconomic scale, joined more recently by many at the higher ends of that scale as a result of the mounting divorce rates. But in this time also, *present* fathers began to appear in new roles. Some of those returning absentees of the 1940s and 1950s began to take part in new ways in the shared nurturing of their small children. This too gets reflected in more recent literature, including all sorts of how-to books and articles written especially for fathers. A late addition to this sequence is the appearance of divorced or never-married fathers as heads of single-parent families being created by what are called changing life-styles. One way or another, this appearance of the father in a nurturing role is a "new" fact of uncertain dimension, durability, and meaning, a harbinger perhaps, though of none-can-yet-say-what. Bibliographically speaking, however, this new nurturant father gets swamped in the much greater flood of more recent writing about fathers who inflict many kinds of trauma, wounds, and disabilities on their children in matters of sex, alcoholism, drugs, neurosis, mental illness, etc. Whether they are benign or otherwise, all this literature, with only the rarest exceptions, deals with fathers only in relation to small children and adolescents.

There would be very little use or point for me to try here to review or examine in any detail the results of the bibliographical prospecting that I have done, or had done for me, from time to time in parts of this social scientific territory. Still, it is worth reporting that it covered quite a bit of ground. It includes a check of the tables of contents of a number of journals for the years 1930-1964, the Cumulative Book Index for 1928-1965, and Psychological Abstracts for 1936 to 1963. In 1970 I had a culling done of the treatment of the father-subject in the twelve then most currently used psychology textbooks and readers. Reporting the overwhelmingly heavy focus in all these works on the childhood years, my searcher dryly remarked in her report: "Psychology textbooks lose track of the individual at an early age."

As a result of a chance conversation, I undertook quite recently to expand and update this hand-dug file by seeing what would turn up if I put my question to a computerized data bank. Whatever else was not impressive about this search, the numbers surely were. They dwarfed those in my earlier tries. My question now went to a machine that had stored in its memory a total of 240,000 Psychological Abstracts taken from some 900 periodicals and 1,500 books and reports published since 1967; 490,000 references "from the 1,000 most important social science journals throughout the world" published since 1972; and 80,000 Sociological Abstracts taken from more than 1,200 journals published since 1963. This stored mass testifies to the enormous inflation of the quantity of such work over these years without any provision in the machine itself for anything resembling quality control.

The problem, however, was not the quantity or even the quality. The problem was my question. What I sought, I explained to the M.I.T. librarian, were titles bearing on relations between fathers and adolescent and grown sons written from the father's point of view, that is, as seen through the father's eyes. I would also be glad, I added (waxing eager and greedy at the thought of all that massed stuff in the computer's brain), to have anything similarly on relations between fathers and daughters, mothers and sons, mothers and daughters, again dealt with in each case from the father's or mother's point of view. The librarian patiently explained that there was no way of posing such a question to the mindless machine at the other end. It could provide only what assorted indexers had supplied it, and there was no indication in the index manuals before her that any had ever thought of my subject in quite that way. I had to add, as the ultimate drawback, that I doubted whether any writers had ever thought of it this way either.

The exercise produced some interesting if not very usable numbers. By one indicator among the Psychological Abstracts, for example, we learned there were 4,860 entries on "parents," 2,889 on "mothers," and 937 on "fathers." In another combination of items in the index, the mother count outdid the father count 5,241 to 2,104. There was no way of knowing, however, what these numbers actually represented. By a process of trying to "tease out" some index "descriptors" that might apply, we got, in two forays at the machine, a total of 1,329 citations from the Psychological Abstracts, 406 from the Sociological Abstracts, and 291 from the "social science" bank. This great fallout of titles and reference included a mass of subjects I had tried to get the machine to exclude. I learned that while you might ask it not to send you any titles about "absent fathers" it would send you everything it had on "father absence." You could ask it to pass over anything about babies, infants, preschool or school-age children or preadolescents, but it would still give you all it could about "two-year-olds" or "four-year-olds" or any-year-olds. You could exclude "drug abuse" but still get any title that mentioned fathers along with "LSD" or "heroin" or "cocaine." I tried not to get titles about "mental illness," but I did get dozens about "schizophrenia." It was at least reassuring to discover that artificial intelligence is, so far, considerably less intelligent than the other kind.

The librarian had asked at the outset whether I had an "ideal article" to base my inquiry on. If so, the machine could more or less instantly produce for me a list of every book or article in which the "ideal" item had ever been footnoted, thereby supplying me with material that had to fall somewhere in my territory. Unfortunately, I had no "ideal article" and indeed had no idea at that point that a few months later, at the instance of the editor of *Daedalus*, I would be trying to write the beginning of one.

A first scan of this immense mountain of material turns up nothing even remotely "ideal," no nuggets, only a few glints in the gravel. There is more here than anyone is ever likely to need to know about how the literature of the clinical and social sciences have dealt with the father theme in these years in these places. As I pore over the massed titles, summaries, abstracts and go digging now and then into the heaps of xeroxed articles that are also part of this file, I must assume that I might yet, poking at it all with my small handpick, suddenly hit it rich, hit the father-lode, so to speak, come upon some father writing, perhaps even some mother writing, to put alongside all these huge piles produced by so many sons and daughters. But I have to confess that as I peer uncertainly up and down these Sierra Madre-like slopes, the configurations do not look encouraging.

The glints in the computer's gravel were there, 42 titles out of the 1,329 received that looked as though they might in some way brush my inquiry with at least a glancing reply, or perhaps simply be worth reading for their own sake. And indeed, after being dug out the old-fashioned way, "by hand," a few did, a few were—11 to be exact. One most promising title, "Imitation in the Family: A Study of Older Parents and Their Older Sons," unhappily delivered nothing on the promise. Another, "Fathers and Sons: The Interlocking Crises of Integrity and Identity," reported, as though it were a brand-new discovery, that in 11 cases of family therapy the therapists recognized that the boy's crisis was taking place at the same time as the middle-aged father's crisis of integrity. Two enterprising students from Taiwan examined the family story themes in 200 traditional Chinese operas, coming up with the information that mother-son stories, full of warmth and affection, outnumbered the father-son stories, full of mutual hostility, and that husband-wife stories, full of troubles, outnumbered them all. A study of the childhood of Vissarion Belinsky, described as the model for the central character of Bazarov in Turgenev's *Fathers and Sons*, makes the point that "the warm nurturant attitude of the elder Bazarov stands in stark contrast to the cold, distant, even hostile attitude characteristic of Russian fathers in the 19th century."

An essay entitled "Understanding Fathers in Jewish Fiction," drawing on assorted son novels by Jewish writers, argues that the Jewish mother has not, as rumored, replaced the Jewish father, who remains a sympathetic figure, even in failure and rejection, and is still the transmitter of the moral tradition that sets the sons on the path to becoming fathers themselves. (In *World of Our Fathers*, which is altogether a son's loving memoir to a whole generation of fathers, Irving Howe deals all too briefly with the intense father-son conflict generated by the wrenching culture shifts between the migrant fathers and their swiftly assimilating sons. "The distance between generations came to be like a chasm of silence which neither affection nor goodwill could bridge," Howe writes, reporting the experience almost entirely in the words of sons, among them this haunting passage about a silent father from a story called "My Father Sits in the Dark," by Jerome Weidman: "A son speaks, troubled that each night his immigrant father 'sits in the dark, alone, smoking, staring straight ahead of him.' The father sits in the kitchen on an uncomfortable chair. 'What are you thinking about, Pa?' 'Nothing.' 'Is something wrong, Pop?' 'Nothing, son, nothing at all.' " Coming home late one night, the son "can see the deeper darkness of his [father's] hunched shape. He is sitting in the same chair, his elbows on his knees, his cold pipe in his teeth, his unblinking eyes staring straight ahead. There is nothing to be said, neither quarrel nor reconciliation. 'What do you think about, Pop?' 'Nothing,' answers the father, 'nothing special.' ")[13]

The items that had the closest bearing on my question were several articles written generally in the psychoanalytic tradition though from several different points of view. The single most relevant glint among these occurs in "The Father-Son Conflict in *Prometheus Unbound*," by Leon Waldoff. Shelley's son poem came out of his unresolved conflict with his father which, the author points out, colored his whole life and underlay much of his poetry. What gleamed here for

me, however, was not Waldoff's psychoanalytic interpretation of the Prometheus story or Shelley's treatment of it, but his unusual remarks about son
writing itself. That we get what we think we know about father-son conflicts
almost entirely from the testimony of sons is something that is rarely noted.
Waldoff not only notes it, but provides a psychoanalytic explanation for it. In
Shelley's poem, he writes,

> we are taken into the consciousness of the son only. In Aeschylus' *Prometheus
> Bound*, Zeus makes no appearance, and in Shelley's play only a brief one. In most
> literary father-son conflicts, from *Oedipus Rex* to the autobiographies and *Bil-
> dungsromane* of the last two centuries, we are given an account of the son's suf-
> ferings only. The reason, of course, is that literature has been written primarily by
> sons, or by that anguished, tortured, "bound" side of the adult self that still feels
> and thinks like a child. Though fathers may begin the hostility, as Jupiter and
> Laius did, the essential burden of the conflict falls inevitably on the son. The
> father cannot solve his son's Oedipal problems for him, even if he should want, not
> even by dying, or perhaps especially not by dying. As a result, literary heroes are
> almost invariably sons, and the dragons they slay, or the tyrants they overcome, or
> the moral and social problems they solve, are often symbols of paternal tyranny.[14]

This touchés close to the core of my inquiry. Oedipus, the literary hero of
Oedipus Rex, the Oedipus of the Complex, the central character in the human
story as written for us by Freud, is a *son*. Oedipus is the son who killed his
father at that crossroads and who went on to commit incest with his mother. In
the psychodrama that Freud fashioned out of this ancient myth, Laius, the slain
father, remains a most marginal figure, playing only a bit role. As Erich Fromm
and others began pointing out many years ago, Freud based his use of the myth
solely on the first play of the Sophocles trilogy, *Oedipus the King*. Even so, he
"ignored" the key fact fully unfolded in that play, namely that at the beginning
of the story, to escape the oracle's curse that his son would be his slayer, Laius
cast the infant Oedipus out to die. In Freud, Laius simply became the father
whose son killed him, as those first sons killed that father in Freud's primal
horde, as sons forever after, in the Complex, would at a tender age want to "kill"
their fathers for "love" of their mothers.

Freud not only ignored that father of Oedipus but also ignored Oedipus as
father himself, the tragic, indomitable figure of the second play, *Oedipus at Co-
lonnus*, cruelly abandoned by his sons to die in his wandering blindness, hating
them unforgivingly for it, fiercely rejecting responsibility for the crimes he had
so unwittingly committed—an "innocence" denied to him in the Freudian unconscious but granted to him at the end by his gods—attended only by faithful
daughters to whom his last words were about love and whose future care was
his final concern. Freud similarly "overlooked" the reprise of the bitterly violent
father-son theme in the third play, *Antigone*.

The formula that Freud created so selectively out of this ancient material
became one of the most commonly used and most loosely understood code-
words in our culture for the complexities of the generational experience. It has
been challenged and modified by critics[15] and by virtually all but the most
faithful practitioners of the rules Freud had handed down on his tablets. The
sheer weight of the greatness of Freud's core achievement—making us conscious
of the unconscious—has kept the Oedipus complex proof, in name if not in

substance, against numerous efforts to supplement or balance or displace it with other "complexes" drawn from the same myth, or variations of it borrowed from other ancient sources. Every educated person in the Western world, and many beyond it, knows about the "Oedipus complex" although for the most part the way they know it would hardly please or satisfy its creator. But who knows or has ever, outside a tiny circle, heard of the Laius complex, the Jocasta complex, the Polyneices complex, the Medea complex, the Orestes complex, the Electra complex, the Lear complex, the Abraham complex, the Isaac complex, or the Joseph complex? How many readers of Matthew Arnold's son poem "Sohrab and Rustum" know that one of Freud's more recent challengers has made a "Rustum complex" out of it? Yet all of these, and who knows how many others, have been nominated at one time or another to stand alongside or dislodge Freud's still-ruling Oedipus complex. So far as I could discover, they continue to exist only in their own slender critical tradition, preserved in seldom-consulted journal volumes or stored away in the infinitely capacious darkened innards of computerized data banks.[16]

One common theme in this critical literature places father-son conflict, not incest, at the center of the complexity.[17] Another puts the Oedipus myth in the setting of that titanic struggle through which the mother gods and matriarchal society were displaced by father gods and the patriarchal society.[18] Another major argument is that the burden placed by Freud on sons belongs more accurately on fathers, that fathers' hostility toward sons (based on fear of death, displacement) is far more salient in the human story than sons' hostility toward fathers (based, as Freud would have it, on rivalry for the mother, castration fear, or on the reach for power). This argument draws heavily on the generational myths of the gods from Uranus to Cronus to Zeus and is traced through similar themes in the mythologies and histories of many cultures.[19] One author who holds for father hostility as the true centerpiece of human experience—he is the creator of the "Rustum complex"—carries the matter down into our own time, arguing that the Oedipus complex has helped "to provide an aura of scientific support for the adult generation's attempt to present generational conflict in terms of the faults and failings of the young." He applies this reading not only to how the father reacts to his "son's hostile emotions during the Oedipal stage" but also to adult reaction to the youth movements of recent years.[20]

What strikes me most strongly on reading such material now in its many varieties is the sense of how much else there is in the universe of father experience and feeling that is simply not included here. There is more in it, if I may use a phrase from a great son play that encroaches on the psychoanalytic method itself, than these practitioners apparently dream of, and one can be sure they dream a great deal. The distortion comes partly no doubt from the clinically focused purposes in much of this work, the concern being with pathology and its sources, not with the health that surprisingly many people do manage to maintain in matters of love and generation, in marriages and in families. Part of the skew also comes from the generalizing so irresistibly produced by the effort to create all-inclusive formulas to explain the whole human experience. Too much of the reality continues to drop through great holes in the nets in which the formula-makers—even great ones like Freud or Marx—try to catch it all.

This includes much of the reality in the varieties of father experience. These may often be lived out more in pain than in pleasure, but still there is a lot more than "son-hostility" or "father-hostility" in what lies between fathers and sons, far more than the fear of displacement or death in the weave of what a father makes of his relations with a son as that son moves on from childhood into his own adulthood.[21]

In this question-raising exercise, I have referred, by no measure adequately or conclusively, only to literature of the academic and clinical disciplines. I did this for several reasons, but mainly because I could not yet at this point deal with real literature, or the literature of the real world, from which I expect and intend to discover a great deal more. To have drawn from it now, I would have had to rely on what I could remember of the reading of many years. Memory is, in general, untrustworthy, but to rely on it in this case would have hopelessly defeated my purpose. For it is precisely my point that it would never have occurred to me to raise my present question when I first read the shaping works of our literary tradition, because when I did, my perceptions were still those of a *son*. That is why I propose now to retrace my way and reread all that I can to see what I discover in them with my sixty-eight-year-old vision that I simply did not see when I passed that way many years ago as boy, youth, man of middling years. Some people are wise enough to keep rereading all their lives long; having been less wise, I will have to do mine in that period of time when, by Erikson's design for our years, the final chance offers to strike a balance between integrity and despair or disgust and, thereby indeed, to grow wiser. Given the lateness of the pursuit, I count on *Daedalus* readers to show me speedily how much and where I have missed about father outlooks in all the kinds of this reading, to direct me to where the buried treasure is to be found, or more likely to show me where it lies scattered right on top of the open ground where I so heedlessly passed it by. In return, I promise faithfully to share whatever I find.

REFERENCES

[1]Lucian Pye, *Mao-Tse-tung, The Man in the Leader* (New York, 1976), chap. 8.

[2]Cf. Harold R. Isaacs, "Fathers and Sons and Daughters and National Development," in Richard J. Samuels, ed., *Political Generations and Political Development* (Lexington, Mass., 1977).

[3]Robert Graves, *The Greek Myths*, vol. 1 (New York, 1957), pp. 312-313.

[4]Quoted in Patrick Mullahy, *Oedipus, Myth and Complex, A Review of Psychoanalytic Theory* (New York, 1948), p. 152.

[5]Erik Erikson, "Reflections on Dr. Borg's Life Cycle," *Daedalus* (Spring 1976): 6

[6]*Four Screenplays of Ingmar Bergman* (New York, 1960) pp. 224-225.

[7]Ibid., p. 19

[8]"Reflections on Dr. Borg's Life Cycle," p. 4

[9]Erik Erikson, "On 'Psycho-Historical' Evidence," in *Life History and and the Historical Moment* (New York, 1975), p. 142

[10]" 'Identity Crisis' in Perspective," ibid., pp. 29-31

[11]Ibid., pp. 29, 147

[12]John Nash, "The Father in Contemporary Culture and Current Psychological Literature," *Child Development* (March, 1965): 36:1.

[13]Irving Howe, *World of Our Fathers* (New York, 1976), p. 255.

[14]Leon Waldoff, "The Father-Son Conflict in *Prometheus Unbound*," *Psychoanalytic Review*, 62(1) (1975): 85. A somewhat obliquely relevant remark is made by Paul Roazen: "The Oedipus complex should not be presented only from the point of view of the son. How does a father react to murderous hate?" p. 100 in *Brother Animal: The Story of Freud and Tausk* (New York, 1969). The point is also

noted by Daniel J. Levinson: "The difficulties between parents and their youthful offspring have been examined almost entirely from the viewpoint of the offspring," p. 255 in *The Seasons of a Man's Life*, (New York, 1978). This recent work, incidentally, offers as "theory" an elaborate redo of Erikson's life cycle sequence sliced into dozens more Capitalized Stages (e.g., The Dream, Entering the Adult World, Becoming One's Own Man, Early Settling Down, Late Settling Down, etc.) without adding significantly to the insights provided by Erikson, with whom the authors here rather oddly seek to claim a kind of separate but equal status. The "theory" is supported empirically by the life stories of forty men aged thirty-five to forty-five. The authors say at the end of the book that "fatherhood was tremendously important for most of the men in our study" (p. 333). If it was, they do not make it apparent either in the life stories, where the subject appears only most fleetingly in all but one, or in the "theory" chapters where it is only glancingly mentioned. The only fathers that appear in most of the life stories are the subjects' own fathers, who figure in their accounts of their own earlier years, giving us again son stories as recorded by son-interviewers.

15Cf. Mullahy, *Oedipus, Myth and Complex*.

16Cf. Leon Shaskolsky Sheleff, "Beyond the Oedipus Complex: A Perspective on the Myth and Reality of Generational Conflict," *Theory and Society*, 3(1) (Spring 1976): notes 22, 23, 82; Mullahy, *Oedipus, Myth and Complex*, p. 136; Matthew Besdine, "The Jocasta Complex, Mothering and Genius," Part 1, *Psychoanalytic Review* 55(2) (1968): 259-276; Part 2, 55(4) (1968-1969): 574-600.

17Mullahy, *Oedipus, Myth and Complex*, p. 271.

18E.g, Marian Tolpin, "Aeschylus: Oresteia, A Cure in Fifth Century Athens," *Journal of the American Psychoanalytic Association*, 17(2) (1959): 511-527.

19E.g., Wolfgang Lederer, "Historical Consequences of Father-Son Hostility," *Psychoanalytic Review* 54(2) (1967): 52-80.

20Sheleff, "Beyond the Oedipus Complex," p. 6.

21As in two father books of a particular kind, both about loss of sons, James P. Wechsler's *In A Darkness* (New York, 1972) and John Gunther's *Death Be Not Proud* (New York, 1949).

Notes on Contributors

NOEL ANNAN, born in 1916, is Vice-Chancellor of the University of London. Among his publications are *Leslie Stephen: His Thought and Character in Relation to His Time* (1951), *Roxburgh of Stowe* (1965), *Report of Essex University* (1974), and the *Report of the Committee on the Future of Broadcasting* (1977).

DOUGLAS BUSH, born in 1896 in Morrisburg, Ontario, is Gurney Professor of English Literature emeritus at Harvard University. Since being named Gold Medalist in Classics at the University of Toronto in 1920, he has edited and written many books on English literature, including *English Literature in the Earlier Seventeenth Century* (1945, rev. ed., 1962), *Mythology and the Renaissance Tradition in English Poetry* (1932, 1957, rev. ed., 1963), *John Milton: A Sketch of His Life and Writings* (1964), and *Matthew Arnold: A Survey of His Poetry and Prose* (1971).

MARY DOUGLAS, born in 1921 in San Remo, Italy, is resident scholar and director of the Culture Program at the Russell Sage Foundation. Her publications include *The Lele of the Kasai* (1963), *Purity and Danger* (1966), *Natural Symbols* (1970), *Implicit Meaning* (1976), and, as general editor, *The Illustrated Golden Bough* (1978).

TAMARA K. HAREVEN, born in 1937 in Czernautz, Rumania, is professor of history at Clark University, research associate at the Center for Population Studies, Harvard University, and editor of the *Journal of Family History*. She is author of *Eleanor Roosevelt: An American Conscience* (1968), *Amoskeag, Life and Work in an American Factory City* (1978), and *Transitions: The Family and the Life Course in Historical Perspective* (1978).

HAROLD R. ISAACS, born in 1910 in New York City, is professor emeritus of political science at the Massachusetts Institute of Technology. His publications, written both as foreign correspondent for *Newsweek*, 1943-1950, and as political scientist, include *The Tragedy of the Chinese Revolution* (1938), *Scratches on Our Minds: American Images of China and India* (1958), and *Idols of the Tribe: Group Identity and Political Change* (1975).

MORTON KELLER, born in 1929 in Brooklyn, New York, is Spector Professor of History at Brandeis University. He is author of *The Life Insurance Enterprise, 1855-1910: A Study in the Limits of Corporate Power* (1963), *The Art and Politics of Thomas Nast* (1968), and *Affairs of State: Public Life in Late Nineteenth-Century America* (1977).

ANNIE KRIEGEL, born in 1926 in Paris, is professor of political sociology at the University of Paris, Nanterre. Among her many books on working class and minority affairs are *Aux origines du communisme français* (1964), *Les juifs et le monde moderne* (1977), and *Un autre communisme? Eurocommunisme* (1977).

JONATHAN LEAR, born in 1948 in New York City, is assistant professor of philosophy at Yale University. He has been a graduate fellow at the Rockefeller University, a Fellow at Trinity Hall, Cambridge University, and is currently writing a book on Aristotle's logic.

SHIRLEY ROBIN LETWIN, born in 1924, is author of *The Pursuit of Certainty: David Hume, Jeremy Bentham, John Stuart Mill, Beatrice Webb* (1965). She has written monographs on moral and political philosophy and law, and is currently completing a book entitled *Trollope's Gentleman*.

LAURA L. NASH, born in 1948 in Madison, Wisconsin, is visiting assistant professor of classics at Brown University. She has published several articles in learned journals, is currently completing (with Cedric H. Whitman) a commentary on Pindar, and is beginning a study of youthful heroes in Greek and Roman mythology.

MATILDA WHITE RILEY, born in 1911 in Boston, is Daniel B. Fayerweather Professor of Political Economy and Sociology at Bowdoin College. Her several publications include *Sociological Research* (2 volumes, 1963) and *Aging and Society* (3 volumes, 1968, 1969, 1972). She is currently at the Center for Advanced Study in the Behavioral Sciences in Palo Alto, California, where she is working on a book on the sociology of age.

CARL E. SCHORSKE, born in 1915 in New York City, is Dayton-Stockton Professor of History and director of the European Cultural Studies Program at Princeton University. His publications include *The Problem of Germany* (1947), *German Social Democracy, 1905-1917* (1950), and *Vienna. Culture and Politics in the Fin de Siècle* (forthcoming).

ROBERT SKIDELSKY, born in 1939 in China, is professor of international studies at Warwick University, England. He is author of *Politicians and the Slump* (1967), *English Progressive Schools* (1969), and *Oswald Mosley* (1975), and is currently writing a biography of John Maynard Keynes.

Index